Decision Making with Insight

Includes Insight.xla 2.0

Sam L. Savage

Stanford University

THOMSON

BROOKS/COLE

Australia • Canada • Mexico • Singapore • Spain
United Kingdom • United States

Publisher: *Curt Hinrichs*
Assistant Editor: *Ann Day*
Editorial Assistant: *Katherine Brayton*
Technology Project Manager: *Burke Taft*
Marketing Manager: *Joseph Rogove*
Marketing Assistant: *Jessica Perry*
Print/Media Buyer: *Jessica Reed*
Permissions Editor: *Elizabeth Zuber*

Production Service: *Pat Brito*
Text Designer: *Pat Brito*
Copy Editor: *Geraldine Hraban*
Illustrators: *Roxanna Morales and Robin Gold*
Cover Image: *Bay Graphics Design, Inc.*
Compositor: *Pat Brito*
Printer: *Webcom*

Printed in Canada
1 2 3 4 5 6 7 06 05 04 03 02

ISBN 0-534-38639-3

For more information about our products,
contact us at:
   Thomson Learning
   Academic Resource Center
   1-800-423-0563
For permission to use material from this
text, contact us by:
   Phone: 1-800-730-2214
   Fax: 1-800-730-2215
   Web: http://www.thomsonrights.com

Brooks/Cole—Thomson Learning
10 Davis Drive
Belmont, CA 94002
USA

Asia
Thomson Learning
5 Shenton Way #01-01
Singapore 068808

Australia/New Zealand
Thomson Learning
102 Dodds Street
Southbank, Victoria 3006
Australia

Canada
Nelson
1120 Birchmount Road
Toronto, Ontario M1K 5G4
Canada

Europe/Middle East/Africa
Thomson Learning
High Holbor House
50/51 Bedford Row
London WCIR 4LR
United Kingdom

Latin America
Thomson Learning
Seneca, 53
Colonia Polanco
11560 Mexico D.F.
Mexico

Spain/Portugal
Paraninfo
Calle/Magallanes, 25
28015 Madrid, Spain

Foreword

Professor Savage concedes up front that the use of spreadsheets for business analysis has some weaknesses (as compared to statistical and optimization packages, simulation languages, and handcrafted programs). He then proceeds to demonstrate a remarkably wide range of spreadsheet capabilities for statistical analysis, discrete-event simulation, and optimization, partly through skillful use of basic capabilities of spreadsheets—specifically Excel—and partly through add-ins supplied with DECISION MAKING WITH INSIGHT.

Along the way, Professor Savage provides valuable advice concerning the use of various analysis methods. Rarely has such sound theory been provided in such an entertaining manner. DECISION MAKING WITH INSIGHT is a must read for those who analyze business problems, are comfortable with Excel, and are not otherwise supplied with all the statistical, simulation, and optimization tools needed for analysis.

Harry Markowitz
Nobel Laureate in Economics

About the Author

After receiving his Ph.D. in computer science from Yale University, Sam Savage spent a year at General Motors Research Laboratory. He joined the faculty of the University of Chicago Graduate School of Business in 1974, where he taught regular classes until 1990. He then developed a popular executive seminar series on Management Science in Spreadsheets.

In 1985, he led the development of the first widely marketed spreadsheet optimization package, What's*Best!*®, which won *PC Magazine's* Technical Excellence Award. In its review of the first edition of *Decision Making with Insight*, *OR/MS Today* stated, "Without question, the leader of the management science in spreadsheets movement is Sam Savage."

Dr. Savage is currently a Consulting Professor in the School of Engineering at Stanford University, where he teaches courses in Interactive Management Science. He consults and lectures extensively to business and government agencies, and is the founder and president of AnalyCorp Inc. (www.AnalyCorp.com), a firm that develops executive education programs and software for improving business analysis. He has been published in both refereed journals and the popular press—with recent articles in the *Harvard Business Review* and the *Journal of Portfolio Management*.

Dr. Savage's home page is www.stanford.edu/~savage.

Dedicated to

Russell, Jacob and Daryl, and to the memory of my parents.

"I have never let my schooling interfere with my education"

MARK TWAIN

Preface

In the mid 1970's I started teaching Management Science to MBA students. I soon discovered that only about 10 percent of them understood the material, and of those that did, only 10 percent went on to apply it. There was a fundamental problem in the way the subject was taught to business students: The approach was so abstract and mathematical that an *algebraic curtain* separated Management from Management Science.

Since then, three revolutions have reshaped the technology and process of decision making. First, the explosive proliferation of microcomputers set the stage for computational rather than algebraic solutions. Second, the electronic spreadsheet created a common analytical vernacular for millions of managers. Third, the Internet is now integrating decision makers, data, and analytical tools in ways never before possible. Today, better business decisions in such diverse areas as risk management, resource allocation, and finance are being guided by analytical spreadsheet models without abstract mathematical formulations. The *algebraic curtain* is coming down.

The goal of the first edition of *DECISION MAKING WITH INSIGHT*[1] and the accompanying *INSIGHT.xla* addins for Microsoft Excel was to provide decision makers with intuition into practical problem solving through concrete examples, concepts, and tutorials. This edition attempts to further the same goal through enhancements in both text and software. No previous training in mathematics or statistics is required; however, I have assumed that the user can create and copy simple spreadsheet formulas.[2] For those with statistics or mathematics experience, it is hoped that this package will rekindle the embers of abstract knowledge obtained, perhaps long ago, in school.

DECISION MAKING WITH INSIGHT has been designed for both the classroom, and individual use in the workplace. In the classroom, it can be used to teach Quantitative Analysis, Management Science, Operations Research, and Production and Operations

---

[1] At that time the book/software combination was called Insight.xla.

[2] For those with no spreadsheet experience, put this package down and go out and learn. Basic spreadsheet skills are important in today's business environment and comprise a significant step toward analytical skills as well.

Management. Instructors may wish to use it in conjunction with a traditional textbook. However, I have used it as the sole text and courseware in university classes and executive education seminars. In the workplace, *DECISION MAKING WITH INSIGHT* can be used on an as-needed basis, where I hope it can guide the development of analytic solutions to business and engineering problems.

Most of the sections stand alone, so the material can be covered in any order. Chapter 1 introduces some important general spreadsheet skills such as creating scaleable formulas and data tables. Chapter 2 introduces Monte Carlo simulation as a method of modeling uncertainty. In particular, random variables and diversification are explored experientially. Chapter 3 extends simulation to general spreadsheet models with uncertain inputs. Examples include inventory lot size, bidding problems, and stock options among others. Chapter 4 covers discrete event simulation for modeling waiting lines and Markov chains for analyzing evolving systems such as competitive markets and populations in health care systems. Chapter 5 is concerned with forecasting, and covers regression and time-series analysis. Chapter 6 introduces decision trees and the value of information. A spreadsheet-based probability wheel is used to define subjective probability. Chapter 7 is devoted to simple optimization models such as product mix, blending, transportation and staffing. Chapter 8 describes integrated, integer, and stochastic models including portfolio optimization, and combinatorial optimization.

In the 1950's my father, L. J. Savage, wrote in his preface to *The Foundations of Statistics* that when reading technical material, "Pencil and paper are nearly indispensable; for there are always figures to be sketched and steps in the argument to be verified by calculation." Instead of pencil and paper, today I recommend a computer with a blank worksheet for the same purpose.

Changes in the Second Edition

The primary changes in the second edition involve the add-in software. There are now two versions of software available: the Standard version, ideal for education and a quick introduction to analytical concepts, and the Commercial version with increased computational power. The text is the same for both versions. The various modules and changes in the second edition are outlined in the two summaries below.

Text Change Summary

An overview and roadmap of the entire package have been added, along with a table of analytical techniques and applications.

Chapter 1 includes an expanded discussion of the role of models in decision making.

Chapters 2 and 3 have been updated to reflect the additional capabilities of the current
Monte Carlo software (XLSim®). New examples include failure analysis and hypothesis testing.

Chapter 4 adds a discussion of the Extend™ Discrete Event Simulation software, and how it can be coupled to Excel.

Chapter 5 has been updated to reflect the new forecasting software (XLForecast™) which has improved modeling of seasonality. The concept of Autocorrelation is also explored.

Chapter 6 has been updated to reflect the new features of the tree software (XLTree™), including tree flipping with updated probabilities.

Chapters 7 and 8 contain additional examples of optimization problems that highlight software advances introduced since the first edition. These include the automatic linearization of logical statements by Lindo System's What's*Best!*® and a heuristic solution of the Traveling Salesman Problem with Frontline System's Evolutionary Solver.

In addition, new exercises have been added throughout.

Software Change Summary

Monte Carlo Simulation

SIM.xla has been replaced by XLSim® which is upward compatible but significantly more powerful. New features are listed below.

■ Freeze/Thaw command: Allows SIM.xla models from first edition to be seamlessly updated to XLSim. Also allows XLSim models to be easily exported and shared with those who do not have the add-in.

■ New distributions include: Multi-variate Normal and Lognormal, Permutations, Myerson's generalized Lognormal.

■ Blitzogram™ Interactive Histograms allows a sequence of distributions to be viewed as an animation.

■ Data Range command allows histograms and other statistics to be quickly derived from spreadsheet data.

Limitations

Iterations: 10,000 (Standard), 1 Million (Commercial)

Output cells: 5(Standard), up to 100 (Commercial)

Parameters for Pameretized Simulation: 5 (Standard), up to 100 (Commercial)

Decision Trees

TREE.xla has been replaced by XLTree™, which includes the following new features.

■ Display Mode: Creates graphical trees with numerous formatting options.

■ Grow Tree: Allows large symmetric trees to be grown from a tree built only on left-most nodes.

- Flip Tree: Allows levels within tree to be interchanged while updating the probabilities.

Limitations

Branching: 3 Branches per node (Standard), limited only by Excel (Commercial).
Maximum depth: 4 levels (Standard), limited only by Excel (Commercial).
State Variables: 4 (Standard), limited only by Excel (Commercial).

Forecasting

FORECAST.xla has been replaced by XLForecast™. Changes include new user interface. Arbitrary seasonality (not just 12 month).

Other Modules

Other modules are unchanged from the first edition except for minor edits.

Acknowledgments

This work grew out of a series of executive seminars on Management Science in Spreadsheets that I initiated through the University of Chicago, Graduate School of Business in 1990. I am indebted to John P. Gould, then dean, whose support enabled the seminar series and its spin-offs to get off the ground. I also owe a great deal to Linus Schrage, who has supplied me for decades with insights into everything from linear programming to simulation.

Since 1990, I have been associated with Stanford University's School of Engineering where I have benefited from continual interaction with the faculty. In particular George Dantzig, Peter Glynn, Ron Howard, Gerd Infanger, David Luenberger, Ross Shachter, and Arthur Veinott have all left their mark on this work. The forecasting routines are based on the ideas of Everette Gardner at the University of Houston who is a master of the spreadsheet in his own right. I have also been influenced by Ben Ball of MIT who adheres to the uncommon notion that applied mathematics should actually be applied to something. Matthew Raphaelson of Wells Fargo Bank, who has developed a keen intuition into the flaw of averages, contributed to several examples in this edition.

David Empey and Anton Rowe provided inspired programming in Visual Basic and C as well as many design improvements along the way. Christian Peccei played a central role in both the design and implementation of the new simulation, tree and forecasting routines introduced in this edition. John Wilde assisted in testing and refining the current software, as well as integrating it into the text. I am indebted to David Zalkind of George Washington University, who has been a continual source of beneficial feedback and suggestions. Special thanks to Tom Liu, Rajit Marwah, and Pearl Woon-Tai for their Markov model based on MINV.

Valuable comments on early drafts of the software and manuscript were provided by Robert L. Armacost, University of Central Florida; David Ashley, University of Missouri; Mark N. Broadie, Columbia University; George D. Brower, Moravian College; Jim Collier, Southern Arkansas University; Byron Finch, Miami University of Ohio; Samuel B. Graves, Boston College; Tom Groleau, Bethel College; Victoria Mabin, University of Wellington; Richard H. McClure, Miami University of Ohio; Pierre Ndilikilikesha, Duke University; Stephen G. Powell, Dartmouth College; Robert M. Saltzman, San Francisco State University; Ken Saydan, University of North Carolina; Carl Schultz, University of New Mexico; Rick L. Wilson, Oklahoma State University; Wayne Winston, Indiana University; and Martin Young, University of Michigan. Alexander Tonsky of Pacific Telesis suggested some nice enhancements to the queuing models. Suggestions for the 2nd edition were made by John Charnes, University of Kansas; Roger Grinde, University of New Hampshire; Tom Grossman; University of Calgary; and Sephan Scholtes, Cambridge University.

In terms of getting the package out the door, Curt Hinrichs of Duxbury Press combined persistence with patience to maintain momentum through thick and thin. For the first edition, copy editing and suggestions from Rebecca Lee and Charles Seiter filled in numerous holes and smoothed off some rough edges. Robin Gold of Forbes Mill Press did the final layout and made numerous detail improvements to the flow. For this edition, Geraldine Hraban did an excellent job of editing, and Pat Brito and Roxanna Morales worked tirelessly on redesign, typesetting, graphics and other production related issues.

An enjoyable source of wisdom came from my uncle, I. R. Savage, whose detailed comments on the first edition yielded many improvements throughout. Finally, to my wife Daryl, who read through the entire first edition manuscript, and to whom I promised in 1998: "no more books (at least for a while)," I say thanks again for your love and support, and how was I supposed to know that a new edition would be as much work as a whole new book?

Palo Alto, 2002

Contents

Fundamental Concepts

Exercises

Tutorials

Road Map

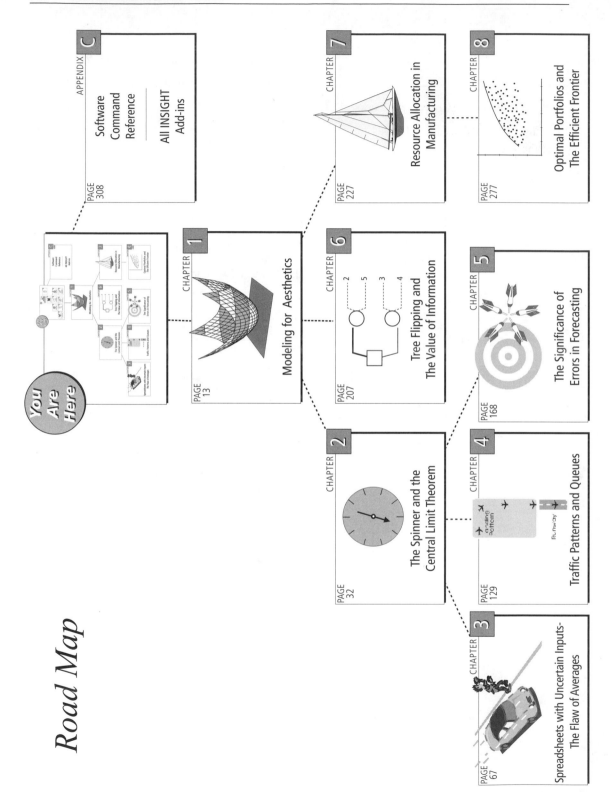

You Are Here

APPENDIX C
PAGE 308
Software Command Reference
All INSIGHT Add-ins

CHAPTER 1
PAGE 13
Modeling for Aesthetics

CHAPTER 2
PAGE 32
The Spinner and the Central Limit Theorem

CHAPTER 3
PAGE 67
Spreadsheets with Uncertain Inputs-The Flaw of Averages

CHAPTER 4
PAGE 129
Traffic Patterns and Queues

CHAPTER 5
PAGE 168
The Significance of Errors in Forecasting

CHAPTER 6
PAGE 207
Tree Flipping and The Value of Information

CHAPTER 7
PAGE 227
Resource Allocation in Manufacturing

CHAPTER 8
PAGE 277
Optimal Portfolios and The Efficient Frontier

Overview of Decision Making with Insight and INSIGHT.xla 2.0

Just as flying a plane requires both an understanding of the flight manuals and a physical feel for the aircraft, Management Science has both an intellectual and experiential side. *Decision Making with Insight* and **INSIGHT.xla** are analogous to a flight manual and light aircraft. Together they can help connect the seat of the intellect to the seat of the pants.

Decision Making with Insight has eight chapters covering various aspects of analytical modeling as outlined below. These chapters do not need to be studied in any particular order, however the roadmap above suggests some scenic routes through the material along with selected landmarks. If you wish to bypass the text and learn the commands of various modules of **INSIGHT.xla**, proceed directly to Appendix C.

Chapter

1. *Analytical Modeling in Spreadsheets.* This chapter discusses analytical modeling in general, and introduces some techniques of spreadsheet modeling that are important in any context, for example, **data tables** and the **sumproduct formula.**

2. *The Building Blocks of Uncertainty: Random Variables.* Virtually all business decisions are made in the light of uncertainty. **Monte Carlo simulation** with XLSim® is introduced as a means of building intuition into **probability distributions** and the **central limit theorem. Blitzogram™** interactive histograms are introduced.

3. *The Buildings of Uncertainty: Functions of Random Variables.* When estimates of uncertain numbers are plugged into even relatively simple spreadsheet models the results can be very misleading. The **flaw of averages** is discussed and **parameterized simulation** with XLSim is introduced as a means for **experimentation under uncertainty.**

4. *Uncertainties that Evolve Over Time.* Commuter traffic jams, airline flight delays, slow internet response and many other daily inconveniences are the realm of **queuing theory.** For those problems that cannot be solved theoretically, **Discrete Event simulation** can provide insight. The **Extend™** simulation package is introduced. Situations with evolving populations such as credit card customers or groups covered by a health maintenance organization can sometimes be modeled as **Markov chains.**

5. *Forecasting.* **Causal forecasting** is discussed. Then **XLForecast™** is introduced in a presentation of **time series** analysis covering **Exponential Smoothing, trends** and **seasonality.** The importance of tracking and making use of errors is stressed; in particular it is shown how forecasting errors may be incorporated into simulations of the future.

6. *Decision Trees.* Decisions between a few alternatives are often modeled with **decision trees. XLTree™** is introduced, along with a **probability wheel** for assessing probabilities from management. **State variables** are presented as an aid to calculating utility values. **Tree flipping** and the **value of information** are also discussed.

7. *Overview of Optimization.* Virtually all endeavors in business and government entail the allocation of limited resources towards achieving some stated objective. For a broad class of such problems, known as **linear programs,** specialized software can quickly arrive at an optimal course of action that might never be discovered by hand. Several examples are presented in the areas of manufacturing, scheduling, finance and transportation. The **Premium Excel Solver** and **What's Best!®** are introduced.

8. *Extensions of Optimization.* There are many ways in which the concept of linear programming may be extended. Examples include the addition of **logical conditions,** which can now be solved automatically by **What's Best!,** problems that extend into **multiple time periods,** and **stochastic optimization** problems in which the underlying data is uncertain. A **Combinatorial** problem is introduced and solved using the **evolutionary** mode of Frontline Systems's Premium Solver. **Non-linear optimization** is also explored. In particular, the **Markowitz portfolio model** is presented along with its relationship to the **efficient frontier** in investing.

Application Matrix

	Ch	Finance	Supply Chain	Production & Operations Management	Human Resources	Marketing	Health Care	National Security
Monte Carlo Simulation	2,3	Profit Tutorial 21 Risk and Diversification 32–40 Investments 48 Pro Forma Cash Flow 68 Stock Options 75 Correlated Investments 92 Value of Petroleum Reserve 107 Funding a New Business 107 Bottom-up Budgeting 108 Real Estate Credit Risk 108 Asian Option 109 Investment Growth 109 Retirement Planning 109	Inventory Costs 57 Optimal Stocking level 71	Project Duration 68 Production Quantity 69 Failure Analysis 80 Optimal Inventory Level 71 Quality Control 106	Overtime Expenses 69 Optimal Staffing Level 74	Competitive Bidding 74 Yield Management 84 Advertising Effectiveness 103	Competitive Bidding 74 Testing for a Disease Cluster 101	
Discrete Event Simulation	4			Toll Booth 119 Assembly Line 127 Capacity Planning 151	Servers 128 Air Traffic 129 Call Center 151			Forest Fire 114
Markov Chains	4	Managing Receivables 152		Machine Replacement 146		Market Share 141 CRM 152 Effects of Advertising 159	Screening for Disease 148	
Regression	5							
Time Series Analysis	5		Forecasting Future Sales 165 Simulating the Distribution of Sales 166,175	Seasonality 182				
Decision Trees	6	Settle or Litigate 220		Deciding on a Purchase 185, 201 Choosing a Route 159,185,201 Drilling for Oil 213		Market Elasticity 218 Marketing Campaign 220	Pharmaceutical R&D 186 Medical Testing 205	Protective Armor for Fighter Aircraft 221 Assess ng Threats of Terrorism 221
Optimization	7,8	Markowitz Portfolio Optimization 74 Efficient Frontier 278	Transportation Problem 245 Network Flow 247 Two Stage Supply Chain 265 Integration of Supply and Production 268 Supply Chain with Uncertain Demand 270 Optimal Plant Location 295	Product Mix 227, 237 Blending 237, 240 Cutting Stock 244 Stamping Parts 253 Truck Loading 256 Fixed Costs 258 Multi-period Model 263 Plant Location 295 Traveling Salesman 278	Staff Scheduling 240, 242	Optimal Advertising Mix 252	Operation of a Healthcare Facility 293	Disaster Relief 247 Allocating Peace-keeping Units 252 Optimal Airlift of Supplies 296

1 ■■■■■■■■■■■■■■■■■■■■■■■■■■■■

Analytical Modeling in Spreadsheets

I hear, I forget
I see, I remember
I do, I understand

CHINESE PROVERB

The unprecedented strategic and operational problems of World War II ushered in an analytical approach to decision making, known as operations research, based on mathematical models of the real world.

Today, the millions of people who enter their own formulas into an electronic spreadsheet are doing mathematical modeling, whether they know it or not. It requires only a small further step to build analytical models that can improve the way decisions are made.

It is not enough to hear about analytical models, nor to merely see models that have been developed by someone else. As the proverb suggests, you will only understand analytical models by building them on your own.

This chapter introduces some aspects of spreadsheet modeling that are important in the analytical techniques that appear in subsequent chapters. It also presents some comments of experienced modelers, to provide perspective.

■ ■ ■ **OVERVIEW**

Introduction

This section contains instructions for installing the INSIGHT software, followed by a brief introduction to the technology of decision making and analytical modeling.

Tutorial: A Manufacturing Example

We start with the problem of modeling the manufacture of boats from a set of limited raw materials. Within this context, the concepts of scalable models and data tables are introduced.

The Voices of Experience

We present observations of several experienced model builders.

The Pros and Cons of Spreadsheet Modeling

The pros and cons of modeling in this environment are briefly summarized.

INTRODUCTION

To install INSIGHT, place the disk in your CD drive, then run SETUP. This program will then step you through the complete installation of INSIGHT onto your hard disk.

The Technology of Decision Making

After World War II, operations research was adapted to the needs of general industry, and the field of management science emerged. Such techniques as simulation, forecasting, decision analysis, and linear programming were adopted by industry in the 1960s and 1970s to solve problems in manufacturing, transportation, marketing, and finance. As the power and cost of computers skyrocketed and plummeted, respectively, the field continued to grow. Layers of programmers and mathematicians still formed an "algebraic curtain," however, separating most managers from management science.

In the 1980s millions adopted the electronic spreadsheet as the quantitative tool of choice. Mathematical modeling, once the exotic domain of the theoretician, was now the vernacular of management. Many analytical methods of the past migrated quickly to this new interactive environment. The algebraic curtain was coming down.

As we enter the new millennium, the field is poised for yet another revolution as the Internet ties together decision makers, data, and analytical techniques.

Disciplined Intuition: A Philosophy

Some subjects, like ancient history, can only be learned from books, videos and other forms of observation. This is a purely intellectual activity. Skills such as riding a bicycle, on the other hand, can't be explained at all intellectually. Instead we must interact with a bicycle through the seat of our pants until riding it becomes intuitive. Most interesting pursuits require both an intellectual and intuitive understanding.

This became vividly clear to me when I learned to fly a sailplane. I studied flight manuals by night and wrestled with the controls by day with little success in connecting what I read to what I did in the air. Eventually, however, a dialog was established between the seat of my intellect and the seat of my pants, and I soared with the hawks. I had developed intuition into flying. But unlike learning to ride a bike through trial and error, this intuition was based on a disciplined regimen of theory and practice. I call this *Disciplined Intuition,* and it serves as the philosophy of this work.

There are many fine books on Operations Research and Management Science that cover their subjects in both greater breadth and depth than DECISION MAKING WITH INSIGHT. In contrast, I have attempted to address both the intellectual and intuitive aspects of the subject through the use of interactive models. Some may wish to use this book and software as a companion piece to a traditional text that provides more rigorous theoretical explanations. Others may wish to use it alone. In either case, the success of this work must be measured in terms of the improvement in the user's intuition, and the extent to which that intuition remains disciplined.

Analytical Models

An analytical model approximates the real world but gives us the freedom to experiment. As an example, PROFIT = REVENUE – EXPENSE is a very simple analytical model of almost any business. A more complex model might be used to help forecast future sales, allocate scarce resources among competing projects, or make a decision to acquire another firm.

The reasons people build analytical models of management situations before making managerial decisions are much the same reasons that people build models of airplanes before making engineering decisions. In fact, the Wright Brother's development of the first airplane illustrates several important benefits of model building. See Friedman (1991).

■ **It is much less costly to make mistakes in a model than in the real world.** The Wright brothers built a series of kites before they spent money or risked their lives on their first manned glider.

- **A model can yield unexpected insights into real world problems.** The absent-minded twisting of a bicycle inner tube box supposedly inspired the Wright's unique wing warping system that allowed their plane to bank.

- **A model allows you to apply analytical tools not available in the real world.** For the Wright brothers the analytical tool was the wind tunnel that allowed them to experiment with models of different wing geometries in search of an optimal design.

- **The discipline of building a model forces you to better understand the relationships being modeled and the data required for analysis.** The Wright brothers built a sequence of three gliders over three years. Each of these was designed to attack a problem they were already aware of, but each illuminated a new problem that they were unaware of.

- **A model serves as a means of communication.** The Wright brothers were exploring new phenomena for which they may have had no words, but since they both observed the behavior of the same models, they shared the same perceptions of reality.

TUTORIAL: IMPORTANT MODELING TECHNIQUES

The following tutorial contains a detailed discussion of some important spreadsheet modeling techniques, including:

- Range Names
- Data Tables
- Sumproduct
- Auditing Tools

Note: The casual reader may wish to skip the next few pages and resume at Exercise 1.3 later in this chapter. You may return to this tutorial at any point to see illustrations of the above topics, as they arise in future chapters.

The tutorial is based on the following business example. A manufacturer produces two types of fiberglass boats: a large sailboat with a profit per unit of $1,200, and a motor boat with a profit per unit of $1,000.

Although many raw materials are required to manufacture the boats, three are currently in short supply: sailcloth, used only for the sailboat; glass fiber, used in both boats; and engines, used only in the motor boat. The boats' profit, raw material requirements, and quantity of raw materials on hand are specified in BOAT.xls, shown in the following figure:

	A	B	C	D	E
1			Large Sailboat	Motor Boat	
2	Production Quantity		0	0	
3	Profit Per Unit		$1,200	$1,000	
4					
5					
6			Large Sailboat	Motor Boat	
7	Raw Materials		Requirements by product		On Hand
8	Sailcloth		4	0	400
9	Glass Fiber		8	4	1000
10	Engines		0	1	120

Starting with BOAT.xls, which you should open now, we will construct a production planning model of this situation.

Understanding the Elements of a Worksheet Model

Worksheet models contain two fundamental types of elements:

■ Numbers that might or might not be under managerial control

■ Formulas that specify functional relationships between the numbers

BOAT.xls contains all the numbers needed for this model (don't confuse it with BOATS.xls, which will be used in later chapters). In the following tutorial you will fill in formulas for total profit and quantities of resources used for a given level of production.

Separation of Data and Formulas

Profit

The total profit is found by summing the profit per unit multiplied by the associated production quantity. A possible formula for profit is =C2*1200+D2*1000. However, this is not a good approach. If the profit per unit changes, the formula must be modified.

A better plan is to keep the data and formulas separate with the formula =C2*C3+D2*D3. Enter this in cell B4 of the worksheet. Type "Total Profit" into cell A4. Now if the profit numbers change, they can simply be updated in cells C3 and D3. As a general rule, data should never be typed directly into a formula.

Note: Always test formulas after entering them. This not only verifies your model as it is being built, but also results in a bit of gratification when you see it work correctly.

Type the number 1 into cell C2, and total profit should be $1,200. Now type 1 into cell D2 and profit should rise to $2,200, as shown in the following figure:

B4			=C2*C3+D2*D3	
	A	B	C	D
1			Large Sailboat	Motor Boat
2	Production Quantity		1	1
3	Profit Per Unit		$1,200	$1,000
4	Total Profit	$2,200		

Resource Utilization

Total usage of sailcloth is calculated by using a formula similar to the one for profit: =C$2*C8+D$2*D8. Enter this formula in cell B8 and the label "Used" in B7. The $ signs before the row numbers indicate an absolute reference that allows the formula to be copied to cells B9:B10, yielding the remaining materials' total usage. Copy the formula now by selecting cell B8, placing the cursor over the small black square in the lower right corner of the cell, and dragging down to B10. The worksheet should appear as shown in the following figure:

B8			=C$2*C8+D$2*D8		
	A	B	C	D	E
1			Large Sailboat	Motor Boat	
2	Production Quantity		1	1	
3	Profit Per Unit		$1,200	$1,000	
4	Total Profit	$2,200			
5					
6			Large Sailboat	Motor Boat	
7	Raw Materials	Used	Requirements by product		On Hand
8	Sailcloth	4	4	0	400
9	Glass Fiber	12	8	4	1000
10	Engines	1	0	1	120

As always, test the model by changing the input cells and verifying that you are getting the right results.

Making Sure the Model is Scalable

This worksheet gives correct values for profit and resource utilization if non-negative production quantities are entered in cells C2 and D2. But what if the manufacturer introduces additional types of raw materials or boats?

Additional Types of Materials

The model can be expanded to include an additional material type by adding new information in columns A, C, D, and E of row 11 and then copying the formula in cell B10 to B11.

Additional Types of Boats and the SUMPRODUCT Formula

You could insert a column in the worksheet for the new boat type with the **Insert Column** command, then profit and requirement data could be entered. But if you did that, all the formulas would need to be modified! Not only is this very tedious, but it is also likely to introduce errors into the model.

A more scalable model can be achieved using the SUMPRODUCT formula. The profit formula C2*C3+D2*D3 can be replaced by the formula =SUMPRODUCT(C2:D2,C3:D3).

SUMPRODUCT performs exactly the same calculation, but, it has the advantage of automatically including additional columns inserted between C and D. The calculations for resource utilization should similarly be changed to SUMPRODUCT formulas. Don't forget to use $ signs on the arguments ($C$2:$D$2) so you can copy the formula correctly. A convenient way to apply $ signs to the correct arguments is to toggle the F4 key while you edit the formula. Save your model before proceeding.

Range Names

It is useful to give names to certain ranges of cells in your model. In this case we will name cells C2:D2 QUANTITY, cells C3:D3 PROFIT_PER_UNIT, and cell B4 TOTAL_PROFIT.

This can be done by selecting the range, then invoking the **Insert Name Define** command and typing the desired name. Another way is to select the range, type the name into the name box in the left of the formula bar, and press the Enter key.

■ FUNDAMENTAL 1-1

SUMPRODUCT

- *SUMPRODUCT* is an important formula in analytical modeling. It is known mathematically as the *vector inner product*.

- *SUMPRODUCT* is an example of a *scalable* formula. That is, the formula need not be modified to handle problems of different sizes. Any formula that takes a range of cells as an argument has this property. Other common scalable formulas are SUM, MAX, and MIN.

Name Box →

	A	B	C	D
			Large Sailboat	Motor Boat
1				
2	Production Quantity		1	1
3	Profit Per Unit		$1,200	$1,000

Once you have defined range C2:D2 as QUANTITY, name the range C3:D3 as PROFIT_PER_UNIT, and B4 as TOTAL_PROFIT. At this point you can either click on the little triangle to the right of the name box or press the F5 key to see all the names currently in the sheet.

Names can be used in formulas either by typing them or, more conveniently, by using the F5 key or the name box and selecting the desired name from the list. Edit the formula for profit to use range names. It should now appear as shown in the following equation:

=SUMPRODUCT (QUANTITY,PROFIT_PER_UNIT)

Experimenting with the Model

Feasibility Checking

Although this model is simple, it can yield important insights. As we experiment with various production figures, we must remember to check that they are feasible. That is, we must not consume more raw materials than we have on hand. We can use logical formulas that compare the quantity of raw materials used with the quantity on hand. Enter the formula =E8>=B8 in cell F8. This formula returns the logical value TRUE if cell E8 (the quantity of sailcloth) is greater than or equal to cell B8 (the amount used), and FALSE otherwise. Copy cell F8 to F9:F10 and enter the label "Feasible" in cell F7. Your model should appear as shown in the following figure:

F8		=E8>=B8			
	B	C	D	E	F
7	**Used**	Requirements by product		**On Hand**	Feasible
8	4	4	0	400	TRUE
9	12	8	4	1000	TRUE
10	1	0	1	120	TRUE

"What If" Analysis

Given a spreadsheet model such as this, you can experiment with the inputs by hand. This is often known as "what if" analysis. Start by setting both boat production quantities to zero. Now how many sailboats can you produce? By trying various guesses in cell C2, you will find that a maximum of 100 sail boats can be produced before sail cloth is depleted. This results in profit of $120,000 and leaves $1000 - 800 = 200$ units of glass fiber and 120 engines. Now, increase production of motor boats to 50, and glass fiber will be depleted. This should result in a $170,000 profit and a remaining inventory of $120 - 50 = 70$ engines. Because all sail cloth and glass fiber have been exhausted, it is not possible to increase the production of either type of boat; but we have a healthy profit. It is tempting to stop here, but next we will apply a more analytical approach.

Data Tables

Data tables require a bit of setup but provide a more thorough form of analysis. You might have used spreadsheets for years without ever having used this powerful command. A data table allows you to repeatedly evaluate a particular formula within the model while systematically varying one or two input cells on which the formula depends.

We will now set up a data table to repeatedly calculate profit while varying the production quantities of both types of boat.

The Formula That Drives the Table. Because the table will have narrow columns, we will express profit in 000's so that the numbers will fit. To accomplish this, divide total profit by 1000. The formula in cell B4 should now look like the following equation:

=SUMPRODUCT (QUANTITY,PROFIT_PER_UNIT)/1000

Also, we must only print the profit value if the production quantities are feasible; that is, if all the cells F8:F10 are TRUE. This is expressed in Excel as AND(F8:10). We will now enter the formula that drives the table. This formula, which should be entered in G6, will return the total profit in thousands for every combination of production quantities that is feasible. Otherwise, it will return a blank. This will require an IF statement, the general syntax of which is

=IF(logical_test, value_if_true, value_if_false).

In our case the logical test is whether the production quantities are feasible. That is, AND(F8:F10) is TRUE. The value if true is TOTAL_PROFIT; the value if false is blank, or " ". The formula to type into G6 is thus

= IF(AND(F8:F10),TOTAL_PROFIT," ")

Test the formula by changing the production quantities in cells C2 and D2.

Specifying the Quantities to Evaluate. Now that the formula is in place, we must specify the production quantities that we want to evaluate in the table.

The production quantities of sailboats will be stored in row 6 starting in column H. We will experiment with all numbers and from 0 through 150, in increments of 5. Start by placing 0 in cell H6 and 5 in I6.

Next select cells H6 and I6 and drag the small box in the lower right corner of the selected region to column AL while holding down the mouse key. This should result in the array of values as shown in the following figure.

The production quantities of motor boats will be stored in column G, starting in row 7. This time we will start at 150 and go to 0. Start by placing 150 in cell G7 and 145 in G8. Again select the two cells. Then drag them to row 37. Now you should have the numbers 0 to 150, in increments of 5, running from H6 to AL6, and the numbers 150 to 0, in decrements of 5, running from G7 to G37.

TUTORIAL: USING THE DATA TABLE COMMAND

1   Select the entire range of the table (G6:AL37). Then invoke the **Data Table** command. The Data Table dialog box appears.

2   Place the cursor in the **Row Input** field of the dialog box, then click on cell C2. That is, C2 is the cell into which the row of sail boat quantities at the top of the table will be plugged.

3   Place the cursor in the **Column Input** field and click on cell D2, the cell for the quantity of motor boats. The dialog box should appear as shown below.

4   Click **OK**, and the entire table will be filled in.

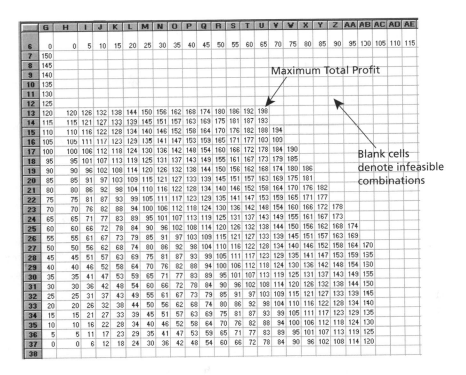

Maximum Total Profit

Blank cells denote infeasible combinations

	G	H	I	J	K	L	M	N	O	P	Q	R	S	T	U	V	W	X	Y	Z	AA	AB	AC	AD	AE
6	0	0	5	10	15	20	25	30	35	40	45	50	55	60	65	70	75	80	85	90	95	100	105	110	115
7	150																								
8	145																								
9	140																								
10	135																								
11	130																								
12	125																								
13	120	120	126	132	138	144	150	156	162	168	174	180	186	192	198										
14	115	115	121	127	133	139	145	151	157	163	169	175	181	187	193										
15	110	110	116	122	128	134	140	146	152	158	164	170	176	182	188	194									
16	105	105	111	117	123	129	135	141	147	153	159	165	171	177	183	189									
17	100	100	106	112	118	124	130	136	142	148	154	160	166	172	178	184	190								
18	95	95	101	107	113	119	125	131	137	143	149	155	161	167	173	179	185								
19	90	90	96	102	108	114	120	126	132	138	144	150	156	162	168	174	180	186							
20	85	85	91	97	103	109	115	121	127	133	139	145	151	157	163	169	175	181							
21	80	80	86	92	98	104	110	116	122	128	134	140	146	152	158	164	170	176	182						
22	75	75	81	87	93	99	105	111	117	123	129	135	141	147	153	159	165	171	177						
23	70	70	76	82	88	94	100	106	112	118	124	130	136	142	148	154	160	166	172	178					
24	65	65	71	77	83	89	95	101	107	113	119	125	131	137	143	149	155	161	167	173					
25	60	60	66	72	78	84	90	96	102	108	114	120	126	132	138	144	150	156	162	168	174				
26	55	55	61	67	73	79	85	91	97	103	109	115	121	127	133	139	145	151	157	163	169				
27	50	50	56	62	68	74	80	86	92	98	104	110	116	122	128	134	140	146	152	158	164	170			
28	45	45	51	57	63	69	75	81	87	93	99	105	111	117	123	129	135	141	147	153	159	165			
29	40	40	46	52	58	64	70	76	82	88	94	100	106	112	118	124	130	136	142	148	154	160			
30	35	35	41	47	53	59	65	71	77	83	89	95	101	107	113	119	125	131	137	143	149	155			
31	30	30	36	42	48	54	60	66	72	78	84	90	96	102	108	114	120	126	132	138	144	150			
32	25	25	31	37	43	49	55	61	67	73	79	85	91	97	103	109	115	121	127	133	139	145			
33	20	20	26	32	38	44	50	56	62	68	74	80	86	92	98	104	110	116	122	128	134	140			
34	15	15	21	27	33	39	45	51	57	63	69	75	81	87	93	99	105	111	117	123	129	135			
35	10	10	16	22	28	34	40	46	52	58	64	70	76	82	88	94	100	106	112	118	124	130			
36	5	5	11	17	23	29	35	41	47	53	59	65	71	77	83	89	95	101	107	113	119	125			
37	0	0	6	12	18	24	30	36	42	48	54	60	66	72	78	84	90	96	102	108	114	120			
38																									

This table provides a great deal of information. Among other things it shows that a profit of $198,000 is possible by producing 65 sailboats and 120 motor boats. Notice that this occurs at a corner of the area of feasible production figures.

EXERCISE 1.1

EXPERIMENTING WITH THE ASSUMPTIONS OF THE PRODUCTION MODEL

a. Suppose the number of engines available were only 100 units. What would be the maximum profit, and for what production quantities would it occur?

b. Return the number of engines to 120. Now reduce the profit per unit of motor boats below $800 until the maximum profit occurs in multiple cells. What is the profit, and how many cells does it appear in? Continue reducing the profit per unit of motor boats. Now how many cells does the optimal profit appear in?

1.2 DOCUMENTING AND AUDITING THE MODEL

Documentation is especially important for models that will be used by more than one person. Because the formulas in a worksheet model are hidden, it is easy to lose track of the flow of the calculations.

a. Use the **Insert Comment** command to place a comment in cell F8 that explains the meaning of the TRUE or FALSE that appears there. Moving the cross shaped cursor over the cell will cause the comment to appear.

b. The auditing tools track the flow of calculations. Place the cursor in cell G6, the formula that drives the table. Then repeatedly invoke the **Tools Auditing Trace Precedents** command. You will see the cells that G6 depends on, the cells that they depend on, and so on. Next bring up the auditing toolbar, shown below, with the **Tools Auditing Show Auditing Toolbar** command.

It is useful to keep this auditing tool bar on screen when you are either creating a new model, or investigating a model created by someone else. These tools automate the generation of worksheet flow diagrams defined in Savage [1992].

THE VOICES OF EXPERIENCE

If you made your way through the previous tutorial, you witnessed the step-by-step development of a small analytical model including a data table. Even if you skipped the tutorial, the next exercise, which is recommended for all readers, will provide you with a feeling for the power of the data table.

1.3 PURE AESTHETICS

The file 3DGRAPH.xls uses a data table to graph an arbitrary function of two variables. Cells K28 and L28 are named X and Y respectively. The function of X and Y is typed into K26, creating the graph. It is shown in the following figure for $F(X,Y) = X^2+Y^2$.

Make sure that your spreadsheet's calculation is set to automatic under **Tools Options**. Open the file and start by changing the formula to X^2+Y^3. Then make as aesthetically pleasing a picture as you can by trying different functions of X and Y in cell K26.

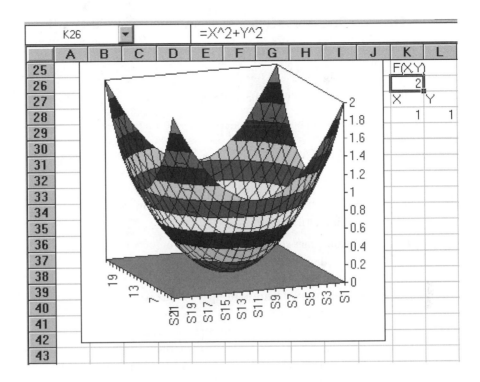

People with significant training in mathematics quickly learn how to get any number of shapes out of 3DGRAPH.xls. Even those with little formal background can, through trial and error, arrive at an aesthetic design. If you found this process illuminating then you have learned from the model. In any event the above exercise allowed you to experience interaction with a mathematical model.

And speaking of experience, what follows are a number of observations by experienced analytical modelers, which together offer a perspective of the big picture of the subject.

"A Successful Model Tells You Things You Didn't Tell it to Tell You" — Jerry P. Brashear

Jerry P. Brashear, an energy consultant, hit the analytical nail on the head with the above statement. Recall that the success of the Wright brothers depended on a sequence of models, each of which resulted in new unexpected results that led them to additional models, and ultimately to their goal.

The Five Stages of Model Development—Donald Knuth

Donald Knuth, a Stanford computer scientist, discovered that computer program development generally goes through five stages. I have paraphrased these since they apply equally to analytical modeling:

1. Decide what you want the model to do.

2. Decide how to build the model.

3. Build the model.

4. Debug the model.

5. Trash stages 1 through 4 and start again, now that you know what you really wanted in the first place.

Once you realize that stage 5 is inevitable, you become more willing to discard bad models early rather than to continually patch them up.

"Spreadsheets are Dimensionally Arthritic"
—Arthur Geoffrion

Arthur Geoffrion, a UCLA management scientist, has investigated the properties of modeling environments. By Geoffrion's criteria the biggest drawbacks of the spreadsheet involve scaling a small prototype model to industrial size. For example, in the boat production model of the tutorial, if we had not been careful, it would have been difficult to add new types of boats.

A more serious problem is that spreadsheet models are fundamentally two-dimensional. Suppose we wanted to model production in each of 12 consecutive months. This would require adding a new dimension to the model for time. Conceptually we could do this by making 11 more copies of the original model. Now suppose we need to model production in two separate plants. We must make two copies of the 12 models we have already made. I refer to changing the dimensionality of a model as *hyperscaling*. Now imagine adding a new boat type to all 24 sub-models described and you will understand what Geoffrion means by dimensional arthritis.

Three things that can reduce dimensional arthritis are

1. Keep data separate from formulas. This will save you from having to modify the model when the data changes.

2. Use scalable range formulas such as SUMPRODUCT that can expand with your model. If you are successful in this regard, your small initial models can be expanded more easily to address larger scale problems.

3. Use multiple worksheets to represent a third dimension beyond rows and columns.

"A Pencil is a Crutch, a Calculator is a Wheelchair, and a Computer is an Ambulance"—Gene Woolsey

Gene Woolsey, a professor of Economics and Business at the Colorado School of Mines, points out that the mechanical act of calculation is not the same as thinking about a problem and can even interfere with the thought process. There is not time to build an analytical model to back up every business decision, and you must usually rely on intuition. Perhaps the greatest value to be derived from analytical modeling is the extent to which it improves your intuition.

"All Models Are Wrong, Some Models Are Useful" —W. Edward Deming

Deming, the father of modern quality control, is reputed to have made this remark. It reminds us that even the best analytical model is a little like telling a lie. And what's worse than telling a lie? Telling multiple lies. With this in mind you can appreciate the importance of simplicity in model building.

The "Inter-Ocular Trauma Test" of Joe Berkson

Even if you learn something important from an analytical model, it is not of much use if you can't communicate the result to others. Joe Berkson, a bio-statistician at the Mayo Clinic, stressed the use of graphs. For a result to be really useful the graph must pass the *Inter Ocular Trauma Test*. That is, it must hit you between the eyes. Spreadsheets have extensive graphing facilities that should be used to communicate results.

"Clear and Precise Seeing Becomes as One with Clear and Precise Thinking"—Edward Tufte

Now that we are on the subject of graphics, Edward Tufte, a Yale professor, has made a career of studying effective visual display. A scatter plot similar to the one in the following figure appears in his book *Visual Explanations*.[1] Although you don't yet know what this chart represents, make a guess at the y value that would correspond to the x value indicated by the question mark.

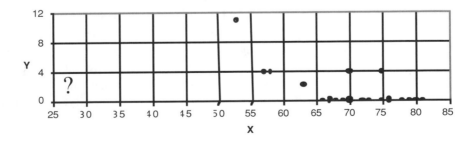

---

[1]Edward Tufte, *Visual Explanations,* Graphics Press, 1996.

We might reasonably expect a high value of *y,* perhaps a good deal higher than any observed so far.

Now for the story that goes with this graph as related by Tufte: Before the launch of the ill-fated space shuttle Challenger, there was concern that unusually low temperatures at Cape Canaveral might cause O-Rings in the booster rockets to leak, leading to catastrophic failure. Analysts attempting to resolve this issue shortly before the launch had access to extensive data on O-Ring damage in previous launches. According to Tufte, although this data was studied in detail, it was never used to create a simple scatter plot of temperature versus the degree of O-Ring damage. If this had been done, the analysts would have observed the previous chart, where x and y represent the temperature and O-Ring damage observed in previous launches, and the question mark denotes the predicted temperature for the Challenger launch. Given the prior concern over O-Ring problems at low temperature, this chart might have convinced those in charge to postpone the launch. Instead, the Challenger exploded because of O-Ring failure, killing all on board.

"It's Dumb to Be Too Smart"—Sam L. Savage

Faced with determining the effect of temperature on O-Ring performance, we could create a complex statistical model resulting in confidence intervals and R^2 coefficients. You would have to be pretty smart to develop such a model and to interpret its results. A relatively dumb person could have created and understood the scatter plot that passed Berkson's Inter-Ocular Trauma Test, and thus saved the Challenger.

Someone who builds a mathematical model can get carried away with all the clever things that can be done with it. The model becomes a safe little world, free from anxiety and office politics, rewarding in its own right. This often results in a very clever model that has little to do with reality. Resist the temptation to be too smart in building a model. Take small model building steps interspersed with healthy doses of reality.

"Because of My Training, I Think About Problems Differently" —William J. Perry

William J. Perry, former U.S. Secretary of Defense, has a B.S, M.S. and Ph.D. all in Mathematics. He was once asked if, during his tenure at the Pentagon, he had ever personally built a mathematical model to answer some pressing question. "No," he replied "there was never enough time or data to build an actual model, but because of my training I think about problems differently." Often analytical models are expected to provide the *right answers*. I believe that Perry describes an even more important role: one in which the model changes the way we think, thereby enabling us to ask the *right questions*.

THE PROS AND CONS OF SPREADSHEET MODELING

Spreadsheets have both strengths and weaknesses. Here we summarize the pros and cons of using this environment for analytical modeling.

First the Cons

Documentability—Spreadsheet models are notoriously difficult to document because all the formulas are hidden. The cell Comments and Auditing Tools can mitigate this problem, but errors often slip through anyway.

Scalability—Before typing a formula into a spreadsheet model, you should ask yourself how it will scale if the quantity of data changes. Range formulas such as SUM and SUMPRODUCT help you scale your model.

Hyperscalability—I use the term hyperscaling to describe the addition of new dimensions to a model. Because spreadsheets are fundamentally two dimensional, adding new dimensions requires copying models multiple times. This is awkward at best, and a show stopper at worst.

The cons are summarized in the following figure:

Now the Pros

The pros of spreadsheet models are shown in the following figure. Despite their drawbacks, spreadsheets have overwhelmingly become the analytical vernacular of management.

END OF CHAPTER EXERCISES

1.4   **EXPERIMENTING WITH A MODEL**

A firm is uncertain about both the demand for a product and the price at which it will sell. It wishes to calculate the total revenue that would be derived from selling 1000, 2000, 3000, 4000, or 5000 units, given a price of $8, $9, or $10 per unit. Use a Data Table to determine revenue for each of these combinations of price and demand.

1.5   **MAKING A MODEL SCALABLE**

The spreadsheet below has been developed to calculate the total cost of parts purchases for a manufacturing facility.

C6		*fx* =B2*C2+B3*C3+B4*C4		
	A	B	C	D	E
1	Part	Cost	Ordered		
2	A	$15	300		
3	B	$20	175		
4	C	$5	450		
5					
6		Total Cost	$10,250		

Cell C6 calculates the total cost with B2*C2+B3*C3+B4*C4

a.   Explain why the total cost formula is not scalable with the addition of new part types.

b.   How can it be made scalable?

2 ■■■■■■■■■■■■■■■■■■■■■■■■■■

The Building Blocks of Uncertainty: Random Variables

The only certainty is that nothing is certain.

PLINY THE ELDER, A ROMAN SCHOLAR

Some 2000 years later, it's a safe bet that Pliny the Elder was right. Everyone must deal with uncertainty.

- What will the temperature be this afternoon?

- What will the price of my favorite stock be tomorrow?

- What number will show up the next time I roll a pair of dice?

In the case of the dice, you can learn a lot about the outcomes by throwing them hundreds of times while recording the results. This is the basic idea behind a computer procedure known as Monte Carlo simulation, which uses the computer to throw a bunch of random inputs into a model. The result is somewhat analogous to shaking a ladder before climbing it, to determine how stable it is.

■ ■ ■ **OVERVIEW**

Introduction

This section contains a short introduction to simulation and instructions for installing and running XLSim®, a Monte Carlo simulation add-in for Excel.

Tutorial: Estimating Profit with Monte Carlo Simulation

The concept of Monte Carlo simulation is introduced in the context of estimating profit given uncertain demand and production costs. We are also introduced to the boss who, when faced with uncertainty, always demands "a number."

The Building Blocks of Uncertainty

This section introduces the basic building blocks for modeling uncertainty and risk. Simulation is used throughout to provide an experiential understanding of such fundamental concepts as uncertain numbers, the Central Limit Theorem, distributions, and risk management.

INTRODUCTION

From Manhattan Project to Wall Street

Developed during the Manhattan (Atomic Bomb) Project in the 1940s, Monte Carlo simulation involves feeding a large number of random inputs into a model while recording the range of outputs. The random inputs are analogous to rolls of dice or spins of a roulette wheel at a casino, hence the name.

As early as 30 years ago, simulation was suggested as an analytical tool for business by David Hertz (1979), while Simon, Atkinson, and Shevokas had proposed it as an intuitive technique for teaching statistics (1976). Efron and Tibshirani and others have used simulation to expand the theoretical scope of statistics (1993).

Today, commercial software packages such as @RISK™ and Crystal Ball®[1] have brought sophisticated Monte Carlo simulation to spreadsheets, adding to its popularity in areas as diverse as accounting, finance, logistics, marketing, operations management, risk management, and strategy.

---

[1]@RISK is trademarked by Palisade Corporation. Crystal Ball is a registered trademark of Decisioneering, Inc.

XLSim®

XLSim is a simple Monte Carlo simulation package for Excel 97 and higher. It is easy to install and learn, and as a Visual Basic Add-in, is at home in either Windows® or Macintosh® environments. You may upgrade to a more powerful version of XLSim at www.AnalyCorp.com.

Running XLSim. Launch Excel and open XLSim.xla from the File menu. A **Simulate** menu will be added to the Excel menu bar.

Auto Load Option. If you want XLSim.xla to load every time you launch Excel, follow these steps:

1. Select **Add-ins** from the **Tools** menu in Excel.

2. Select XLSim.xla from list of add-ins and click **OK**.

   A **Simulate** menu will be added to the Excel menu bar.

   You can later go back and deselect XLSim.xla from the **Add-in** menu to prevent Excel from loading it automatically.

TUTORIAL: ESTIMATING PROFIT WITH MONTE CARLO SIMULATION

An Example: Uncertain Profit

A firm is introducing a product into a new market. Imagine that as marketing manager, you are trying to estimate the profit that will result from the product introduction. The items on which profit depends are

■ Sales in units.

■ Price per unit.

■ Unit cost: The marginal cost per unit of production, marketing, and sales.

■ Fixed costs: Fixed overhead, advertising, and so on. These are known to be $30,000.

   The calculation for profit is as follows:

   Profit = Sales * (Price – Unit Cost) – Fixed Cost

Market Scenarios

Because this is a new market, there is significant uncertainty. For purposes of this tutorial we will assume that either a low or high volume market can occur with equal likelihood: If there is a low volume market, sales of roughly 60,000 units are expected at a price of $10 per unit. If there is a high volume market, the good news is that your company's sales are expected to be roughly 100,000 units. The bad news is that under this scenario, the market is so hot that it brings in competitors. This, in turn, drives the expected price down to $8 per unit.

These market scenarios are summarized in the following table:

	Market Scenarios		
	Low Volume	High Volume	Average
Probability	50%	50%	
Units	60,000	100,000	80,00
Price	$10	$8	$9

Note: In a more refined model we might have 200 or 2 thousand scenarios instead of 2, but the basic steps would be the same.

Unit Cost

The VP of production believes that the cost per unit will be $7.50. But you have been advised that, depending on the cost of raw materials and actual production experience, this cost might be as low as $6.00 or as high as $9.00. This uncertainty is summarized in the following table.

Low	Most Likely	High	Average
$6.00	$7.50	$9.00	$7.50

Enter the Boss

Typically, managers entrusted to work on problems like these have bosses who ask questions such as the following:

The Boss: What is the profit going to be for the new product?

You: I'm not sure what profit's going to be because I don't know what sales or prices or costs are going to be.

The Boss: What are we paying you for? GIVE ME A NUMBER. I want it now, 15 minutes at the latest!

So back you go to your desk to come up with a number.

Enter the Worksheet

Luckily you have been building a worksheet model called PROFIT.xls to help you answer this question. Open this file now, as well as XLSim.xla, and follow this example on your own computer.

The boss needs the number now, so you do the simplest thing that comes to mind. You plug in averages of all the uncertain inputs in cells B5:B7 and fixed cost, the one number you are certain of, in cell B8 as shown in the following figure:

	A	B	C	D	E	F	G
1	PROFIT.XLS						
2					Market Scenarios		
3	Financials				Low Volume	High Volume	Average
4				Prob.	50%	50%	
5	Sales in Units	80,000		Units	60,000	100,000	80,000
6	Price per Unit	$ 9.00		Price	$10	$8	$9
7	Unit_Cost	$ 7.50					
8	Fixed_Costs	$ 30,000		Unit Cost Scenarios			
9				Low	Most Likely	High	Average
10	Profit	$90,000		$ 6.00	$ 7.50	$ 9.00	$ 7.50

=Sales * (Price – Unit_Cost) – Fixed_Cost

Great! Profit is $90,000, you have a number for the boss and 14 minutes to spare. Actually, that 14 minutes will provide plenty of time to refine your answer with Monte Carlo simulation, as described in the next section.

Monte Carlo Simulation: The Basic Steps

The basic steps of running a Monte Carlo simulation are

1. Build a model of the uncertain situation

2. Specify the simulation setting

3. Run the simulation and examine the results

These steps will now be discussed in detail in the context of the PROFIT example. The first step in creating a simulation is to model the uncertainty you face. In general, this constitutes the bulk of the work and comprises two parts: the worksheet and the uncertain inputs. Once you have developed the model, you will specify the settings for the simulation.

The Worksheet

The worksheet must reflect the relationships between the various numbers of the model, regardless of whether those numbers are certain or uncertain. This step has already been carried out in PROFIT.xls and consists of the formula for Profit in cell B10 shown earlier.

The Uncertainties

The uncertainties are modeled by formulas in the spreadsheet that output random numbers each time they calculate.

TUTORIAL: MODELING MARKET SCENARIOS

We will start by modeling the market scenario uncertainty.

1 In cell D11 enter the formula =RAND(). This is a built-in Excel function that produces numbers randomly between, but not including, 0 and 1. Such a function is known as a random number generator.

2 Press the calculate key (the F9 key in Windows or Command-= in Macintosh) a few times to see how it behaves. Cell D11 is just as likely to be greater than or less than 0.5. We will say that the high volume scenario has occurred when D11 is greater than 0.5, and the low volume scenario has occurred otherwise.

3 In cell B5, type the formula =IF($D$11>0.5,F5,E5), then copy it down one cell to B6. Use the **Edit Paste Special Formulas** command to avoid altering the currency formatting of cell B6. These formulas have the effect of plugging the high or low volume numbers into cells B5 and B6 with equal probabilities. Press the calculate key a few times to make sure it really works. The model should appear as shown below, although the exact numbers will depend on the RAND() function.

=IF($D$11 > 0.5,F5,E5)

	A	B	C	D	E	F	G
1	PROFIT.XLS						
2					**Market Scenarios**		
3	**Financials**				Low Volume	High Volume	Average
4				Prob.	50%	50%	
5	Sales in Units	100,000		Units	60,000	100,000	80,000
6	Price per Unit	$ 8.00		Price	$10	$8	$9
7	Unit_Cost	$ 7.50					
8	Fixed_Costs	$ 30,000		**Unit Cost Scenarios**			
9				Low	Most Likely	High	Average
10	Profit	$20,000		$ 6.00	$ 7.50	$ 9.00	$ 7.50
11				0.5067			

=IF($D$11 > 0.5,F6,E6)   =RAND()

TUTORIAL: MODELING UNIT COST

When you have estimates of a low, most likely, and high value for an uncertainty, it is often reasonable to use a random number generator with what is known as a Triangular Distribution. In this example, the number appearing in the cell will take on random values between $6.00 and $9.00 but not with equal likelihood. The most likely value is $7.50, with linearly decreasing probability as the values go to the extremes.

1 If you have not yet loaded XLSim.xla, do so now. Then, with the cursor in the Unit Cost cell B7, click on the function icon. The Function menu will appear. *Note*: The appearance of this menu varies with different versions of Excel.

Function Icon

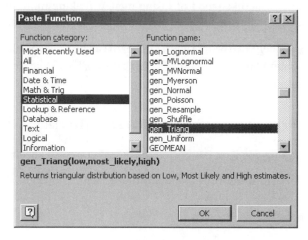

2 Select **Statistical** from the left menu, **gen_Triang** from the right menu, and click **OK***. (*Note:* for demonstrations of all the XLSim random number generators, see the file gen_Functions.xls). The following dialog box opens.

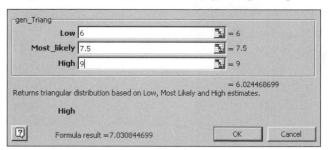

3 Fill in the **Low, Most_likely,** and **High** values as shown in the previous figure and click **OK.** As an alternative to entering numbers, you can place the cursor in the boxes in the dialog box, then click on the cell in the spreadsheet in which the desired number is stored, cells D10, E10, and F10 in this case. Unlike the market uncertainty that was modeled to give two discrete possibilities, high volume or low volume, unit cost can have a continuum of outcomes in our model. *Note*: Uncertainties come in both discrete and continuous varieties, and either or both can appear in a model.

4 Press the calculate key a few times to be sure all of the uncertain input cells are functioning. At first this appears to be a big step backwards. At least before you introduced uncertainties into your worksheet you had a number to give the boss. Now the model behaves like a can of worms.

* Early versions of Excel click **Next.**

At this stage you could perform a Monte Carlo simulation by pressing the calculate key a few hundred times while a friend with a clipboard records the values of profit in cell B10. By analyzing the hundreds of profit values on the clipboard, you could estimate the likelihood of losing money, making more than $10,000, making more than $20,000, and so forth, given that you decide to introduce the new product.

Fortunately, two people and a clipboard can be replaced today by a Visual Basic macro (XLSim.xla) as we will see in the next step. Save your changes to PROFIT.xls before continuing.

TUTORIAL: SPECIFYING THE SETTINGS FOR MONTE CARLO SIMULATION

1

Now that you have completed the model you must specify the simulation settings.

Select **Simulation** from the **Simulate** menu to open the following dialog box:

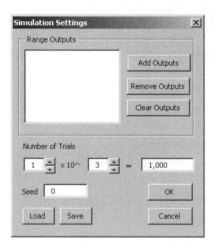

2

Click on the **Add Outputs** button and specify cell B10 in the field labeled Cells. This specifies the cell containing the profit formula as an **Output Cell.**

3

Then in the **Names** field either type "Profit" or specify cell A10, and click **OK**.

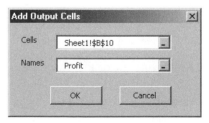

4

Make sure the number of **Trials** is set to 1,000.

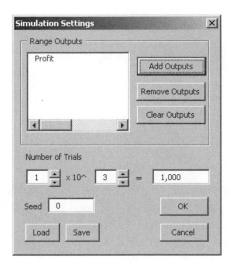

5

Click **OK** to run the simulation. This is equivalent to pressing the calculate key 1000 times while keeping track of each resulting profit.

Simulation Output

Statistics. You will see a count of the number of trials on the status bar until the simulation is finished, then the statistics of the simulation are displayed in a workbook called SimStats.xls. Observe the average profit.

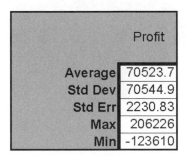

	Profit
Average	70523.7
Std Dev	70544.9
Std Err	2230.83
Max	206226
Min	-123610

Uh Oh! Although results will vary from run to run, the average value of profit for the 1000 trials will be around $70,000. This is considerably less than the $90,000 you were about to tell the boss!

There is also a lot of variability. Look at the maximum and minimum values of profit that occurred in the 1000 trials. The minimum value is probably quite negative, meaning there is a chance you could lose a lot of money. How are you going to explain that to the boss?

The Histogram. Select **Graphs** from the **Simulate** menu to open the **Graph Settings** dialog box:

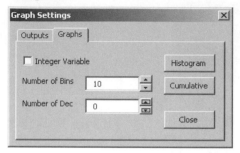

The Histogram button allows you to view the percentage of trials that fall into various intervals or *bins*. Reduce the number of decimal places to 0 and click **Histogram** (and then close). The histogram will be created on its own tab in the SimStats workbook. This graph shows the relative likelihood of profit falling into different ranges.

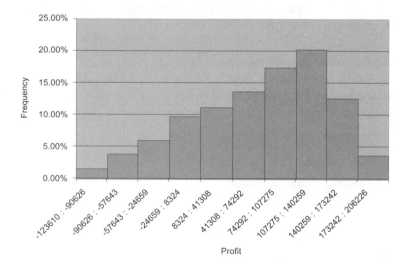

Notice that there is a 4% chance of a profit between roughly $175,000 and $205,000, but there is also a 2% chance of losing between $90,000 and $125,000.

The Cumulative Graph. Open the **Graph Settings** dialog box again, and then click the **Cumulative** button to create the cumulative graph. This shows the percentage of times that profit was less than or equal to the amount shown on the horizontal axis. The average, in this case about $70,000, is shown by a vertical line.

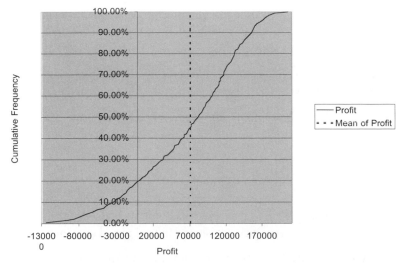

The likelihood of losing money may be determined by locating 0 on the horizontal axis (where the y-axis crosses), then going up to the curve to read the percent of trials that are less than 0, or about 20% in this case. Notice that there is about a 10% chance of losing $30,000 or more.

Back to the Boss

Once you are proficient in using simulation, the previous analysis could easily have been done in 10 minutes, allowing you to get back to the boss 4 minutes early. Let's listen in.

You: Well, Boss, if you average out all the things that might happen with this product, you should expect a profit of about $70,000. But that doesn't tell the whole story.

The Boss: What do you mean, "not the whole story"? I told you I want a number.

You: Well, the $70,000 average includes a 20% chance of losing money, and a 10% chance that we lose over $30,000. Look at this. (You hold up the cumulative graph). If it's a number you want for profit, here are all the numbers between –$130,000 and $200,000 with the probability that profit will be less than or equal to any of them.

The Boss: You mean there's one chance in five of losing money?

You: Right, but also an equal chance of making more than $120,000. You're the one who has to decide whether or not to go ahead with the new product. You need to evaluate the trade-offs between the upside and downside.

> The Boss: I guess you're right. Maybe we should run a simulation taking into account our entire product line to better analyze the total profit picture.

We flash forward one year and, unfortunately, the product has lost money. We first tune in on what would have happened if you hadn't bothered to run the simulation.

> The Boss: You told me we would make $90,000 and we lost money! You're fired!

Consider the scenario in which you ran the simulation.

> You: I'm sorry the product lost money.

> The Boss: Well, I knew the risks going in, and I decided to take the gamble. Even good decisions can lead to bad outcomes.

Of course, the boss might not really want to know about the range of possible outcomes. A manager who is aware that something undesirable can occur is responsible for doing something to prevent it. Thus managers sometimes have incentives to keep themselves in the dark and as far from cumulative probability graphs as possible. If you want to keep your own boss ignorant of legitimate risks, it's your business, but don't do so without considering the consequences.

Back to the Model

In a real problem, you must justify how you model the uncertainties. But even more important than the details of any individual uncertainty is deciding which uncertainties to model in the first place. For example, suppose you were estimating the economic output of an oil well in the Gulf of Mexico. You could spend months modeling the uncertain costs of drilling, the uncertain quantity and quality of oil produced, and the uncertain price of crude at time of delivery. But the precision of all this work is meaningless if you have neglected to take into account the chance that a tanker could collide with the platform causing a massive oil spill. When building a simulation model, think big.

THE BUILDING BLOCKS OF UNCERTAINTY

Now that the concept of Monte Carlo simulation has been introduced as a tool for dealing with uncertain events, we will get back to basics and examine the fundamental building blocks of uncertainty. These include the following:

■ **Uncertain Numbers: Random Variables**. Everyone must deal with numbers they are not certain of. Simulation will be used to demonstrate some of the most basic concepts regarding uncertain numbers, or *random variables*, as they are called.

- **Averages of Uncertain Numbers: Diversification.** As uncertain numbers are averaged, uncertainty is reduced. This is known as *diversification* and is an important manifestation of the *Central Limit Theorem*.

- **Some Important Classes of Uncertain Numbers: Idealized Distributions.** There are several important classes of idealized uncertain numbers. The most important of these are *normal* random variables.

- **Uncertain Numbers and Bad Outcomes: Risk Management.** Uncertainty is an objective feature of the universe. Risk is in the eye of the beholder; it depends on what you are afraid of. Risk management is the attempt to minimize the undesired outcomes of uncertainty.

■ FUNDAMENTALS 2-1

Random Variables

A *random variable* is a precise mathematical description of a number that you are uncertain of. For most practical purposes the term *uncertain number* is a preferable alternative.

Uncertain Numbers: Random Variables

Everyone must deal with numbers they are not certain of. We will use Monte Carlo simulation to demonstrate some of the most basic concepts regarding uncertain numbers. In your statistics course you may have seen this material described in terms of *random variables*.

Your firm's future sales, costs, and project durations are all numbers you don't know yet. While you grapple with this array of uncertainties, your boss, introduced in the previous tutorial, is likely to come in and demand "a number" for next year's profit. This section is devoted to developing a constructive response to such demands.

A Simple Example with a Spinner

As a simple example, consider the number pointed to by a game board spinner like the one simulated in SPINNER.xls. This random variable is also built into every worksheet as the function =RAND(), which behaves just like a spinner, outputting a different number between 0 and 1 every time it calculates.

Type =RAND() into a blank workbook and press the calculate key (the F9 key in Windows and Command-= in Macintosh) a few times to see how it behaves.

■ FUNDAMENTALS 2-2

Continuous and Discrete Random Variables

A random variable, such as the outcome of a spinner, is known as a ***continuous*** random variable because it can take on all values between two extreme values. A random variable, such as the outcome of rolling dice, is known as a ***discrete*** random variable because it can take on only distinct values.

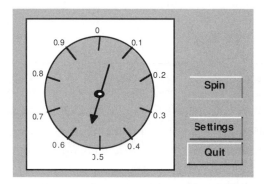

To attach more meaning to the spinner example, imagine that your company's profit for next year displayed the same degree of uncertainty as if someone twirled the spinner and then multiplied the result by $1 million. To make it more interesting, suppose further that if profit is less than $200,000, you will be laid off.

Before running a simulation to analyze profit, test your intuition by trying to answer the following questions:

EXERCISE
2.1   **Test Your Intuition on Random Variables**

a.   If you faced this same situation repeatedly, what profit would you expect, on average?

b.   What is your likelihood of getting laid off?

c.   What should you tell the boss when they demand "a number" for profit?

d.   Starting with the following diagram, create a bar graph that shows the percentage of times that profit in millions is likely to fall between 0 and 0.2, 0.2 and 0.4, and so forth.

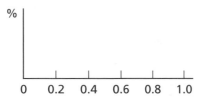

Quickly jot down your answers on a piece of paper, including a sketch for part d, passing over those questions for which you have no ready answer. We will now run a simulation to answer these questions.

Building the Model: Simulation Setting and Output

The first step in creating a worksheet simulation is to model the uncertainty you face. In general, this constitutes the bulk of the work but in this case there is not much to it.

To model profit in millions, simply type =RAND() into a cell such as A1 in a blank workbook. Press the calculate key a few times to observe the random results. This single cell is the whole model.

TUTORIAL: SPECIFYING SIMULATION SETTINGS

1 Select **Simulation** to bring up the following dialog box. If the settings from the previous simulation still appear in the outputs box, you should remove them using the **Clear Outputs** button. Next, press the **Add Outputs** button and specify the cell containing the profit formula as the **Output Cell**. Then type "Profit in Millions" into the Name field and click **OK.**

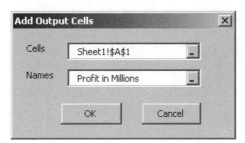

2 Specify 10,000 trials by clicking on the small arrows next to the field on the left.

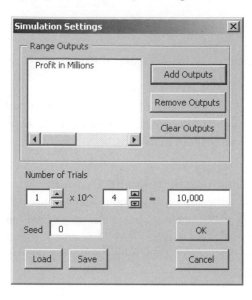

3 Click **OK** to run the simulation.

Statistics. Now let's now examine the simulation we just created. Although results will vary from run to run, the average value over the 5000 trials will be close to 0.5 million as shown, in the following figure. The remaining statistics will be discussed in later examples.

	Profit in Millions
Average	0.497048825
Std Dev	0.290201394
Std Err	0.004104067
Max	0.999747932
Min	0.000170396

Create a histogram with 5 bins using the **Simulate Graphs** command. The graph will be created on its own tab in the SIMSTATS workbook. This shows that roughly equal numbers fell into each of the five intervals 0–0.2, 0.2–0.4, and so forth. If enough trials were run, the bars would be perfectly uniform. In fact, the technical term for RAND() is a *uniform* random variable[2]. This is the shape you should have

---

[2] Although we have used RAND() here for simplicity, the equivalent function built into XLSim (gen_Uniform(0,1)) offers more control, and should be used for serious simulations.

drawn in question d in the previous exercise. Yet a surprising number of people draw something that is clearly higher in some places than others, which would indicate, erroneously, that the arrow of the spinner is more likely to stop in some places than in others.

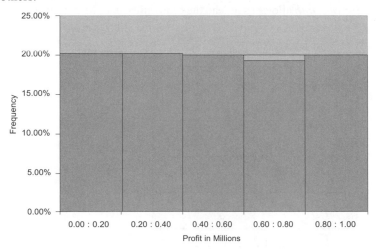

■ FUNDAMENTALS 2-3

Histograms

An uncertain number can be thought of as a shape, known as a *histogram*, which depicts the likelihood that the number will take on different values.

The intervals covered by the bars are called bins. The histogram can have any shape, as long as the bars total 100%. If you think of the bars as blocks of wood sitting on a board, then the *average*, also known as the *mean* or *expected value* of the uncertain number, is the point at which the board would balance.

The more trials you run and the more bins you add, the greater the accuracy of the picture of the uncertain number. If you were to run an extremely large number of trials with extremely narrow bins, your histogram would approach the *probability distribution*, which displays all possible outcomes of the uncertain number.

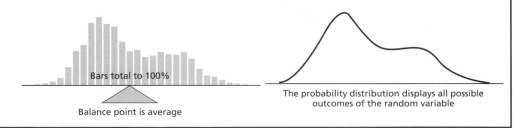

■ **FUNDAMENTALS 2-4**

The Cumulative Graph

The *cumulative graph* allows us to read the probability that the output cell is less than or equal to any particular number. This may be the most useful way to express an uncertainty to your boss.

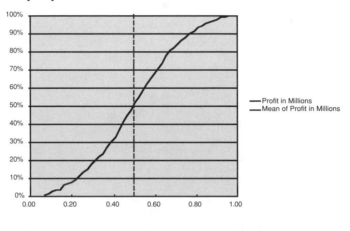

Now on to question 1b: What is your likelihood of getting laid off? Remember that if a number less than 0.2 is spun, you're on the street. Select the **Statistics** tab of the SIMSTATS worksheet, then click on the **Cumulative** button. The likelihood that the output cell will be less than any particular number can be read from the cumulative graph, which is created on its own sheet.

In particular, the likelihood of getting laid off is found by locating 0.2 on the horizontal axis, then going up to the diagonal line and over to the vertical axis to read the percent of trials that were less than 0.2, or 20%.

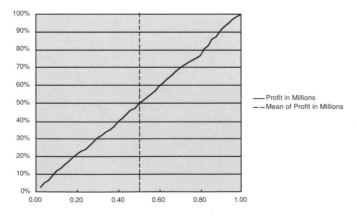

■ **FUNDAMENTALS 2-5**

The Mean, Mode, and Median

The *mean* of an uncertain number can be thought of as the balance point of its histogram. Related concepts are the *mode*, the place with the tallest bar, and the *median*, the bar with equal weight to its right and left. In general the mean, mode, and median will be different unless the histogram is symmetric.

■ **FUNDAMENTALS 2-6**

The Variance and Standard Deviation

Several measures of the spread or degree of uncertainty of a number have been defined. A common calculation used to represent the degree of uncertainty is the *variance*, σ^2. This is calculated by subtracting the average from the uncertain number, squaring that difference, and taking the average of those squared differences.

Because we are squaring the numbers, the variance ends up in squared units. Thus you might have a stock portfolio with expected earnings of $10,000 with the variance in earnings equal to 1 million square dollars. Because squared units are not intuitive, the square root of the variance, known as the *standard deviation*, σ, is often used.

How about question 1c: What do you tell the boss when you are asked for "a number" for profit? As discussed in the tutorial, the cumulative graph shows *all* the possible numbers on the horizontal axis, so that one can immediately determine the likelihood that profit will be less than or equal to any particular number by going up to the line then over to the vertical axis. Of course you should point out that the average would be $500,000 if you faced this situation repeatedly, but it is important for the boss to be aware of the entire range of outcomes as displayed on the cumulative graph.

People often give the boss the mean when "a number" is demanded, but this can be very misleading. For example, if you buy a lottery ticket for $1 that has one chance in a million of paying $2 million, on average you'll be $1 ahead. However, this figure alone hardly expresses the uncertainty of the situation. The mean, mode, median, variance, and standard deviation together provide a more complete picture of the situation, but the real key to understanding uncertain numbers is the shape or distribution.

The Distribution Gives the Complete Picture

The variance and the standard deviation are not very intuitive. Fortunately, the boss doesn't need to understand them to benefit from the complete picture provided by the cumulative distribution. Later, however, we will see that the standard error, which is related to the standard deviation, plays a central role in determining the accuracy of the simulation results.

Consider a parallel in which learning the value of some uncertain number is analogous to apprehending a criminal. The mean and standard deviation are similar to the height and weight of the suspect: They are definitely useful information if it's all you've got. The graphs and percentiles representing the distribution, on the other hand, are analogous to mug shots and DNA samples of the suspect, and provide a complete identification.

Averages of Uncertain Numbers: Diversification and the Central Limit Theorem

As uncertain numbers are averaged together, uncertainty is reduced. This is known as *diversification* and is an important manifestation of the Central Limit Theorem.

It is naive, of course, to think that profit is determined by spinning a spinner and multiplying by a million dollars. Suppose, instead, that profit displays the uncertainty of *two* spins averaged together and then multiplied by a million dollars. As before, a profit of less than $200,000 results in being laid off.

Before proceeding, test your intuition by answering the same questions about this more complicated example.

EXERCISE
2.2

TEST YOUR INTUITION ON RANDOM VARIABLES AGAIN

a.   If you faced this same situation repeatedly, what would profit be on average?

b.   What is your likelihood of getting laid off?

c.   What should you tell the boss when they demand" a number" for profit?

d.   Starting with the following diagram, create a bar graph that shows the percentage of times profit is likely to fall between 0 and 0.2, 0.2 and 0.4, and so on.

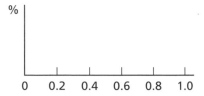

Actually, we'll answer question 2.2c right away. In most situations involving uncertain numbers, you should train your boss to start asking, "What's the distribution?" instead of "What's the number?"

Now simulate the average of two spins:

1. Return to the workbook containing the cell that models profit and replace =RAND() with =(RAND()+RAND())/2 or =AVERAGE(RAND(),RAND()). Be sure to get the parentheses right.

2. Specify the settings exactly as in the single spinner example.

3. Generate simulation statistics, histogram, and cumulative distribution, as in the single spinner example.

The Central Limit Theorem

The simulation yields an average profit of about 0.5 million, so that the answer to question 2a remains unchanged from the case of the single spin.

Output Name	Profit in Millions
Average	0.50107
Std Dev	0.21256
Std Err	0.00951
Max	0.96908
Min	0.01883

Now look at the histogram. It goes *up* in the middle with two spins. If you drew anything that went up in the middle for question 2d, give yourself full credit. We will discuss the actual shape later. But first, why did it go up in the middle, and more important, so what?

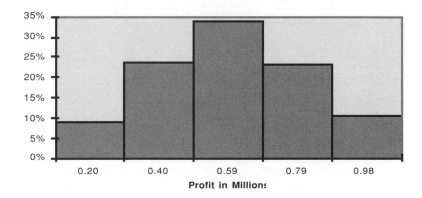

The answer to the question "so what?" is provided immediately by the histogram. The bars must total 100%, so the fact that the graph got taller in the center means that it must have shrunk on the ends. Therefore the chance of getting laid off has been reduced. This is one of the principle manifestations of *diversification* and is at the heart of the Central Limit Theorem, which will be discussed shortly.

■ **FUNDAMENTALS 2-7**

Diversification and Variance Reduction

When uncertain numbers are averaged together, the distribution of the average goes up in the middle and down on the ends, becoming more centralized. This centralizing of the distribution is the primary manifestation of ***diversification***.

The width or narrowness of a distribution defines the range of uncertainty of the number. The wider the distribution, the greater the variance, standard deviation, and uncertainty; the narrower the distribution, the smaller the variance, standard deviation, and uncertainty.

Evaluating the Results

The likelihood that the average of the two spins is less than 0.2 is read from the cumulative graph. This confirms that the probability of getting laid off has dropped sharply from what it was in the case of the single spin. In fact, it has dropped from 20% to about 8%.

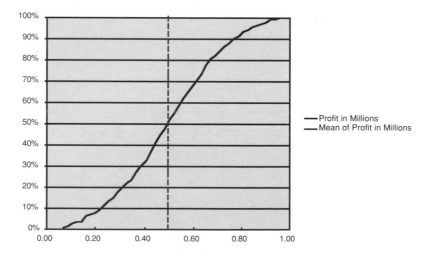

Why Did the Histogram Go Up in the Middle? Consider what happens when you roll a die: You can get any number between 1 and 6 with equal probabilities of 1/6. The histogram looks like the following figure:

When you roll two dice, you can get any number between 2 and 12, but still with equal probability? If you think so, you'd better stay out of Las Vegas! There is only one way to get a 2 or 12, but six ways to get a 7 and intermediate numbers of ways to get the values in between.

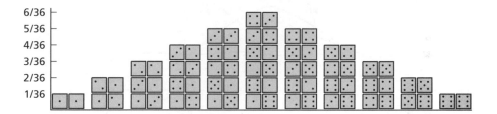

Now back to the average of two spinners: Imagine that the spinner moved in increments of 1/100th. Then the only way for the average of two spins to equal zero is for both spins to be zero. On the other hand, for two spins to average 0.5, you could spin 0 and 1, .01 and .99, .02 and .98, and so on. This change in the shape of the distribution as uncertain numbers are added together or averaged is at the heart of the most important result in probability theory: the Central Limit Theorem.

The Central Limit Theorem does not apply only to spinners For an example involving the return on investments in the Hollywood film industry see Savage (2001b).

■ FUNDAMENTALS 2-8

The Central Limit Theorem

Simulation can be used to visualize the effect of averaging uncertain numbers. The figure below, created by running thousands of trials and using the Common Graph option for all outputs, compares the distributions of RAND() and the averages of 2 RAND()s, 3 RAND()s, and 12 RAND()s.

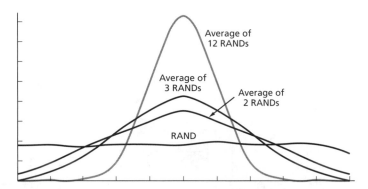

By the time 12 RAND()s have been averaged the resulting distribution is virtually indistinguishable from the famous *Normal* distribution or ***bell-shaped curve***. The precise manner in which this occurs is the subject of the ***Central Limit Theorem***, which states that if enough independent samples of almost any distribution (not just RAND()'s) are averaged together, that the resulting distribution is normal.

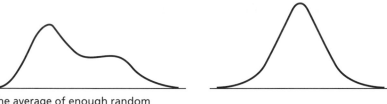

The average of enough random variables that look like this (or almost anything else for that matter) . . .

looks like this.

EXERCISE
2.3   THE DISTRIBUTION OF THE MAXIMUM OF TWO UNIFORM RANDOM VARIABLES

What is the shape of the distribution of the maximum of two independent uniform random variables? *Hint*: Simulate this using the RAND() and the MAX() functions.

EXERCISE
2.4   SIMULATING DICE

a. Create a cell in the worksheet that simulates the roll of a single die starting with the RAND() formula. *Hint*: Use the INT() function. When creating the histogram of a discrete random variable such as this that takes on integer values, it is best to select the **Integer Variable** option.

b. Simulate the sum of the roll of two dice and compare the histogram to that of the single die. What do you observe?

Creating Histograms in Excel

It is often useful to display the histogram of data stored in Excel. A convenient way to do this is through the **Simulate Data Range** command of XLSim. Simply select the range containing the data, and (optionally) give it a name, then click OK.

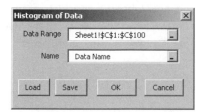

A statistical report, Histogram and Cumulative graph are then available as if you had run a simulation of a single output cell. The exercises that follow describe some additional ways to create histograms in Excel.

EXERCISE
2.5   CREATING AN INTERACTIVE HISTOGRAM USING =FREQUENCY

The Excel function =FREQUENCY(data_array, bins_array) returns the count of numbers in **data_array** that lie in each of a set of intervals specified in **bins_array**. This is known as a frequency distribution, the graph of which is a histogram. The FREQUENCY function is an array formula, which makes it a little tricky to use, but it is very powerful. Refer to the Excel Help system to learn how to enter array formulas, then create a histogram of =RAND() as follows.

a. Type =RAND() into a cell A1 in a blank worksheet and copy it down to A50. This will be the data array. In cells B1:B5 type the numbers 0.2, 0.4, 0.6, 0.8, and 1. This will be the bin array. Select cells C1:C5 to hold the frequency array. Next click the Function Wizard and select Statistical from the left menu and FREQUENCY from the right menu. Fill in the data_array and bins_array, then click **OK**. Even though you clicked **OK**, you are NOT FINISHED! Your worksheet should now appear as shown in the following figure.

C1		=FREQUENCY(A1:A50,B1:B5)		
	A	**B**	**C**	**D**
1	0.147701	0.2	10	
2	0.781992	0.4		
3	0.153136	0.6		
4	0.160842	0.8		
5	0.843211	1		

b. Be sure cells C1:C5 are selected. If they are not, select them now. Next click in the formula bar to go into edit mode, then press **Shift-Ctrl-Enter** (**Command-Enter** on the Macintosh®)[3]. The array C1:C5 should be filled in, and {}s should appear around the function in the formula bar. This signifies that you have correctly entered the function as an array formula. Press the calculate key a few times and observe frequency count change as you generate random numbers.

c. Graph C1:C5 to produce a histogram. Observe the histogram changes as you press the calculate key a few times. I refer to a live or interactive histogram as a *Blitzogram* Savage(2001a,b). Save this file, then go on to the next exercise.

EXERCISE
2.6 CREATING SIMULATIONS WITH DATA TABLES

The Data Table is a very powerful but seldom used spreadsheet command. Among its many other applications, it can be used to do simple simulations as follows. (**Warning!** This approach will sometimes crash certain versions of Excel.)

a. Starting with the worksheet developed in the last exercise, place the cursor in column A and insert a column with the **Insert Column** command. Next erase all the RAND() formulas (now in column B) except the one in the first row. Now select cells A1:B50 and invoke the **Data Table** command. Then place the cursor in the Column Input Cell field of the dialog box, click on

---

[3] Array formulas are powerful, but require careful application. The complicated set of keystrokes required to use them is analogous to using a baby proof cap on a medicine bottle.

any cell in the worksheet and press enter. Cells B2:B50 should fill up with new trials of the RAND() formula in cell B1. Press the calculate key a few times, and observe the histogram.

b.   Next, replace the formula in cell B1 with =(RAND()+RAND())/2 and observe the change in the histogram. Save the worksheet and go on to the next exercise.

c.   Your current histogram can handle any random number between 0 and 1. Modify the bin range so that the histogram can handle numbers in column B with an arbitrary maximum and minimum value.

EXERCISE 2.7

USING THE HISTOGRAM COMMAND FROM THE DATA ANALYSIS TOOLS

Another way to create histograms is with the Data Analysis Tools. Invoke the **Tools Data Analysis** command, then select Histogram from the menu. Find actual data on the world wide web, then create a histogram, first using the Excel **Histogram** command, then using the **Data Range** command in XLSim.

Important Classes of Uncertain Numbers: Idealized Distributions

In reality, every uncertain number has its own distribution. However, the theory of probability has led to important classes of idealized distributions that approximate the behavior of many real world random variables. Given the implications of the Central Limit Theorem, it is not surprising that a lot of random variables are approximately normally distributed. A discussion of applications of the Normal distribution along with other important idealized distributions follows.

■   The *Normal* distribution plays a fundamental role in virtually all branches of science. Some simplified examples follow:

Physics

The velocity of a given air molecule is determined by adding up the results of all the collisions it has had with other air molecules. Hence air molecule velocities are normally distributed.

Biology

The size of a given animal involves averages of the sizes of all its ancestors. Hence the size of animals of a given species (along with almost everything else you can measure in biology) tends to be normally distributed.

■ **FUNDAMENTALS 2-9**

The Normal Distribution

The *Normal distribution* is an idealization of the result of averaging a large number of identical, independent random variables.

All Normal distributions look basically the same. They differ from each other in only two respects: where they are centered and how wide they are. They are centered at their mean or average, often referred to as μ. Their width is measured by the *standard deviation*, σ, the square root of the variance.

You may think of σ as one-sixth of the distance that spans 99% of all occurrences of the random variable. That is, 99% of the time, a normal random variable will be within 3σ above or below its mean. Also, 95% and 68% of the distribution lies between plus and minus 2σ and 1σ around the mean, respectively.

These percentages hold only for the Normal distribution. If you run a simulation, however, you can determine such percentiles from the statistics screen and cumulative graph for any type of distribution.

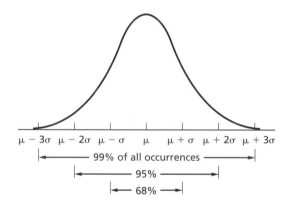

Finance

Consider an initial investment I that over time gets repeatedly multiplied by random growth factors. Suppose, for example, that in the first month it grew by a factor of 1.1, then shrank by a factor of .97 in the second month, and grew by a factor of 1.2 in the third month. The value at the end of three months would be I*1.1*0.97*1.2. If you have studied logarithms you may remember that they transform multiplication to addition. So the logarithm of the value after three months is

Log(I)+Log(1.1)+Log(.97)+Log(1.2). And therefore the log of the value of the investment after a large number of periods is the sum of a large quantity of random numbers, and is hence approximately normally distributed. An uncertain number whose logarithm is normally distributed is known as *Lognormal*. This is why investment prices are often modeled as Lognormal random variables, as will be demonstrated in the next chapter.

■ The *Binomial* distribution models a process like a sequence of coin flips in which you are concerned with the total number of heads. For example, suppose your firm has produced a batch of 50 circuit boards, each of which has a 2% chance of being defective. The total number of defective boards in the batch can be modeled with a binomial distribution. We will see the Binomial distribution again in the next chapter.

■ The *Poisson* distribution models a process such as the number of phone calls arriving per minute at a call center, or the monthly number of orders for a product or service.

■ The *Exponential* distribution models the time between phone calls or orders of a product or service. The Poisson and Exponential distribution will appear again in the discussion of waiting lines in Chapter 4.

XLSim.xla provides formulas for generating random variables from several idealized distributions, as described in the technical reference and demonstrated in gen_Functions.xls. The following example involves a normal random variable.

An Investment Example

The percentage returns on certain financial investments are modeled by normal random variables. As discussed, Normal distributions can be fully specified by their means and standard deviations, and a wealth of on-line financial data is available to help you estimate these. In this example, we will explore the effect of splitting an investment budget between two similar but independent funds.

Suppose that you are managing the financial portfolio of a large municipality and must allocate all your investment between a domestic and foreign mutual fund. Imagine that the returns of the two funds are very similar, but independent. That is, the likelihood of either one going up or down is not affected by what the other one does. Analysis indicates that the percentage return of each is normally distributed with a mean of 10% and a standard deviation of 10%. That is, the return from each fund is shaped like the picture on the next page. This implies that you should expect to earn 10 cents for each dollar invested. There is also a chance of losing money, however, in which case the municipality will default on the salaries of teachers and fire fighters.

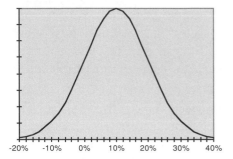

We can find the probability of losing money with either of these funds as follows: Use the following Excel formula for the Normal distribution to calculate the probability of making 0 or less (that is, losing money) from an investment with a mean and standard deviation of 10%.

=NORMDIST(0, 0.1, 0.1, TRUE)

The first argument indicates that you are calculating the probability of 0 dollars or less. The next two arguments are the mean and standard deviation respectively. The last argument of this function is TRUE indicating the cumulative form of the distribution. This calculation indicates a 16% chance of losing money.

Although this Excel formula allowed us to analyze a single investment, additional knowledge of probability theory would be required to determine the likelihood of losing money with an investment split between both funds. However, it is easy to simulate the returns on the following three strategies:

1. Invest all in the domestic fund.

2. Invest all in the foreign fund.

3. Split investment between the two funds.

EXERCISE
2.8   **TEST YOUR INTUITION ABOUT INVESTMENTS**

Perhaps you are ready to answer the following questions:

a. How do the average returns of the three investments compare?

b. What is the relative likelihood of losing money for each of the three investments?

TUTORIAL: SIMULATING THE RETURNS

Model the return of the domestic fund, the foreign fund, and an investment split between the two by following these steps:

Make sure that XLSim.xla is loaded, then open a blank workbook. Place the cursor in cell A3 where we will model the return of the domestic fund, then click on the function icon. The Paste Function dialog box, shown below, opens.

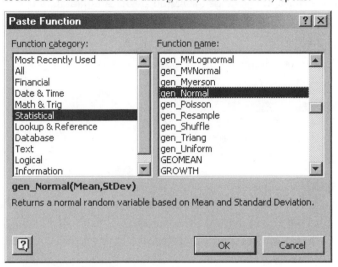

Select **Statistical** from the left menu and **gen_Normal** from the right menu, and click **OK**, which opens the following dialog box:

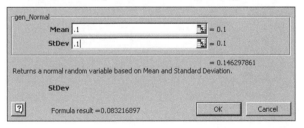

Type .1 for both the mean and the standard deviation and click **OK**. Press the calculate key a few times to be sure the cell is properly generating random numbers. *Note:* XLSim's random number generator functions all start with "gen_". Before opening an Excel workbook that uses these functions, you should first open XLSim.xla[4]. Do not confuse these functions with the built-in distribution functions in Excel such as the NORMDIST function discussed earlier. NORMDIST does not return random numbers at all, but is an on-line table of the Normal distribution useful in statistical calculations.

---

[4] Be sure you learn how to use the Freeze and Thaw commands as discussed in Appendix C.

4

Copy the domestic fund formula to cell B3 to model the foreign fund, which has the same distribution of returns as the domestic fund. Again, press the calculate key a few times. You should see the two numbers vary independently.

Note: Although the domestic and foreign returns have the same distribution, you must not place **gen_Normal** (0.1, 0.1) in a single cell which is then referred to by both funds. This would result in the two funds moving in lock step, which would be extremely unrealistic and invalidate the results of the simulation.

5

If we were to split the investment equally between the domestic and foreign funds, the return would be the average of the two returns. So create a new cell with this result, (A3+B3)/2, as shown in the following figure:

	C3	↧		=(A3+B3)/2	
	A	**B**	**C**	**D**
1	Domestic	Foreign	Split	
2	Return	Return	Return	
3	0.282127	-0.00445	0.138839	
4				

6

In this example we will monitor more than one output cell. Click **Add Outputs** from the **Simulation Settings** dialog box. Select the range A3:C3 in the **Cells** box and the range A1:C1 in the **Names** box. The names can also be entered directly, separated by commas. Click **OK** and the setup screen should appear as shown in the following figure. Run 1000 trials.

Evaluating Simulation Output

The Statistics. The simulation statistics display the average returns of each strategy along with other useful statistics.

The average return of each of the three investments is the same: around 10%. However, the standard deviation of the split investment is significantly lower than the other two (about 7% compared with 10%). Notice the maximum and minimum values over the thousand trials.

		Domestic	Foreign	Split
Average return of investments →	**Average**	0.101464	0.09665	0.09906
Standard deviation of investments →	**Std Dev**	0.100641	0.10029	0.07079
	Std Err	0.003183	0.00317	0.00224
Maximum to minimum →	**Max**	0.426738	0.51631	0.31639
range of invertments →	**Min**	-0.224845	-0.2298	-0.0961

Clearly the outcomes of the pure investments are more uncertain than is that of the split. This is a double-edged sword; in this example, the only way to reduce the downside risk of a big loss is to forego the opportunity of a large gain.

The Percentiles. The percentiles contain the same information as the cumulative graphs but in numeric form. For example, the 25th percentile of the domestic fund (in the first column) is roughly .03. This means that we would expect the domestic fund to have a return of 3% or less with a chance of 25%.

The table shows that the two pure investments (columns 1 and 2) made essentially no money or less about 15% of the time. The split investment, on the other hand, made 0 or less with a chance of 5%. This is three times less likely to lose money than either of the pure investments.

Percentiles			
5%	-0.064233	-0.0637	-0.0178
10%	-0.029925	-0.0341	0.01026
15%	-0.005275	-0.0094	0.02467
20%	0.017673	0.0135	0.03765
25%	0.032521	0.03063	0.0505
30%	0.047177	0.04827	0.06077
35%	0.063222	0.05701	0.07236
40%	0.076823	0.07096	0.0817
45%	0.089416	0.08571	0.09075
50%	0.102941	0.09673	0.09801

At the other end of the spectrum, the pure investments returned about 22% or more 10% (100%–90%) of the time, whereas the split made more than 22% less than 5% of the time.

90%	0.226779	0.22532	0.19076
95%	0.263721	0.26417	0.21273
100%	0.426738	0.51631	0.31639

The Histogram. Because we are interested in the comparative anatomy of these different investments, select **Common Graphs** from the **Simulate** menu. On the **Outputs** tab check the boxes for the variables you want to show on the common graph.

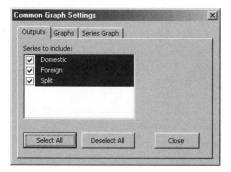

Interactive. On the **Graphs** tab select the **Interactive Blitzogram**™ type and click the **Histogram** button. This creates a histogram for each output on separate worksheets. You can see how the histogram changes shape, output by output, by using the **Ctrl+PgUp** and **Ctrl+PgDn** keys.

2D Line. You can also see the histograms superimposed by using the 2D Line Graph. On the **Graphs** tab select a **2D Line** histogram type and check the **Smoothed** box which becomes visible after the **2D Line** option is selected, as shown below. Click the **Histogram** button.

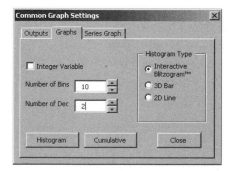

Because of the smoothing, the numerical results of the smoothed histograms are not dependable, and they should be used for qualitative comparisons only. For quantitative results, use either the percentiles or the common cumulative graph as described later.

The domestic and foreign investments have nearly the same shape, whereas the split investment clearly shows how diversification leads to a narrower distribution.

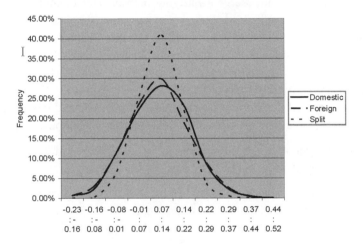

The Common Cumulative Graph. This again shows a single average of 10% for all three investments, nearly identical distributions for the domestic and foreign outcomes, and the narrower distribution of the split investment. The probabilities of making a given amount (or less) in each case can be read by going to the desired amount on the horizontal axis, then up to the appropriate curve and over to the vertical axis.

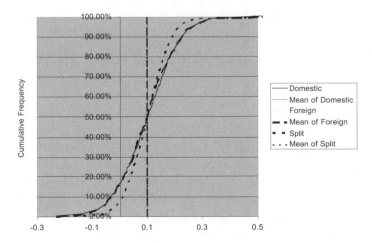

All graphs are generated within Excel and can be edited using the Chart Wizard as we did earlier.

Risk vs. Uncertainty: Risk Management

Risk management involves the systematic study of the uncertainties facing an organization for the purpose of identifying both undesirable outcomes and managerial steps that reduce their likelihood of occurrence. Simulation can play a central role in this activity, as we will see in the next chapter. This chapter will end with a brief discussion of risk vs. uncertainty to lay the groundwork.

Risk is in the Eye of the Beholder

The words *risk* and *uncertainty* are often used imprecisely and interchangeably. For the purposes of this discussion I will make following distinction.

Uncertainty is an objective feature of the universe. The position of a spinner or the price of a given stock cannot be known exactly in advance.

Risk is a subjective measure of how one feels about the various possible outcomes of an uncertain event. For those who are long on a particular stock, the risk is that the price will go down. For those who have shorted the stock, the risk is that the price will go up.

Risk Attitude measures the degree to which an individual or organization tolerates risk. An extremely risk averse individual may be concerned about choking on their breakfast cereal. At the other extreme, a thrill seeker getting out of bed on the same morning might be worried about being late for their sky diving lesson.

Value at Risk: Managing Risk in the Investment Example

Case 1: Downside Risk. In the previous investment example there would be serious consequences if the investment lost money. If this is the risk that concerns you, it would be sound risk management to split the investment rather than invest purely in either the domestic or the foreign fund. This reduces the likelihood of losing money from 15% to 5%, keeping the average return at 10%.

Case 2: Upside Risk. Imagine that you are investing privately, have plenty of money in the bank, and few obligations to others. You are not worried about losing money, but will be upset if you don't make at least 22% on your investment. With this risk attitude, you would choose either the pure domestic or foreign fund because each presents a 10% chance of achieving your goal compared with less than 5% for the split investment as read from the percentile table of the simulation.

Value at Risk. A downside risk measurement that is gaining in popularity is known as Value at Risk or VaR. Suppose that the amount to be invested in the previous example had been $100,000. Then looking back at the percentiles we see that 5% of the time with the domestic fund we would have lost 6.2% or more. Thus, the *value at risk* at the 5% level for the domestic fund is $6,200. By comparison, the value at risk at the 5% level for the split fund is only about $1,400.

Conclusion

In this chapter we introduced the concept of Monte Carlo simulation in the context of a tutorial involving uncertain profit. We then used this powerful technique to explore some general properties of uncertain numbers, or random variables as they are known. The chapter closed with a short discussion of risk management. In the next chapter we will investigate more complex models involving uncertainty.

END OF CHAPTER 2 EXERCISES

2.9 ANALYZING DATA

For the following set of numbers: (3, 2, 1, 2, 3, 1, 3, 3, 2, 1)

a. Create a histogram

b. Create the cumulative graph

c. Find the Average, Median and Mode

2.10 COMBINATION OF THREE DICE

a. List the combinations on three dice that would result in each of the numbers from 3 to 18.

b. Make a bar chart of the results with the numbers 3 through 18 on the x axis, and the number of combinations on the y axis.

2.11 EXPLORING FOR REAL DATA

Collect data from the Internet on each of the following and investigate their distributions using the **Data Range** command in XLSim.

a. Daily stock prices.

b. Batting averages of major league baseball players.

c. Distances in light-years of various stars from the earth.

Explain any differences that you observe.

3 ■■■■■■■■■■■■■■■■■■■■■■■■■■■■■■

The Buildings of Uncertainty: Functions of Random Variables

If a man will begin with certainties, he shall end in doubts, but if he will be content to begin with doubts, he shall end in certainties.

FRANCIS BACON, ENGLISH PHILOSOPHER

Every day millions of managers input uncertain numbers into elaborate spreadsheet models.

- Marketing directors input uncertain levels of customer satisfaction into models to predict profitability.

- Logistics managers input uncertain demands into models that specify inventory levels.

- Investors input uncertain security prices into investment models.

- Personnel directors input uncertain workload requirements into models to estimate labor cost.

The uncertain outputs of worksheet models with uncertain inputs are known technically as functions of random variables. It is tempting to plug "best guesses" as inputs into such models, in the hope that what comes out are the "best guesses" for the outputs. According to Francis Bacon (and confirmed by probability theory), it is doubtful that this hope is realized. Monte Carlo simulation, on the other hand, begins with doubts. That is, instead of plugging in a single "best guess," it keeps the full range of uncertain inputs alive, providing results that are ultimately more certain.

∎ ∎ ∎ OVERVIEW

We discuss more complex spreadsheet models involving uncertain inputs.

Tutorial: Estimating Inventory Costs Given Uncertain Demand

We examine an inventory model with uncertain demand and investigate the implications of using "best guesses" or point estimates as inputs. Two general techniques for estimating input distributions are introduced: resampling past data and generating triangular random variables.

The Buildings of Uncertainty

If uncertain numbers (random variables) are the building blocks of uncertainty, then worksheet models with uncertain inputs are buildings of uncertainty. Technically these are known as functions of random variables. This section describes some important business examples, and simple ways to analyze them with Monte Carlo simulation. Also discussed are uncertain numbers that depend on other uncertain numbers. These are known as dependent random variables.

INTRODUCTION

In the last chapter we addressed very simple models containing at most one formula beyond the random inputs. Furthermore, we assumed that the random variable inputs were from known idealized distributions: uniform in the spinner examples and normal in the investment example.

In real world situations, the worksheet models are far more complex, and worse, unless you are a statistician, you will have difficulty in specifying idealized distributions for the input cells. Even if you *are* a statistician and know how to use some distribution with an exotic sounding name, you might have difficulty justifying your assumption to the boss. This is the stage at which people often throw up their hands and pull "a number" out of thin air.

TUTORIAL: ESTIMATING INVENTORY COSTS GIVEN UNCERTAIN DEMAND

In this tutorial, we use an example that shows how even a simulation based on informal assumptions can provide valuable insights. Be sure XLSim.xla is loaded before proceeding.

An Inventory Problem

A pharmaceutical supply firm inventories cases of a perishable drug for which demand is uncertain, as represented by 36 months of historical data. The average demand has been 5 cases per month, so this is the number the firm currently stocks.

The operating cost of maintaining the inventory has two components:

■ If at the end of the month the demand has been less than the number stocked, the excess cases will have expired and must be destroyed at a loss of $50 per unit.

■ If the demand is greater than the number stocked, the additional units must be air freighted at additional cost. The air freight rate fluctuates depending on the capacity of the carrier. Although good records have not been kept, the shipping clerk indicates that it is most likely $150 per unit. However, he admits it can range from a low of $100 to a high of $300.

This situation is modeled in INVNTORY.xls, which you should open now. The formulas are displayed below (cells C5, C6, and C8). Notice in the following figure that some of the cells have been named for clarity.

	A	B	C	D	E	F	G	H
1	Demand		Amt Stocked					
2	5		5					
3								
4	Costs	Per Unit	Total					
5	Expiration Cost	$50.00	=IF(Amt_Stocked>Demand,(Amt_Stocked-Demand)*Exp_Cost,0)					
6	Air Freight	$150.00	=IF(Amt_Stocked<Demand,(Demand-Amt_Stocked)*F_Cost,0)					
7								
8	Overall Cost		=C5+C6					

The sheet also contains 36 months of historical demand data starting in cell B14. Note the average demand of 5 calculated in cell C14.

C14		=AVERAGE(B14:B49)
	A	B	C
12	Historical Data		
13	Month	Demand	Average
14	1	10	5
15	2	6	
16	3	10	
17	4	8	
18	5	7	
19	:	:	

Try plugging some of the numbers from the demand column into cell A2 to see how the total cost is affected.

This time the boss says, "What is inventory operating cost going to be next month? I know it might vary, so just give me the average, and be quick about it." It is common in situations like this to plug in the average of the uncertain inputs, then read the corresponding "average" outputs from the model. This is known as using *point estimates* because you have used single points (5 and 150 in this case) as "best guesses" to represent the entire ranges of demand and freight cost. Plug in 5 and 150 for demand and freight cost, respectively. You should see an overall cost of 0.

Therefore, you might want to tell the boss: "As long as you understand that cost will vary, if it's just the average cost you want, then 0 is my best guess." Or, then again, you might want to confirm this with a simulation first.

EXERCISE 3.1 TEST YOUR INTUITION ABOUT POINT ESTIMATES

a. What are the advantages of using point estimates in this case?

b. What are the disadvantages?

Simulating the Cost

The Uncertainties

The relationships between the inputs and overall cost have already been modeled in INVNTORY.xls. What remains is to model the random nature of the input cells: Demand and Air Freight. Unlike the previous example, we have no basis on which to assume some idealized distribution such as uniform or normal.

We will use a separate approach for each input cell: *resampling historical data* to model random demand and generating *triangular random variables* to model freight cost.

TUTORIAL: RESAMPLING HISTORICAL DATA

This simple but powerful approach to modeling uncertainty works as follows. Imagine 36 ping pong balls, each with one of the 36 historical demands painted on it. Place these in the type of rotating basket used for lottery drawings. To model demand, simply rotate the basket, draw out a ball, type the number on that ball into cell A2 (the Demand cell), then replace the ball in the basket. Repeat this for as many trials as you like. You will find that doing this with XLSim.xla is a lot easier than painting numbers on ping pong balls and using a rotating basket. Unlike the methods of classical statistics, which require you to begin with the assumption of an idealized distribution, resampling lets you pull yourself up as if by your own bootstraps. In fact, it is the basis for a powerful new perspective on statistical analysis known as **bootstrapping** (Efron and Tibshirani, 1993, and Simon, 1974).

To resample historical data, use the **gen_Resample** function as follows:

1 With the cursor in the Demand cell, A2, click on the function icon. The Paste Function dialog box opens.

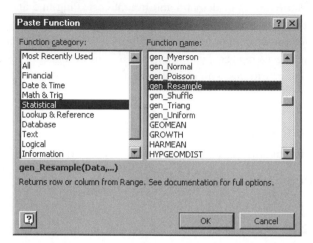

2 Select **Statistical** from the left menu and **gen_Resample** from the right menu. Click **OK**. The following dialog box opens.

3 Select the cells containing the 36 historical data points, and click **OK**. This places the **gen_Resample** formula in cell A2.

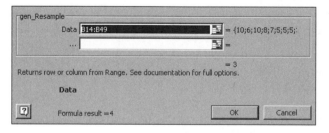

4 Press **Home** to get to the top of the sheet, then press the calculate key (F9) a few times to be sure the cell is functioning properly.

Tutorial: Triangular Distribution

With air freight costs, all we have is the recollection of the shipping clerk and no time to research the subject. Few things in life have a truly triangular distribution. Nonetheless, it provides a quick and dirty way to specify high, low, and most likely values as indicated by opinion.

Note: The most likely value of the distribution, also known as the ***mode,*** is not the average in this case because the distribution is not symmetric around its average, as shown in the following figure.

To generate triangular random variables, use the function **gen_Triang** and follow these steps:

1 With the cursor in the Air Freight cell, B6, click on the function icon. The Paste Function dialog box opens.

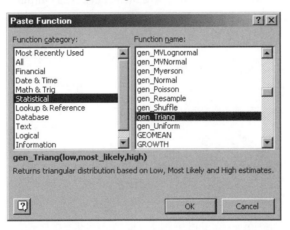

2 Select **Statistical** from the left menu and **gen_Triang** from the right menu, then click **OK**. The following dialog box opens:

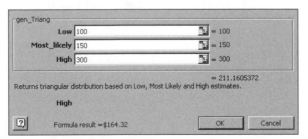

3 Fill in the **Low, Most_likely**, and **High** values and click **OK**. This places the **gen_Triang** formula in cell B6.

4
Press the calculate key a few times to be sure the cell is functioning properly. Because the model you created uses functions that are not part of the standard Excel library, for other users to work with your model XLSim must be installed on their computer. The **Freeze** and **Thaw** commands under the **Simulate** menu are useful for sharing your models. If you intend to share a workbook with another user use the **Freeze** command just before saving the workbook. This copies any formulas containing XLSim gen_functions into the comment area of that cell and replaces the formula with the last random number generated. The model can then be shared with others. If the next user also has XLSim, they should use the **Thaw** command to reactivate these formulas[1]. Once the random input formulas have been specified, save INVNTORY.xls so you do not have to repeat these steps for future experiments. When you reopen the model at a later time, be sure that XLSim.xla is opened first and remember to use the **Thaw** command to reactivate the formulas if you have frozen them.

5
After selecting **Simulation** from the **Simulate** menu click Add Outputs. Then specify C8, Overall Cost, as the output cell, and A8 as the output cell name in the following dialog box and click **OK**.

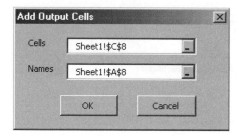

6
Click **OK** once more to run a simulation of 1,000 trials.

---

[1] This procedure is necessary because Excel would normally save the file path for the XLSim functions, but this path may not be the same for all users.

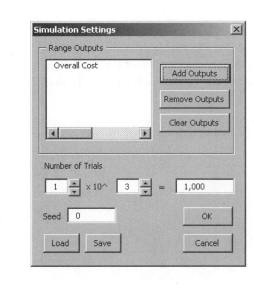

Simulation Results

Statistics. You will recall that plugging in point estimates of 5 for demand and 150 for air freight yielded an overall cost of 0. How does this compare with the average of overall cost on the simulation statistics screen? Remember, because the results are based on random numbers, you might not get exactly the same result twice.

The Histogram. Create a histogram using the **Simulate Graphs** command specifying 0 decimal places. Your histogram should look similar to the following figure.

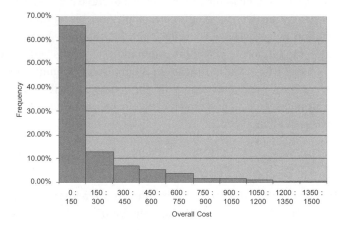

Recall that the average is the point at which this figure would balance if the histogram were made of blocks sitting on a board. Clearly, it would not balance all the way to the left at 0. A cost penalty is incurred regardless of whether demand is above or below average. It should now be obvious that cost will often be greater than 0 but can never be less than 0.

The Cumulative Graph. The cumulative graph shows that the average cost is almost $200 with a 20% chance of a cost over $400. This is a far cry from 0!

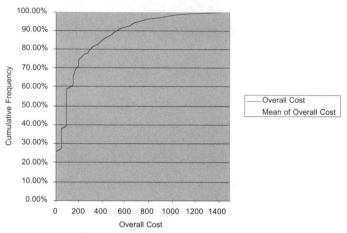

The Flaw of Averages

This leads us to one of the most important lessons of this book: that contrary to popular opinion, *Average inputs don't always yield average outputs.*[2] I refer to this widely held misconception as the ***Flaw of Averages*** (Savage 2000, 2002). With this in mind we will answer question 3.1a: What are the advantages of using point estimates in this case? Answer: *NONE!*

We have just gained the important insight that average overall cost is not the cost associated with average demand. And we accomplished this by running a simulation for which we did not even have accurate input distributions. Like horseshoes and hand grenades, being close counts with simulation, too. This refutes a commonly expressed view that Monte Carlo simulation is not a valid technique unless the input distributions are known with precision. With approximate distributions, although it is not possible to make precise probabilistic statements, important qualitative results may nonetheless be illuminated.

**EXERCISE
3.2**   INCREASING THE BINS OF A HISTOGRAM

Run the simulation with 10,000 iterations and create a histogram with 100 bins. What is the probability that cost will actually be 0?

---

[2] The only time average inputs yield average outputs is when the model is *linear*. And even those few people who know what linear means can't easily tell if a worksheet has this property.

THE BUILDINGS OF UNCERTAINTY

Even if you are in the small minority who knew that plugging in "best guess" inputs was worthless in the inventory example, you probably work with people for whom this is a time-honored tradition. This should be enough motivation to explore in more detail what happens when the building blocks of uncertainty (random variables) are combined into more complex models with uncertain inputs. The resulting buildings of uncertainty, known technically as functions of random variables, display a number of non-intuitive features that can be understood through Monte Carlo simulation.

In this section, we examine the following topics:

■ **Worksheet models based on uncertain numbers: Functions of random variables**. Worksheet models usually have a number of uncertain input cells. Typically "best guesses" are plugged into these cells, leading to answers that are just plain wrong. Monte Carlo simulation can provide a clear picture of the effects of uncertainty, such as hidden costs and unnecessary risks.

■ **Experimenting under uncertainty: Parameterized simulation**. Repeated simulation experiments can determine managerial steps that can simultaneously improve average performance and reduce risk.

■ **Uncertain numbers that are related to each other: Statistical dependence**. A company might be uncertain about its future need for cash and its future ability to borrow. These uncertainties are related to each other, in that when a company has the most pressing need for cash, it will also find it the most difficult to borrow. The relationships between these uncertainties must be correctly understood and simulated for accurate planning.

■ **How many trials are enough? Convergence**. Simulation might never give the same answer twice. The longer a simulation is run, the more dependable the results. How many trials are needed?

■ **Sensitivity analysis: The big picture**. Simulation can yield insight into the relationships between various aspects of a complex model. This can provide a big picture of what is going on.

■ **Hypothesis Testing: Did it happen by chance?** Hypothesis testing attempts to distinguish true relationships in data from patterns that occur by chance. Although classical statistical methods have been used to address these issues in the past, recent simulation-based techniques, such as bootstrapping, provide more generality and better intuition for those not technically trained.

Worksheet Models Based on Uncertain Numbers: Functions of Random Variables

We will start by formalizing the notion of a function of random variables. (See Fundamentals Box 3-1.)

■ **FUNDAMENTALS 3-1**

A Function of Random Variables

An output that depends on random variable inputs is known as a ***function of random variables***. Thus, any cell in a worksheet that depends directly or indirectly on any other cells that contain uncertain numbers is a function of random variables.

■ **FUNDAMENTALS 3-2**

Linear Model

In a ***linear model***, the random inputs can be multiplied by constants and added together. Virtually nothing else, including IF, MAX, and MIN formulas, look up tables, nor many other formulas present in most worksheet models, are allowed in a linear model.

In the inventory example, the random variables were demand and air freight rate. The function of these random variables of interest was the overall operating cost. We found through simulation that plugging in "best guesses" or point estimates of demand and air freight did *NOT* result in the "best guess" for overall cost.

There is a special class of models, however, known as linear models, for which average inputs do yield average outputs (see Fundamentals Box 3-2).

For instance, suppose that a company has two divisions: A and B. A simple model for the company's total profit *is* linear:

Total Profit = Division A's Profit + Division B's Profit

So in this case, plugging in the average values of the uncertain inputs (profits of Divisions A and B) does result in the average output (total profit of the firm)—that is,

Expected Total Profit = Division A's Expected Profit + Division B's Expected Profit

In general, however, it is difficult to determine whether a large worksheet is linear. It is always safe to assume it is not linear, and run a simulation to determine the distribution of the outputs.

We formally state the Flaw of Averages in Fundamentals Box 3-3.

■ FUNDAMENTALS 3-3

The Flaw of Averages

In general, plugging average values of uncertain inputs into a function of random variables **does not** result in the average value of the function. For the special case of *linear* functions, average inputs **do** result in average outputs. In probability or statistics books you might see this written as

$$F(E(x)) \neq E(F(x))$$

unless F is linear, where x is the uncertain number, F is the function, and E is the expected or average value. A more detailed version of this statement is known as Jensen's inequality.

A Sobering Example of the Flaw of Averages. Point estimates of average inputs are used erroneously in many contexts. This problem can be compared to the fate of a drunk, wandering back and forth on a busy highway. The random *input* is the drunk's position; the *output* is the drunk's fate.

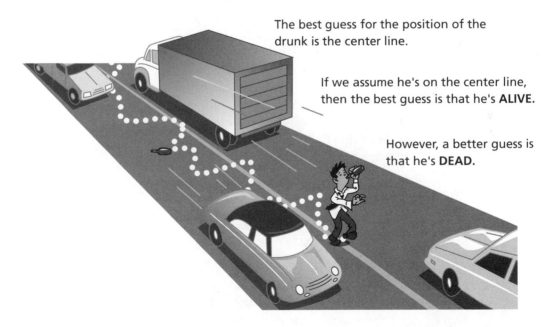

The best guess for the position of the drunk is the center line.

If we assume he's on the center line, then the best guess is that he's **ALIVE**.

However, a better guess is that he's **DEAD**.

Some Business Examples. There are numerous examples in business where the use of point estimates leads to erroneous results. A few are described in the following exercises, which are designed to help you identify such situations on your own while you improve your skills with XLSim.xla.

ESTIMATING PROJECT DURATION

The printing of a sales brochure has been split between two printing firms so the failure of any one firm will not completely shut down the sales campaign. Each firm estimates that their half of the brochures will take 20 hours to print. Past experience indicates that the estimates from both firms are accurate on average. However, actual completion time has been normally distributed around the average with a standard deviation equal to 15% of the estimated time.

a. What is the expected amount of time to complete all of the brochures? *Hint:* Use the MAX function.

b. What are the chances that all brochures will be completed in 20 hours or less?

c. What is the expected time to complete half the brochures? *Hint:* Use the MIN function.

d. What are the chances that half the brochures will be completed in 20 hours or less?

A PRO FORMA CASH FLOW STATEMENT

Business plans involving anything from bank loans to venture capital often forecast net cash position through a pro forma cash flow statement. Starting with an initial cash position, subsequent positions are calculated by adding expected sources and subtracting expected cash outlay for each month. PROFORMA.xls, shown in the following figure, models the rosy picture of a business that starts with $250,000 and turns it into more than $1.5 million in just 12 months.

C6	↓		=B6+C4-C5		
A	**B**	**C**	**D**	**E**	**F**
1		Pro Forma Cash Flow Statement			
2		$000's			
3		Jan	Feb	Mar	Apr	May
4 Cash in	$500	$500	$500	$500	$500
5 Cash Out	$400	$400	$400	$400	$400
6 Net Cash	$350	$450	$550	$650	$750
7					
8 Initial	$250				
9 Cash					

Needless to say, the actual sources and outlays of cash are not always forecast with great accuracy. Suppose that all the projected sources and outlays (but not initial cash) in PROFORMA.xls are normally distributed around their estimated values with standard deviations equal to 25% of the estimated value.

a. What is the minimum net cash position we should expect any time during the 12 months?

b. What are the chances that the minimum will actually be negative, which implies bankruptcy?

EXERCISE 3.5

ESTIMATING PRODUCTION QUANTITY

A firm manufactures television coaxial cable from four components that it orders from outside suppliers. A single wire forms the center conductor, a woven wire mesh forms the outer conductor, and two types of plastic are used for the inner and outer insulation. Orders have been placed for each component in quantities required for 5000 feet. On average, each supplier has delivered the ordered amount with a uniform variation ranging between plus or minus 100 feet.

a. How much cable should the manufacturer expect to be able to produce?

b. What are the chances it will be less than 5,000 feet?

Hint: Model the amount delivered by each supplier with **gen_Uniform.**

EXERCISE 3.6

ESTIMATING OVERTIME EXPENSES

A health care facility is planning its personnel budget for the coming year. One nurse with a salary of $1,000 per week is required for every 5 patients. The average patient census is 300, as shown in the file CENSUS.xls, which contains 52 weeks of census data. Therefore, it is estimated that 60 nurses will be needed at an average cost of $60,000 per week. This translates to an estimated annual budget of $3,120,000 for nurse salaries.

On those weeks when the census is below the average of 300, the nurses must be paid full salary anyway. On those weeks when the census is exceeded, $500 in overtime expense is incurred per patient in excess of 300. For example, if the census were 310, an additional $5,000 would be incurred that week.

a. Create a histogram of the census data using the **Simulate Data Range** command.

b. What is the average weekly nursing cost?

c. What is the chance that on any given week actual expenses will be less than or equal to that budgeted? *Hint:* Create an output cell that equals 1 if expense is less than or equal to the budget. Such a formula is known as an *indicator.* The average of the indicator is just the likelihood that the budget was met for the week.

d. Given your answer to part c, what is the chance that the overall nursing budget will be met for the year?

**EXERCISE
3.7**

Create One of Your Own

Develop a worksheet based on your own experience of a situation in which averages of uncertain numbers have been inappropriately plugged into a model.

Experimenting Under Uncertainty: Parameterized Simulation

People facing uncertainty have generally achieved one of the following levels of enlightenment:

■ *Level 0: Dumb.* When the boss asks what the output of some model will be, this person throws up his or her hands and says, "I don't know because I don't know what the inputs will be."

■ *Level Minus 1: Dumber.* One step down from dumb, these people plug best guesses into the model and confidently proclaim that they have the best guess for the output.

■ *Level 1: Smart.* A big step up from dumb, these people run a simulation to find the output's range of uncertainty. In the process, they are forced to learn something about the nature of the uncertain inputs of their model, which makes them smarter still.

■ *Level 2: Proactive.* Even at Level 1, you are simply reporting what is likely to happen. Reaching Level 2 requires a commitment to action given the uncertainty observed at Level 1.

One way to become proactive is through *Parameterized Simulation.* This involves repeating a simulation several times while systematically adjusting some number in the model. Such a number is known as a *parameter*.

Seeking the Optimal Stocking Level

In the inventory example, an obvious question to ask is this: "Who says we should stock 5?" And an obvious way to answer this question is to run the simulation several times while experimenting with different quantities stocked. The penalty for understocking is between $100 to $300 per unit, whereas the penalty for overstocking is only $50 per unit. Therefore, increasing the amount stocked above 5 makes intuitive sense. XLSim.xla allows as many as five such experiments to be run, so we will try stocking 4, 5, 6, 7, and 8. It is important to keep the original number of 5 stocked so we can compare the results with the status quo. The number being changed each time—in this instance, the number of cases stocked—is the parameter.

Seeding the Random Numbers

There is a problem, however. Because of the random nature of simulation, we can expect to get different answers with every run, even with the same number stocked. So, how can we tell if one stocking level is really better than another?

This is analogous to the problem faced by the coach of a minor league baseball team who must choose one of several potential recruits to join the team. To test the players' relative batting abilities, he could put each recruit up against a separate pitcher. But then the coach wouldn't know if the differences in their performance were because of the pitchers or batters. It would be better to test each player against the same pitcher. But the best test of all would be provided by a computerized, laser guided pitching machine programmed to pitch exactly the same sequence of fast balls, slow balls, curves, and so on to each recruit.

This facility is provided in XLSim.xla through the *seed* on the settings screen. Think of the random number generator as a ball machine that sends out a sequence of 2^{31} (2,147,483,648) different pitches before repeating. The various potential stocking levels represent the potential recruits. The seed indicates where in the sequence of pitches the ball machine will start for each recruit. This allows you to repeat the experiments. With a seed of zero you do not know where in the sequence the machine will start, and the results will not be repeatable.

TUTORIAL: RUNNING A PARAMETERIZED SIMULATION OF INVNTORY.XLS

1

We will run a parameterized simulation by using the following steps. The uncertain inputs are the same as in the earlier examples, and no changes are required. This time, however, we will test five different quantities to stock (4, 5, 6, 7, and 8).

Ensure that XLSim.xla is loaded, retrieve INVNTORY.xls as saved from the previous example and use the **Simulate, Thaw** command if you have frozen the file.

2 Enter 4, 5, 6, 7, and 8 in any contiguous range in the worksheet. Cells D2:D6 are used in the example shown below.

B	C	D
	Amt Stocked	
	5	4
		5
Per Unit	Total	6
$50.00	$100.00	7
$223.14	$0.00	8

Now specify the settings for running five separate simulations of 100 trials, one for each parameter value, by following these steps:

3 Select **Parameterized Sim** from the **Simulate** menu. The following dialog box opens:

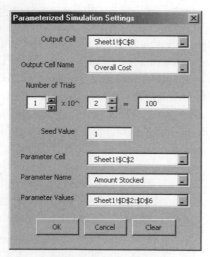

4 Specify C8, Overall Cost, as the output cell.

5 Set the number of trials to 100. This will be enough to allow us to see the effect of different stocking levels. For decisions of economic consequence, however, a larger number of trials is recommended (see the discussion of Standard Error later).

6 Specify a nonzero seed. The number 1 was chosen here, but any positive integer will do.

7 Next specify C2, Amt Stocked, as the parameter cell. The parameter name and outpE§ cell name are optional but useful in interpreting the simulation output.

8 Finally, specify D2:D6 as the range containing the parameter values, then click **OK**.

ng. In a real life situation, with
ow this with a longer run to get

ercentile.

7	8
250	300
300	350
620	413

xpect to incur an overall cost
. This is the *value at risk,* or
ne number stocked goes from
t average cost was 6, but the
gement's risk attitude would
ces would they stock 5.

affing level that minimizes
e cost and the risk of an

at is bidding for a contract
mpany for the following
t $100,000 to provide the
also known to be bidding
now with certainty what
ted high, low, and most

ly to win the contract. If
fitable even if the HMO

nimum average cost—
d on the seed used and

| 14938 |
| 84161 |
| 84161 |
| 94409 |
| 0 |

lect **Common Graphs**
ted on the **Outputs** tab
utton to view the graph.

overall cost is minimized
ttom lines show the range
een the top line (the 95th
dramatically this band of
7. For managing risk, this
n the reduction in average

9
M
5

Simulation Output

The simulation output indicates that stocking 6 results in the minimum average cost—about 10% lower than stocking 5! *Note:* Your results will depend on the seed used and the number of iterations run.

Amt Stocked	4	5	6	7	8
Average	246.970062	180.731567	164.348404	169.017014	190.014938
Std Dev	287.117941	223.429176	157.991974	114.086052	100.484161
Std Err	28.7117941	22.3429176	15.7991974	11.4086052	10.0484161
Max	1240.18323	1033.48596	826.788818	620.091614	413.394409
Min	0	0	0	0	0

This is good news, but a graph provides additional insight. Select **Common Graphs** from the **Simulate** menu. Make sure all the outputs are selected on the **Outputs** tab then move to the **Series Graph** tab. Click the **Series Graph** button to view the graph.

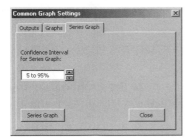

The center line of the graph shows clearly that the mean overall cost is minimized around 6 units stocked. But, more important, the top and bottom lines show the range of the results. That is, 90% of all overall costs were between the top line (the 95th percentile) and bottom line (the 5th percentile). Notice how dramatically this band of uncertainty narrows as the amount stocked goes from 4 to 7. For managing risk, this reduction in uncertainty can be even more important than the reduction in average cost.

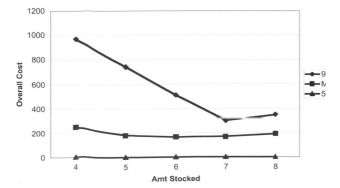

We only ran 100 trials here to get a qualitative feeling. In a real life situation, with results as dramatic as these, it would make sense to follow this with a longer run to get more accurate results.

Go back to the Statistics sheet and view the 95th percentile.

Amt Stocked	4	5	6	7	8
90%	610	447	281	250	300
95%	972	743	511	300	350
100%	1240	1033	827	620	413

Five percent (100% – 95%) of the time we should expect to incur an overall cost greater than or equal to the numbers shown on this line. This is the *value at risk*, or *VaR* at the 5% level, and it is reduced by nearly 50% as the number stocked goes from 5 to 7. In this example, the stocking level with the lowest average cost was 6, but the stocking level with the smallest 5% VaR was 7. Management's risk attitude would dictate whether to stock 6 or 7. But under no circumstances would they stock 5.

EXERCISE

3.8 THE OPTIMAL STAFFING LEVEL

Return to the nursing example and determine the staffing level that minimizes expected cost. Is there a trade off between average cost and the risk of an occasional large cost?

EXERCISE

3.9 COMPETITIVE BIDDING

Consider a Health Maintenance Organization (HMO) that is bidding for a contract to supply health care services to a medium-sized company for the following year. The management of the HMO believes it will cost $100,000 to provide the required health care services. Two competitive firms are also known to be bidding for this contract. Of course, management does not know with certainty what the competitors will bid, but managers have estimated high, low, and most likely bids for each competitor as follows:

Bid Estimates	Competitor A	Competitor B
High	$135,000	$140,000
Most Likely	$110,000	$115,000
Low	$100,000	$105,000

If the HMO bids too high, one of the competitors is likely to win the contract. If it bids too low, the contract will not be sufficiently profitable even if the HMO does win it. Management wants to determine the amount to bid to maximize the expected profit. This situation is modeled in BID.xls, shown in the following figure:

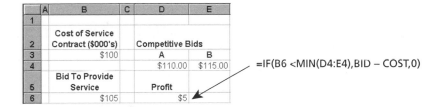

Management is considering the following bids: $100,000, $105,000, $110,000, $115,000, and $120,000.

a. Use parameterized simulation to determine which of these maximizes the expected profit. *Hint:* Use **gen_Triang** to simulate your competitors' bids.

b. Suppose management was also uncertain about the cost of fulfilling the contract. The costs are estimated to be normally distributed with a mean of $100,000 and a standard deviation of $20,000. How would this influence the amount that management would want to bid?

Stock Options: Turning Uncertainty to Advantage

The field of financial engineering has developed numerous techniques for managing and actually exploiting uncertainty. Suppose, for example, you had reason to believe that because of a possible merger a particular stock might increase dramatically in value over the next few weeks. On the other hand, if the merger fell through the stock could also go down dramatically. If you purchase the stock, you have the potential to either make or lose a lot of money. Suppose that you cannot tolerate the risk of such a large loss. Then you can purchase what is known as a Call Option on the stock. This provides you with the right, but not the obligation, to buy the stock at a given price at a future date. This way, if the stock value increases, you can profit by buying it at a low price. If the stock value decreases, you are only out the cost of the option. Although there are many types of options, the most basic options are described here. For a clear explanation of options, see Hull (1991) or Luenberger (1997).

Basic options include the following:

▪   The *American Call Option* provides the right, but not the obligation, to purchase a particular stock option, at a particular price (the strike price), on or before a particular date (the expiration date).

- The *European Call Option* differs from the American Call in that it can be exercised only on the expiration date.

- The *American Put Option* provides the right, but not the obligation, to sell the stock to someone for the strike price on or before a particular date.

- The *European Put Option* differs from the American Put in that it can be exercised only on the expiration date.

To gain insight into how options behave, make sure XLSim.xla is loaded and open the file OPTION.xls. This is a simplified model of a 12-week European Call option with a strike price of $21 for a stock that is selling for $20 today.

Note: To activate the random number generation formulas that have been stored in this workbook select **Thaw** from the **Simulate** menu. The **Freeze** and **Thaw** commands allow different users to share workbooks that have been created using XLSim functions.

Stock price movement is often modeled as a *random walk*; that is, a set of random steps where the mean of each step is based on the last step. In this model the current price of $20 is entered in cell A6 and repeated in B9. The price in each subsequent period is determined by multiplying the price in the previous period by a random growth rate. If this growth rate is greater than 1, the stock price goes up. If it is less than 1, the price goes down.

You don't have to understand the precise nature of this random process to gain insight into the qualitative behavior of call options. For those interested, however, the distribution of growth factors is expressed as the number *e* raised to a normally distributed random variable. Because the natural log of such a variable is normal, it is known as a *lognormal random variable* as we discussed in the last chapter. XLSim can also generate lognormal variables directly. To learn more about lognormal random variables, see gen_Functions.xls, Hull (1991) or Luenberger (1997).

The value of the option at the expiration date (12 weeks out) is determined as follows: If the final stock price in week 12 (FP) is higher than the strike price S, the option is said to be *in the money*. Then you can buy it at S and immediately sell it on the market for FP, pocketing the difference, FP–S. If FP is less than or equal to S, there is no point in exercising the option, and it is worth zero. This is expressed as MAX(Final_Price-Strike,0) in cell H6.

However, the value of the option today must reflect the fact that a dollar in 12 weeks is not worth as much as a dollar today. This is known as the *net present value (NPV)* of the amount in cell H6. Suppose $1 one year from now was worth 5% less than $1 today; that is, the annual rate is 5%. The net present value of $1 in t years for annual rate r can be shown to be e^{-rt}. This has been calculated for the 12 weeks of the option in cell I6.

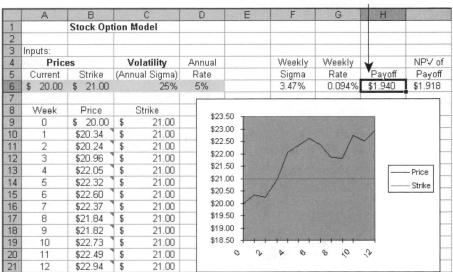

=MAX(Final_Price-Strike,0)

After thawing the model, press the calculate key a few times and observe the graph of the stock price over time and the value of cells H6 and I6.

How Are Options Priced?

It is beyond the scope of this work to explain the theory of option pricing. For a detailed discussion see Hull (1991) or Luenberger (1997). However, for an intuitive starting point, the theoretical price of an option is the expected net present value; that is, the average value of cell I6. Before going on to the next exercise, try to imagine the shape of the distribution of cell I6.

EXERCISE

3.10   OPTION PRICING

a.   Run a simulation with 1000 trials to estimate the expected NPV of the option.

b.   What percent of the time is it in the money? *Hint:* Create an indicator output cell, as discussed in the last section, that equals 1 if the option ends up in the money and zero otherwise. The average value of the indicator is just the percentage of the time the option expires in the money.

The Increase of Option Prices with Uncertainty: Implied Volatility

Another use of parameterized simulation is to estimate the effect of changes in the uncertainty of the inputs. Still working with OPTIONS.xls, we will see what effect the stock's **volatility** (a measure of the uncertainty of its future price contained in cell C6) has on the value of the option. Try replacing the volatility with 0 and then 50%. For each value, press the calculate key a few times to see how the volatility effects the graph's behavior.

Next, run a parameterized simulation of cell I6 with values for Sigma equal to .10, .15, .20, .25, and .30. Create a **Series Graph** with Percentiles set to "None". The resulting graph should appear as follows.

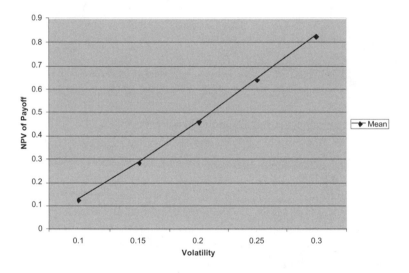

The vertical axis represents the expected NPV of the option, which should approximate its market price. The graph indicates that the value of the option increases with the volatility of the underlying stock. It is often useful for investors to know this volatility. Assuming that the market in options is efficient, we can look up the price of an option in the newspaper and use an equivalent of this graph to determine the **implied volatility** of the stock. In this case, for example, if the price of the option were $0.60, it would imply that the stock's volatility was approximately 25%.

Uncertainty Over Time

It is instructive to observe how the uncertainty of a stock's price increases as you try to predict further and further into the future. We will use the **Series Graph** to demonstrate this as follows. As output cells, select the stock price at time 1, 3, 5, 7, and 9 weeks. Then run 1000 iterations. When the simulation is complete, select **Common Graphs** from the **Simulate** menu, make sure all outputs are selected, and click the **Series Graph** button with Percentiles of 5% to 95%. The 5th and 95th percentile curves clearly show that the uncertainty in price increases over time, but at a decreasing rate. In theory, the shape of these percentiles should approximate the curve of a square root function.

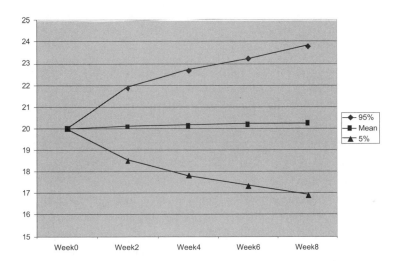

Uncertain Numbers That Are Related to Each Other: Statistical Dependence

The concept of statistical dependence can be illustrated in terms of the person who brings a bomb whenever he or she flies because the chance of two bombs on a plane is negligible. The fallacy here is that the chance of some other nut bringing a bomb is not influenced by bringing your own.

Statistical dependence can be subtle and non-intuitive. For example, if you do manage to get your bomb on board the plane, that implies that security is lax. So you have actually *increased* the chance of another bomb on board!

Ignoring the effects of statistical independence or dependence can have serious consequences, and it is important to take these concepts into account when building simulation models.

Resampling Multivariate Data

In INVNTORY.xls we used **gen_Resample** to generate random inputs from a single column of past data. The next example involves two columns of statistically dependent data. In this situation, when we select a number at random from the first column, we must pick the adjacent one in the second column to preserve the statistical dependence. Instead of using **gen_Resample** as normal formula, this time we will use **gen_Resample** as an array formula to keep the columns synchronized. See the file gen_Functions.xls for examples of **gen_Resample**.

■ **FUNDAMENTALS 3-4**

Statistical Dependence

Two random variables are said to be *statistically independent* if the value of one is of no relevance in determining the value of the other. Two random variables are said to be *statistically dependent* if the value of one is relevant in determining the value of the other.

Failure Analysis

We will start with an example of failure analysis in engineering, by simulating the dependability of a new industrial engine running in an uncertain environment. To keep the engine operating properly, the cooling system must dissipate heat while the oil pump maintains adequate oil pressure. This new engine is lighter and cheaper to produce than its predecessor, but on the downside there is concern that it will be less dependable under extreme operating conditions. If the oil pressure drops below 20 lbs/sq. in. at the same time that the operating temperature exceeds 225 degrees Fahrenheit, it is believed the engine will fail. The problem is to estimate the likelihood of failure given the wide variety of potential operating environments of the new engine. Data from the more robust predecessor engine will be used for this purpose. Temperature and oil pressure for the new engine are expected to be similar to those of the old engine, for which substantial operating data has been recorded.

Tutorial: Estimating Likelihood of Failure

1 Open ENGINE.xls. The Data sheet contains operational data on the predecessor engine. One hundred Temperature/Pressure pairs were recorded over a wide variety of operating environments. The Temperature data is stored in a range called Temp_Data while the associated pressure data is stored in Press_Data. The average temperature and pressure over these environments was 200 degrees and 78 lbs./sq. in. as shown.

X Microsoft Excel - Engine.xls			_ □ ×
	A	B	C
1		Temperature	Pressure
2	Average	200	78
3			
4	Environment	HISTORICAL DATA	
5	1	176	114
6	2	195	93
7	3	191	93
8	4	210	52

Data / Model / XY Chart /

Histograms created for each quantity using the **Simulate Data Range** command indicate that neither is normally distributed, as shown below.

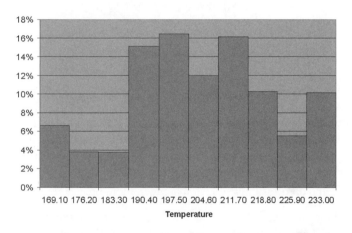

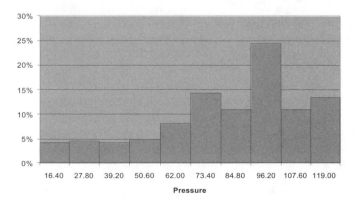

2 Click on the worksheet tab "Model." Here we see that the model of the new engine will indicate failure if the temperature is greater than 225 and the pressure is less than 20. With the average temperature and pressure values in cells A2 and B2, the engine does not fail, but as you should have learned by now, averages are little use in this sort of analysis. Try various values of temperature and pressure. (If the indicator does not turn to "1" for sufficiently high temperatures and low pressures, use the **Tools Options** command to check that your spreadsheet is in Automatic Calculation mode.) This indicator formula will be used during simulation to determine the probability of engine failure.

B5	▾	f_x	=IF(AND(Press<20,Temp>225),1,0)		
	A	B	C	D	E
1	Temperature	Pressure			
2	200	78			
3					
4					
5	Failure Indicator	0			

3 Since the distributions of temperature and pressure are not of any well-known types and are based on substantial data, this is an ideal opportunity to use the resampling technique discussed earlier. We will do this in two ways. First, for practice, we will do the simplest type of resampling, which ignores the dependence of oil pressure on temperature. Unlike using average temperature and pressure, resampling the entire range of temperatures and pressures will at least indicate some possibility of failure. However, it will give an inaccurate estimate of the chance of failure. The second, more accurate, approach will take into account the relation between operating temperature and oil pressure, and lead to a much more precise result.

To perform the first experiment, place the formula **=gen_Resample (Temp_Data)** in cell A2 and **=gen_Resample (Press_Data)** in cell B2 as shown.

Press	▾	f_x	=gen_Resample(Press_Data)	
	A	B	C	D
1	Temperature	Pressure		
2	187	83		

Press the F9 key a few times to make sure the formulas are working correctly.

4 Run a simulation of 1000 trials or more, specifying B5, the failure indicator, as the output cell. You should find an average value of the indicator of around .007. This means that failure occurred in only 0.7% of the trials.

Recall that the average value of an indicator of an event is an estimate of the probability of that event occurring.

5

This gives us our first indication of the risk of failure—but remember, it was based on the naïve assumption that temperature and pressure were unrelated.

In reality, although both temperature and pressure are uncertain, high temperature reduces the viscosity of oil, leading to lower oil pressure. Thus temperature and pressure are *statistically dependent*. This becomes clearly visible in the XY scatterplot of temperature and pressure on the XY Chart tab. *Note:* If the temperature and pressure had not been sampled in pairs, this dependence would not have been preserved. This is an important consideration in collecting the data in the first place.

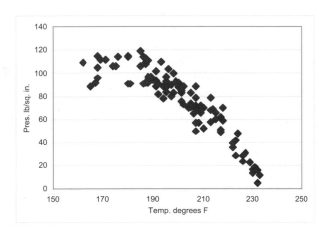

PUZZLE: The way we used gen_Resample in step 3 above did not preserve this statistical dependence. Does this cause the resulting estimate of the likelihood of failure to be too high or too low? Why? You will learn the answer at step 9.

6

We will now use gen_Resample in a more sophisticated manner, which preserves dependence. This uses gen_Resample as an array formula, which is a bit tricky, but worth the trouble. Start by placing the cursor in cell A2 in the Model worksheet. Then, while holding down the left mouse button, also select cell B2. The screen should appear as shown below.

A2	▾	*fx*	=gen_Resample(Temp_Data)	
	A	B	C	D
1	Temperature	Pressure		
2	187	83		

7

The next step is to edit the formula to include the pressure data as a second argument as shown below, but don't press the Enter key yet.

✕ ✓ *fx* =gen_Resample(Temp_Data,Press_Data)

8

Now simultaneously hold down the <Shift> and <Ctrl> keys, then press <Enter> (see Microsoft Excel help on array formulas for more details). If you did everything right, curly brackets will now appear around your formula. Array formulas control multiple cells at once. When gen_Resample is used as an array formula, it assures that the random sample taken from the temperature data in cell A2, is paired with its associated pressure data point in B2. *Note:* It was not necessary to enter the two data ranges individually, separated by ",". It would also have been possible to enter the single combined range as an argument as shown below. Either range names or standard cell addresses may be used as arguments. See gen_Functions.xls for other examples.

{=gen_Resample(Combined_Data)}

9

Run a simulation of the failure indicator with the dependence preserved, and you should find a much higher probability of failure—around 5.5%. That's about eight times higher than the previous result, which ignored dependence.

This tutorial has shown how to use an indicator formula to estimate the probability of an event. It has also demonstrated the array version of gen_Resample to simulate multiple random inputs with statistical dependence.

An Example of Yield Management

On commercial aircraft crossing the Pacific, both high ground temperature at takeoff and strong head winds en route significantly diminish the payload. High temperatures reduce payload because hot air is less dense than cold air and thus there is both less to hold up the wings and less to feed the engines. Strong head winds make the trip take longer, so more fuel must be carried instead of paying passengers. Tables accounting for runway length, temperature, and head winds are used shortly before takeoff to determine the payload. Unfortunately, an airline can't wait until shortly before takeoff to sell tickets for the flight. Therefore, a problem arises in deciding how many seats to sell, given the uncertainties of the weather.

In the hypothetical example that follows, seats on a large aircraft can be sold for $2,000 each. If the number sold exceeds the payload, however, there are severe penalties for overbooking as follows: For the first 10 seats overbooked, it is usually possible to re-book the passengers on other airlines. By the time all the paperwork is done, however, this costs an additional $1,000 beyond the lost revenues. If more than 10 seats have been overbooked, things are much worse. In general, it is not possible to find alternate flights for more than 10 people. Not only are there now hotel and other expenses, but the airline also has a group of angry customers on its hands. Management has assessed the cost of both direct expense and goodwill at $10,000 per overbooked passenger beyond 10 passengers.

PAYLOAD.xls models this situation.

1. Temperature and head wind entered here.

2. Payload calculated in two-way lookup table.

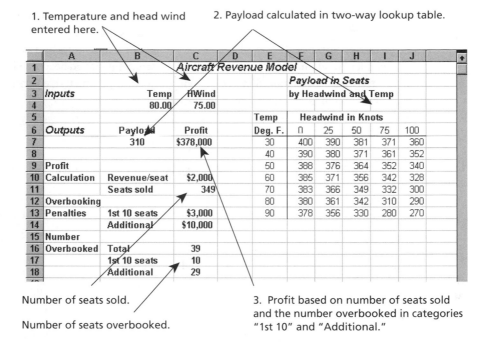

Number of seats sold.

Number of seats overbooked.

3. Profit based on number of seats sold and the number overbooked in categories "1st 10" and "Additional."

The formula in cell B7 calculates the payload for given values of temperature (B4) and head wind (C4). This requires looking up the temperature and head wind in the table. The formula is

=VLOOKUP(B4,$E$7:$J$13,LOOKUP(C4,$F$6:$J$6,$P$2:$T$2))

Hypothetical weather data for the air route in question is contained in the Weather Data sheet as shown in the following figure. The average temperature and head wind are calculated at the top of each column.

	B	C	D
1		Temp	H-Wind
2	Averages	70.5095	53.9822
3			
4		62.71	41.22
5		76.24	58.29
6		75.25	66.6

Experiment with the model by plugging various values for temperature and head wind into cells B4 and C4 of the payload sheet and observing the changes in payload and profit.

We will compare four approaches to estimating the profit. First, we will use a point estimate based on the average temperature and head wind. (By now, you should be suspicious of this approach.) Then, we will model temperature and head wind as independent random inputs. Next, we will model temperature and head wind including their statistical correlation. Finally, we will perform a parameterized simulation to determine the optimal number of seats to sell.

Tutorial: Using a Point Estimate

To use a point estimate, link the average temperature and head wind to cells B4 and C4 as follows:

1 With the cursor in cell B4 of the Payload sheet, press the "=" key to start a formula.

2 Click on the **Weather Data** tab.

3 Click on cell C2 (average temperature) and press **Enter.**

4 Cell B4 of the Payload sheet now contains the formula "='Weather Data'!C2", which yields the average temperature. Copy this to cell C4 for the average head wind.

The results show that the payload under average temperature and wind conditions is 349. If 349 seats are sold and these average conditions occur, then revenue will be $698,000.

Tutorial: Simulating Temperature and Head Wind as Independent Random Inputs

1 We will replace the average temperature and head wind with random samples from the data. Click on the **Weather Data** tab.

2 Replace the **Average** formulas in cells C2 and D2 with **gen_Resample** formulas using the temperature and head wind data as input. *Note:* To paste in a new function using the Paste Function icon, you must first delete the existing formula. The **gen_Resample** function has the effect of drawing a temperature and head wind at random from past data independently. Thus any relationship between temperature and head wind will be lost.

3 Select **Payload** and **Profit** as output cells and run a few hundred trials.

The results should be close to those shown below. Notice that the average payload is higher than 349 (the payload under average weather conditions), but the average profit is lower than $698,000. The minimum profit in this run was only $78,000. Also, profit will be nearly $680,000, or greater, 85% of the time.

Output Name	Payload	Profit
Average	355.48	665388
Std Dev	19.1373	91038.7
Std Err	0.85585	4071.37
Max	390	698000
Min	280	78000
Percentiles		
5%	310	378000
10%	330	578000
15%	342	677000

TUTORIAL: SIMULATING TEMPERATURE AND HEAD WIND AS DEPENDENT RANDOM INPUTS

Is there a relationship between temperature and head wind for the data in question? An XY (scatter) plot of the columns on the **Weather Data** sheet can be easily created with the Excel **Chart Wizard**. The following figure shows a strong relationship in which high temperatures tend to go hand in hand with strong head winds. As will be discussed later, this displays a *positive correlation* between the variables.

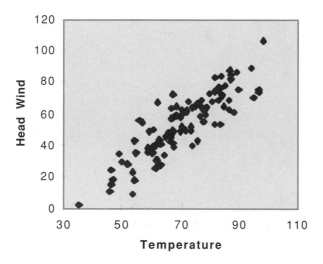

Now simulate the effects of the positive correlation between temperature and head wind by following these steps:

1

Replace the two **gen_Resample** formulas in the **Weather Data** sheet with a single array formula implementation of the **gen_Resample** formula. This pulls a temperature and a head wind at random from past data in tandem. Thus, the hand-in-hand relationship between these two inputs will be preserved.

2

Again, select Payload and Profit as output cells and run a few hundred trials.

The average payload should not have changed too much from the previous run. Average profit on the other hand has dropped by about $30,000—more than 5%. Also, at least one trial actually had negative profit.

Now profit will be only about $380,000 or greater 85% of the time. Or equivalently, 15% of the time, profit will be less than about $380,000, much lower than before. Notice that all three percentiles shown for payload and profit are the same, because the cumulative distribution is very flat in this region.

Output Name	Payload	Profit
Average	351.198	627502
Std Dev	26.4537	161214
Std Err	1.18305	7209.72
Max	400	698000
Min	270	-22000
Percentiles		
5%	310	378000
10%	310	378000
15%	310	378000

Why is profit so dramatically affected by taking positive correlation into account? Now, when one thing goes wrong (say high temperature) the other thing (high head wind) is more likely to go wrong. Had these two effects been negatively correlated (that is, high temperatures implied low head winds, and vice versa) the effect on profit would have been just the opposite.

EXERCISE
3.11   **DETERMINING THE OPTIMAL NUMBER OF SEATS TO SELL**

Run a parameterized simulation to compare the results of selling 320, 330, 340, 350, and 360 seats.

a.   How is average profit affected by number of seats sold?

b.   How is the 15% value at risk affected?

The Language of Statistical Dependence

We were able to model the dependence between head wind and temperature in the previous example by resampling past data. In general, however, data might not be available for resampling, and you might have to explicitly describe the statistical dependence between random variables.

The simplest sort of statistical dependence involves an approximately straight line relation between two or more random variables. Consider the variables x and y whose scatterplot is shown in the following figure. As you can see, a high value of x increases the chance of a high value of y and vice versa.

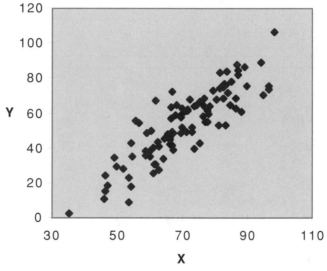

The formula in Fundamentals Box 3-5 does not provide much intuition. However, a geometrical interpretation of covariance might help. Imagine a rectangle with one corner at the point $\bar{x}, \bar{y}$ and another at some point x_i, y_i. Its area (width times height) is $(x_i - \bar{x}) (y_i - \bar{y})$ as shown in the left part of the following figure.

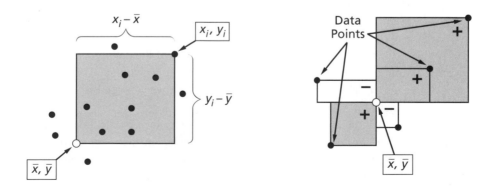

■ **FUNDAMENTALS 3-5**

Covariance

The degree to which x and y go up and down together is quantified by a calculation known as the *covariance* or σ_{xy}. This is defined as

$$\sigma_{xy} = \frac{1}{n} \sum_{i=1} (x_i - \bar{x})(y_i - \bar{y})$$

where n is the number of data points and $\bar{x}$ and $\bar{y}$ denote the average values of x and y respectively. The covariance of two arrays of historical data in Excel can be found using the COVAR(Array1,Array2) formula.

■ **FUNDAMENTALS 3-6**

Correlation

The *correlation, R,* is a measure of the power of x in predicting values of y. It is defined as

$$R = \frac{\sigma_{xy}}{\sigma_x \sigma_y}$$

where σ_{xy} is the covariance, and σ_x and σ_y are the standard deviations of x and y respectively. The correlation can take on any value between -1 and $+1$. R = +1 means that y can be perfectly predicted when x is known and increases when x increases. R = 0 means that y does not change in a predictable linear manner with x. R = -1 means that y can be perfectly predicted when x is known, but decreases when x increases

---

But $(x_i - \bar{x})(y_i - \bar{y})$ is just the term in the definition of the covariance. With this in mind, the covariance can be seen to be the average area of all rectangles starting at point $\bar{x}, \bar{y}$ and ending on a data point. Of course, depending on the signs of $(x_i - \bar{x})$ and $(y_i - \bar{y})$, the areas will be either positive or negative, and can cancel out as shown in the right side of the previous figure. Thus, if the data points lie roughly on a line running between southwest and northeast, the covariance is positive. On the other hand, if they lie roughly on a line running between northwest and southeast, the covariance is negative.

Although nonzero covariance always implies statistical dependence, zero covariance does not always imply statistical independence. For example, the following scatterplot displays an example of random variables that are clearly dependent but have nearly zero covariance:

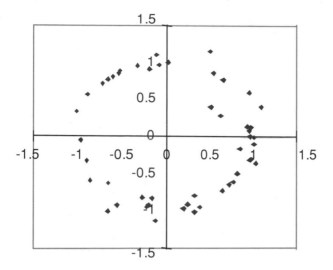

EXERCISE
3.12 THE CORRELATION OF THE HYPOTHETICAL WEATHER DATA

Use the CORREL function within Excel to find the correlation between temperature and head wind on the weather data sheet of PAYLOAD.xls.

The Connection with Linear Regression

A linear regression on the previous data involves fitting a straight line to the points as shown in the following figure.

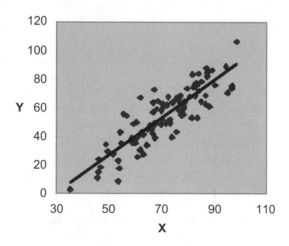

That is, y is expressed as ax + b. The numbers a and b themselves can be expressed in terms of the covariance σ_{xy} as shown in the following equations:

The slope of the line: $a = \dfrac{\sigma_{xy}}{\sigma_x^2}$

The y-intercept: $b = \bar{y} - a\bar{x}$

The predictive power of a regression is usually expressed by a value known as R^2, which is square of the correlation defined in Fundamentals Box 3-6.

Portfolios of Correlated Investments

The concept of random variables is at the heart of the theory of investment portfolios and risk management. In an earlier example we compared pure investments in a domestic and a foreign fund with a diversified investment split between the two funds. Each fund by itself had an expected return of 10% and a standard deviation of 10%. When the investment was split between these two statistically independent funds, the expected return remained the same, but the degree of uncertainty as measured by the standard deviation dropped to roughly 7%. This was a result of diversification alone.

We will now explore what happens when statistically dependent funds are combined. The main result can be stated as in Fundamentals Box 3-7.

Two new funds will be added to the earlier example.

■ FUNDAMENTALS 3-7

Correlated Investments

When *positively* correlated funds are combined, the effects of diversification are **reduced.** When *negatively* correlated funds are combined, the effects of diversification are **increased.**

The International Fund. The returns of this fund, like the domestic and foreign funds, are normally distributed with a mean of 10% and standard deviation of 10%. However, this fund is not independent of the foreign fund. The companies represented by the international and foreign funds are quite similar in nature. Therefore, if one of these funds does well, the other is also likely to do well. Similarly, if one drops in value, the other is likely to drop as well. Thus, there is a positive covariance between these two funds. Suppose it is estimated to be 0.5%.

The Hedge Fund. The hedge fund, like the other funds, has returns that are normally distributed with a mean of 10% and standard deviation of 10%. However, this fund is not independent of the domestic fund. Historically, the investments composing the hedge fund have tended to move in the opposite direction from the domestic fund. Thus, when the domestic goes up, the hedge tends to go down, and vice versa. Therefore, there is a negative covariance between these two funds. Suppose it is estimated to be –0.5%.

The file FUNDS.xls uses the **gen_MVNormal** formula to generate multi-variate normal random variables from a given set of mean returns and covariance matrix.

Domestic	▾	*fx* {=gen_MVNormal(C8:C11,E8:H11)}					
A	B	C	D	E	F	G	H
1	FUNDS.XLS						
2				**Funds**	Domestic	Hedge	Foreign	Internat
3		**Simulated Returns**			10.39%	16.44%	4.05%	8
4								
5								
6						**Covariance Matrix**		
7	**Funds**	**Means**			Domestic	Hedge	Foreign	Internat
8	Domestic	10%	Domestic		0.010	-0.005	0.000	(
9	Hedge	10%	Hedge		-0.005	0.010	0.000	(
10	Foreign	10%	Foreign		0.000	0.000	0.010	(
11	International	10%	International		0.000	0.000	0.005	(

When using this model, keep the following in mind:

■ **gen_MVNormal** is an array formula which has been entered in cells E3:H3 simultaneously, using the <Ctrl> and <Shift> keys. Use the Excel Help command to learn more about array formulas.

■ The covariance, σ_{xy}, of x and y always equals σ_{yx}, so you only have to fill out the diagonal and lower half of the matrix.

■ The diagonal values of .010 are the variances of the funds. Remember that the standard deviations are the square roots of these numbers, or .1.

■ The multivariate normal random variables are generated through a method known as Cholesky Factorization. It is not necessary to understand the details of this process to use the simulation. See Bratley, Fox, and Schrage (1987) and Law and Kelton (1991) for a more thorough explanation of this topic.

Note: Use the **Thaw** command from the **Simulate** menu to activate the random number generation formulas the first time you use the worksheet.

Experimenting with Different Portfolios

Simulating the Individual Funds. Start by running a simulation with one output cell for each of the funds. Run a few thousand trials, and you should find that the distributions of the four funds are virtually indistinguishable. This can be seen clearly by using the **Simulate Common Graphs** command.

Comparing Portfolios. Next we will create three portfolios: domestic combined with hedge, domestic combined with foreign, and foreign combined with international. Place formulas in FUNDS.xls to compute the returns of each pair of funds. For example, the formula for the domestic and hedge portfolio would be .5 * Domestic + .5 * Hedge because we are now splitting our investment between these two funds. These new cells, which you should label D+H, D+F, and F+I, will be your next simulation's output cells. Run a simulation of 10,000 trials. The results should appear as shown in the following figure:

	D+H	D+F	F+I
Average	0.10017	0.10073	0.09944
Std Dev	0.05042	0.0696	0.08628
Std Err	0.0005	0.0007	0.00086
Max	0.29861	0.3544	0.45249
Min	-0.0771	-0.1622	-0.2577
rcentiles			
5%	0.01698	-0.0149	-0.0416
10%	0.03488	0.01142	-0.0096
15%	0.04706	0.02912	0.01024
20%	0.05718	0.04206	0.0273
25%	0.06602	0.05329	0.04114
30%	0.07357	0.06414	0.05387
35%	0.08118	0.07425	0.06553
40%	0.08809	0.08313	0.07651
45%	0.09429	0.09222	0.08811
50%	0.1008	0.10074	0.09944

Simulation Statistics. The simulation statistics show that although on average all three portfolios have the same return, the Value at Risk is lowest for the portfolio comprising the negatively correlated domestic and hedge funds, highest for the positively correlated foreign and international funds, and in between for the uncorrelated domestic and foreign funds.

■ The average returns are the same.

■ Standard deviation reflects degree of uncertainty. Remember, because the returns are normal, 95% of them will lie between plus and minus two standard deviations of the average.

■ Percentiles allow you to calculate the Value at Risk at various levels. For example, if $100,000 were invested, then the 5% of the time the D+H portfolio will make less than $1,698, D+F has a 5% VaR of $1,490, and F+I has a 5% VaR of $4,160.

The Common Graphs. The **Simulate Common Graphs** command is particularly appropriate for comparing investment strategies. Start with the Interactive option and the number of bins set to 30, click **Histogram** (and then close).

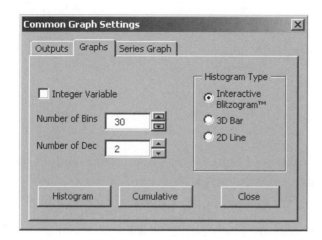

This results in three histograms that can be scrolled through using <Ctrl><PgUp> and <Ctrl><PgDn> to create an animation. The greater the covariance between funds in the portfolio, the wider the distribution.

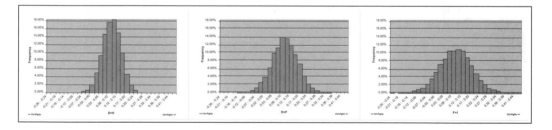

The Blitzogram Interactive Histogram

Next look at the 3D Bar and 2D Line graphs. Notice that the 2D line graph should be used for qualitative results only—as it is not numerically accurate, especially when smoothing is used.

The Common Cumulative Graph. By looking at the previous common histogram, you should be able to figure out which line corresponds to each of the portfolios, even though they are not labeled in the following graph:

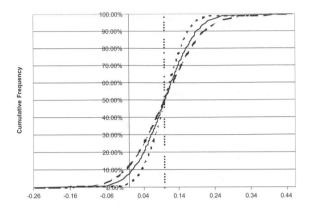

The General Problem of Simulating Correlated Random Variables

As we have seen, **gen_Resample** can be used as an array formula to generate correlated random variables from past data, regardless of their distribution (see gen_Functions.xls for more details).

If you know the means, variances, and covariances of a set of normal random variables, you may generate them in a manner similar to the FUNDS.xls example with the **gen_MVNormal** array formula. Multivariate lognormal variables may similarly be generated with **gen_MVLognormal**. See gen_Functions.xls for more details of **gen_MVNormal** and **gen_MVLognormal**.

Both the @RISK and Crystal Ball programs offer further facilities that allow you to generate correlated random variables from arbitrary distributions using a method known as *rank order correlation*.

How Many Trials Are Enough? Convergence

If you go back to INVNTORY.xls and repeat the simulation several times for 100 trials with a seed of 0, you will get several different estimates for the average cost. This lack of consistency arises from the inherent randomness of Monte Carlo simulation. Run 100 trials of the INVNTORY model. Select **View Trials** from the **Simulate** menu and check the series of interest.

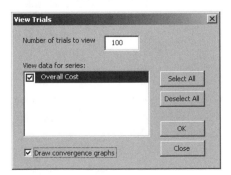

Next, check the **Draw convergence graph** box and click **OK**. A graph similar to the one shown below is generated in a new worksheet within **SimStats**.

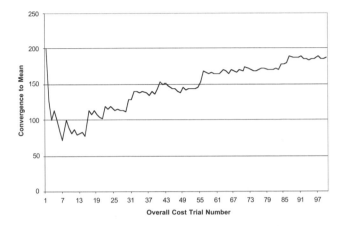

This graph displays the cumulative average of the 100 trials. Note that in this case, after the first few trials, the average overall cost was below 100—but the cost of the 16th trial was a whopper, dragging the average back over 100. You may verify this on the **Trials** sheet of **SimStats**. The simulation is said to have *converged* when this graph becomes flat. This has not yet occurred by 100 trials for this example.

Although the convergence graph provides insight into this process, in practice it can take a long time to generate for a large number of trials. Fortunately, there is another way to estimate the accuracy of the simulation using a number known as the *standard error*.

The Standard Error. If you repeatedly ran this simulation for 100 trials with a seed of 0, you would continue to get varying results. That is, the average of 100 trials of overall cost is a random variable in its own right. How is this average of 100 distributed? According to the **Central Limit Theorem**, it must be approximately normal. The standard error estimates the standard deviation of the distribution of the average of the 100 trials of overall cost. Thus, given the results of this particular run, we can be 95% confident that the true average is 186.5 ± 2x21.7 or between 143 and 230 (see the table on the next page). The greater the number of trials performed, the smaller the standard error will be, but there are diminishing returns. The standard error is, in fact, the standard deviation divided by the square root of the number of trials. Thus, to get twice the accuracy requires four times as many trials; to get three times the accuracy requires nine times as many trials, and so on. Now try running 900 trials and see how smooth the convergence graph becomes. Also the standard error should be roughly 21/3 = 7.

	Overall Cost
Average	186.530059
Std Dev	217.221412
Std Err	21.7221412
Max	1036.61193
Min	0

Note: The standard deviation of 217, displayed above the standard error, refers to the distribution of overall cost (not the average of 100 trials). Because the distribution of overall cost is distinctly not normal (see the histogram of overall cost in the inventory example), it is not true that 95% of the time overall cost will lie in the range 186 ± 2x217. The standard deviation is not a useful concept for such distributions. The probability of overall cost taking on various values should be read from the cumulative graph.

What Is Your Computer Doing Tonight? There are currently at least 100,000,000 computers in the United States. Most of these are idle at least ten hours per day for a total of at least 1 billion wasted computer hours. From the perspective of someone in 1970, when a computer hour cost roughly $1,000, we are squandering the Gross National Product every 24 hours measured in computer power, so feel free to run thousands of trials!

Sensitivity Analysis: The Big Picture

In exploring the effects of uncertainty, it is important to understand the manner in which one uncertainty affects other uncertainties.

TUTORIAL: EXPLORING DEMAND VERSUS OVERALL COST

We will explore the relationship between demand and overall cost in the inventory example worked previously.

1 Return to the simulation of INVNTORY.xls. If you have left Excel, you must first open XLSim, followed by INVNTORY.xls. If you did not save your earlier changes, you must re-specify the random inputs for demand and freight cost. For purposes of this experiment, stock 5 units of inventory even though we now know this is not optimal.

2 This time specify **Demand** as the first output and **Overall Cost** as the second output. Run 50 trials.

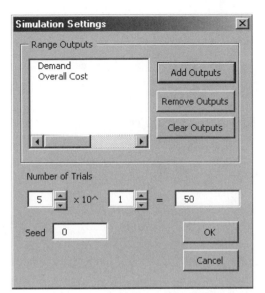

3

When the simulation is complete, select **View Trials** from the **Simulate** menu and select both data series and click **OK**. The trials should appear as shown below:

	A	B	C
1	Demand		Overall Cost
2	4		50
3	7		435.325
4	8		749.01
5	6		191.996
6	5		0
7	1		200

4

Delete column B, then select the entire range of trials and create an XY scatterplot (refer to Excel Help for details).

The resulting graph shows how overall cost (on the vertical axis) varies with demand (on the horizontal axis). It is clear that only cost equals 0 when demand is exactly 5, and that cost increases for both higher and lower values of demand. The vertical stacks such as those above demand = 6 and 8 reflect the various rates of air freight incurred at those demands during the 50 trials.

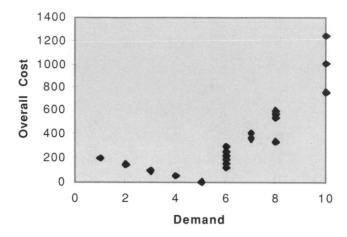

Once you have seen this graph, it is difficult to hold on to the illusion that average overall cost is zero. This picture also helps explain the concept of *linear model*. Had the model been linear, all the points on the scatterplot would have been clustered about a single straight line. In this case, they are clustered about a "V" shaped region.

Hypothesis Testing: Did it Happen by Chance?

It is often difficult to identify causal linkages between events. Does advertising in a local newspaper actually increase sales? Does a cluster of cases of a rare form of cancer indicate an unsafe work environment?

We may explore past data or perform an experiment to generate new data in an attempt to determine causal relationships between events. However, most data displays at least some degree of randomness, which clouds our view of the true relationships.

Hypothesis testing is an effort to distinguish true relationships from patterns in the clouds of randomness inherent in most data. In the final analysis, hypothesis testing helps answer the following question:

Is a true relationship responsible for the perceived pattern, or did it happen by chance?

For example, consider researchers testing a new vaccine who have found fewer cases of the targeted disease among those who have been inoculated than they have among an untreated group. Was the vaccine responsible for the reduction in cases, or did it happen by chance? This is an important question, given that inoculating with the vaccine will be expensive and may bring its own medical risks.

Suppose instead, that the two groups had been treated with smooth vs. chunky peanut butter. One group would undoubtedly have had fewer cases of the disease than the other. Would this have implied that the type of peanut butter had caused the reduction in cases, or could it have happened by chance?

In addition to determining the efficacy of new pharmaceuticals, hypothesis testing applies to relationships between all sorts of data. For example:

■ Are cases of a rare disease that all occurred in the same building due to an unsafe work environment, or did the cluster arise by chance?

■ Was our advertising campaign responsible for the increase in our sales or did it happen by chance?

■ Did on the job experience cause the average number of product defects to decrease over time, or did it happen by chance?

Although these sorts of questions may often be addressed using classical statistical tests, we will use an approach based on simulation that was pioneered separately by Bradley Efron (Efron & Tibshirani, 1993) and Julian Simon (Simon 1974). These computational methods are not only more general than the classical ones, but they also provide far more intuition for those who are not trained in statistics.

Examples

Hypothesis testing is applicable over a wide range of settings. The three examples that follow have been drawn from public health, advertising, and quality control. The examples also display three different types of random sampling. In the first example, the randomness is generated from first principles. In the second, past data is resampled with replacement as in the inventory problem discussed earlier. In the last example, the data is shuffled like a deck of cards.

Disease Clusters

According to the Cancer Information Center of the National Cancer Institute "A disease cluster is the occurrence of a greater than expected number of cases of a particular disease within a group of people, a geographic area, or a period of time." (see http://cis.nci.nih.gov/) Disease clusters can signify the occurrence of an epidemic, a bio-hazard, or some other threat to public health. Therefore they must be taken very seriously. But before panic sets in, one must always ask if the "greater than expected number of cases" could merely have happened by chance.

Consider some horrible non-contagious disease (SHND) that occurs in only 1% of the population. In a particular office building with 250 workers, 5 cases of SHND are reported. Should this raise an alarm concerning the building, or could it have happened by chance?

Make sure that XLSim is loaded, then open BUILDING.xls and execute the Simulate Thaw command. Press the F9 key a few times to make sure the model is working.

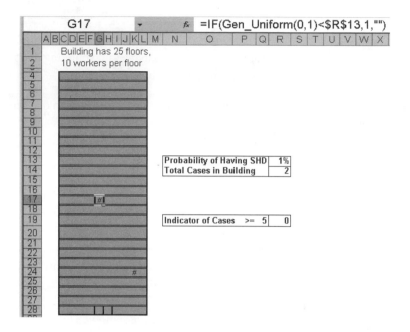

The building, with 25 floors and ten workers per floor, is modeled as follows. For each of the 250 workers, we generate a random number between 0 and 1 with Gen_Uniform(0,1). If the number is less than the population probability of having SHND (in cell R13), the worker is represented by a 1. Otherwise the worker is represented as a Blank. Note that by making the columns narrow and adding decimal places to the 1s, # signs appear on the screen to represent cases of the disease. Since R13 is set at 1%, we would expect one worker in 100 to have the disease, or 2.5 cases on average for a building of this size. Press the calculate key a few times to see the range of outcomes. The indicator in cell R19 is equal to 1 if the total cases in the building equals or exceeds the value in cell Q19 (5 in this case).

Let's assume that the higher than expected number of cases of SHND (5) happened by chance, and thus the building environment was not the cause. This is known as the *null hypothesis* because it assumes that the effect we are concerned about (in this case that of the building) was null. Simulate this model with R14, the total cases in the building, and R19, the indicator of 5 or more cases, as output cells.

Results

You should find that the average number of cases is close to 2.5, which is what we expected in the first place. It is a good idea to include output cells for which you already know the answer, just to verify the model. You should also find that the average value of the indicator, and hence the probability of 5 or more cases is just over 10%[1].

---

[1] For those familiar with the binomial distribution, this result could have been calculated in Excel as 1-BINOMDIST(4,250,0.01,TRUE) which yields 10.8%.

At this stage the alarmists will say: "We told you it was an unsafe building, there is only one chance in ten that the 5 or more cases occurred here by coincidence." This line of reasoning leads to unwarranted hysteria. Suppose the location is in a medium sized city in which there are 100 buildings of this size or greater. You would then expect roughly ten buildings to contain at least 5 workers with SHND. Since the 5 cases could reasonably have happened by chance we had better postpone calling the Center for Disease Control until we learn more.

EXERCISE

3.13 **DISEASE CLUSTER**

Suppose that upon further investigation it is learned that 4 of the 5 cases occurred on the same floor of the building. Does this warrant a call to the CDC, or could this have happened by chance, too?

Advertising Effectiveness

A firm selling a product nation wide has just started experimenting with ads in local newspapers. In the past month they have placed ads in the local papers of 10 of their 30 markets. For each of the 30 markets, the firm has tracked the sales increase from the prior month in which there was no advertising at all. The results are shown in the table below.

Change in Sales from Previous Month				
Markets with Ads		**Markets without Ads**		
Market 1	6.6%	Market 11	-2.8%	
Market 2	9.8%	Market 12	1.9%	
Market 3	8.6%	Market 13	-7.9%	
Market 4	-1.3%	Market 14	8.5%	
Market 5	4.9%	Market 15	4.1%	
Market 6	14.1%	Market 16	3.0%	
Market 7	11.4%	Market 17	3.3%	
Market 8	13.9%	Market 18	1.7%	
Market 9	6.6%	Market 19	6.6%	
Market 10	-1.1%	Market 20	7.0%	
		Market 21	3.4%	
		Market 22	5.0%	
		Market 23	8.2%	
		Market 24	6.6%	
		Market 25	4.1%	
		Market 26	10.1%	
		Market 27	-3.5%	
		Market 28	-1.2%	
		Market 29	10.6%	
		Market 30	9.9%	
				Difference of Averages
Average	**7.35%**	**Average**	**3.93%**	**3.42%**

On average, the sales in the markets with the ads increased 3.42% more than in the markets without ads. Was this increase caused by the ads or did it happen by chance? We will test this with a simulation.

Make sure that XLSim is loaded in Excel, then open Markets.xls and execute the **Simulate Thaw** command.

The Data

The left side of the sheet displays the original data. Cells C3:C12 have been given the range name of AD, while cells E3:E22 have been named NO_AD.

	H3			f_x	=gen_Resample(AD,NO_AD)					
	B	C	D	E	F	G	H	I	J	K
1	Change in Sales from Previous Month						Simulated Changes			
2	Markets with Ads		Markets without Ads				"Left" numbers	"Right" numbers		
3	Market 1	6.6%	Market 11	-2.8%			5.0%	-3.5%		
4	Market 2	9.8%	Market 12	1.9%			-1.2%	3.3%		
5	Market 3	8.6%	Market 13	-7.9%			-7.9%	11.4%		
6	Market 4	-1.3%	Market 14	8.5%			6.6%	4.1%		
7	Market 5	4.9%	Market 15	4.1%			7.0%	1.7%		
8	Market 6	14.1%	Market 16	3.0%			9.8%	-7.9%		
9	Market 7	11.4%	Market 17	3.3%			14.1%	10.1%		
10	Market 8	13.9%	Market 18	1.7%			5.0%	3.3%		
11	Market 9	6.6%	Market 19	6.6%			4.1%	4.9%		
12	Market 10	-1.1%	Market 20	7.0%			3.4%	4.1%		
13			Market 21	3.4%				6.6%		
14			Market 22	5.0%				5.0%		
15			Market 23	8.2%				4.1%		
16			Market 24	6.6%				-1.2%		
17			Market 25	4.1%				9.8%		
18			Market 26	10.1%				5.0%		
19			Market 27	-3.5%				6.6%		
20			Market 28	-1.2%				4.1%		
21			Market 29	10.6%				3.3%		
22			Market 30	9.9%				6.6%		
23					Difference of Averages		Average of "Left"	Average of "Right"	Difference of Averages	Indicator Diff>3.42%
24	Average	7.35%	Average	3.93%	3.42%		4.59%	4.07%	0.52%	0

The Simulation

Cells (H3:H12 and I3:I22) all contain the same gen_Resample formula which draws numbers randomly from both the AD and NO_AD data ranges with replacement. Press the Calculate key a few times to make sure the sheet is working properly. Since we are assuming for the moment that ads make no difference, we can think of the whole data set as being drawn from a single distribution of changes in sales. Therefore we should expect that the average of the left randomized column would often be greater than the average of the right randomized column by 3.42% or more. Note that the indicator in cell K24 tests for this. As mentioned earlier, the process of sampling historical data is known as bootstrapping.

| | | | K24 | ▾ | f_x | =IF(J24>=F24,1,0) |

	H	I	J	K
	Average of "Left" numbers	Average of "Right"	Difference of Averages	Indicator Diff>3.42%
23				
24	4.59%	4.07%	0.52%	0

Run a simulation with K24 as the output cell, and you will find an average of about 5%. This means there is only about a 5% chance of getting a difference of 3.42% or greater at random. Equivalently, there is a 95% chance that the original placement of numbers into the left and right columns *did* make a difference, and hence, that the advertising was probably the cause.

Resampling vs. Shuffling

In the last example, numbers were drawn at random from a data set using **gen_Resample**. This is known as sampling with replacement, because it is equivalent to repeatedly drawing numbered cards from a deck, recording the number, then replacing the cards in the deck. When you view the Markets worksheet and press the Calculate key, the simulated changes (on the right) are generated by drawing and replacing 30 times from the actual changes (on the left). You will see that some data elements may appear more than once in the simulated changes while others may not appear at all.

In the next example, we will create randomness that is analogous to shuffling the cards instead of sampling with replacement. With shuffling, each data element will appear exactly once, but in a different order each time the Calculate key is pressed. This is known as a permutation test, and is it performed using the gen_Shuffle formula. See (Efron & Tibshirani, 1993) and (Simon, 1974) for a further discussion of these techniques.

Quality Improvement

A firm that manufactures 100 circuit boards each week hired a new production manager sixteen weeks ago. They have tracked the number of defective boards per week since then, as shown in the graph below. This appears to indicate a reduction in the average number of defects over time. In another good sign, the consistency from week to week also seems to be improving.

As a quantitative measure, the firm has calculated the average number of defects in both the first and second 8 week periods since the arrival of the new manager. They have also calculated the standard deviation over these two periods, with a lower standard deviation indicating greater consistency. The results are displayed in the table below.

Number of Defects by Week

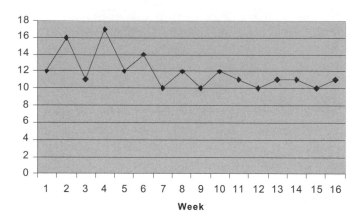

	First eight weeks	Second eight weeks	Improvement
Average no. of Defects	13.00	10.75	2.25
Standard Dev. of Defects	2.45	0.71	1.74

EXERCISE 3.14 **QUALITY CONTROL**

The file DEFECTS.xls contains the data with calculated results. The firm wants to confirm that the apparent improvement is not just due to chance. Use **gen_Shuffle** to randomize the order in which the data appears. Then run a simulation to determine:

a. The chance that the average number of defects could improve by 2.25 or more between the first and second half of the data, if the numbers were ordered randomly.

b. Perform a similar experiment to determine whether the improvement in standard deviation could have happened by chance.

Note: See the file gen_Functions.xls to view an example of **gen_Shuffle**.

Conclusion

Uncertain numbers are common in every aspect of human endeavor. Traditionally, analytical solutions to most such problems were so difficult that managers plugged in "best guesses" for the inputs and hoped for reasonable outputs. As we have seen, this often leads to the flaw of averages. Today's microcomputers allow Monte Carlo simulation to be applied to many of these problems in the managerial vernacular of the spreadsheet, so that everyone in the organization can understand the results.

END OF CHAPTER EXERCISES

3.15 EVALUATING A PETROLEUM PROPERTY

A petroleum firm is considering the purchase of a producing, but marginally profitable oil field. It is known to contain 1 million barrels of oil. However, the pumping cost is an expensive $9 per barrel. The price of oil at the time they are considering the deal is $10 per barrel. Thus if they could pump all the oil right away, the firm would net $1 million. Unfortunately, it will take one year to set up the production system, and by that time the price of oil may have changed. It is estimated that the price of a barrel of oil one year in the future is normally distributed with a mean of $10 and a standard deviation of $3.

The President of the firm says: "since the average price of oil in one year is $10, the average value of the deal is still $1 million."

The Chief Financial Officer says: "because of the uncertainty the expected value must be less than $1 million."

They are both wrong. Prove by means of a simulation that the expected value of the deal is greater than $1 million. *Note:* This is an example of what is known as a Real Option. What does the word option refer to in this example?

3.16 FUNDING A NEW BUSINESS

Imagine that your firm has committed to a new web based service for which you can expect revenue of $100 per customer. There is no marginal cost of providing the service. However, infrastructure must be developed, which will require capital. Specifically, $80 of up-front investment is required for each unit of customer capacity.

To make the accounting easier, assume that the new product will become obsolete after only one month. Furthermore, demand for your one month of business is uncertain, but your best guess is 20,000 customers, with a 95% confidence interval of between 10,000 and 30,000 customers. Therefore, planning for the average case, the firm intends to set up a facility with a capacity of 20,000 customers. This will require an investment of $80 x 20,000 = $1,600,000.

The expected revenue is estimated to be $100 x 20,000 = $2,000,000. Subtract off the investment of $1,600,000, and the expected profit is $400,000. Critique this analysis in terms of the levels of stochastic enlightenment, and suggest an improvement to the plan.

3.17 BOTTOM-UP BUDGETING

A large organization uses a bottom up approach to budgeting. Each of its ten divisional Vice Presidents submits an estimated budget to the CEO, who then makes the final allocation. Needless to say, the Vice Presidents are not completely certain of their needs. Suppose that their cash requirements are independent and normally distributed with a mean of $1 million, and standard deviation of $100,000, and suppose further that each Vice President requested their average requirement of $1 Million. Then by adding these estimates together, the CEO would arrive at $10 Million for the correct average of the total budget. But what Vice President in his or her right mind would submit a budget that had a 50% chance of being exceeded? So instead of submitting the average, one might expect the VPs to submit a number that they were 90% confident would be adequate.

a. Using the Excel function =Normdist, determine the amount that each VP would have to submit in order to be 90% confident of not exceeding the budget.

b. If the CEO arrived at a total budget by adding up these estimates, what would be the probability of exceeding the total budget?

c. If the CEO wished to achieve 90% confidence of not exceeding the total budget, how much ought to be initially allocated to each of the 10 divisions, assuming that funds can be moved between divisions during the year if needed.

Hint: Simulate the cash requirements of each of the ten, along with their sum.

3.18 REAL ESTATE CREDIT RISK

A regional bank has determined that when real estate values fall, the rate of default increases on their home equity loans as shown in the following table.

% Change in Real Estate	Default rate/1000
15%	1
10%	2
5%	2
0%	2
-5%	8
-10%	30
-15%	60
-20%	100

Due to an adverse economy, the region's real estate is expected to drop in value 10% on average over the next year. Thus the bank is planning on a default rate of 30 per thousand. However, it is expected that there will be variation across the region, with a standard deviation of 5% around the mean of 10%. What advice would you give to the managers of the bank?

Hint: Use VLOOKUP to convert change in real estate value percent into default rate. However, this requires sorting the table on the percent column from negative to positive.

3.19 ASIAN OPTION

An Asian stock option differs from a standard option in that the value at maturity is the difference between the strike price and the average stock price during the period, not the *final* stock price. Although the famous Black-Scholes equation provides an analytical way to estimate the value of a normal option, Asian options require simulation.

a. Modify Option.xls to model an Asian **Call Option**.

b. For various strike prices, compare the value of the Asian vs. the standard option.

3.20 GROWTH OF AN INVESTMENT

It is common to simulate the growth of an investment over time. Create an investment model, by modifying Option.xls so that the time period is 10 years instead of 12 weeks.

a. Change cell F6 to contain the formula =**Volatility** to reflect the fact that we are now using annual sigma instead of weekly sigma. Set annual sigma to 15%.

b. Remove all reference to the option calculations (payoff formulas) and strike price.

c. The annual rate is now the expected annual growth rate of the investment, for example 10%. Be sure to change cell G6 to contain =**Rate** to reflect this.

d. Replace Current Price with the amount of the investment.

Run a simulation of the value of the investment in each of the 10 years, and observe how it changes from year to year using the interactive histogram.

3.21 A RETIREMENT PLAN

Starting with the model created for problem 5, simulate a retirement plan in which a fixed amount is withdrawn from the fund each year. Perform a parameterized simulation in which you adjust the amount withdrawn, and determine the probability that the fund will last the full 10 years before being depleted.

3.22 Playing Cards

Simulate drawing five cards from a 52 card deck. Use indicator variables to estimate the probability of drawing:

a. Four of a kind.

b. A flush (all five cards are of the same suit).

c. A Straight (five consecutive numbers).

Hint: Represent the cards by the numbers 1 through 52, and use a table lookup to store the suit and value associated with each number. Use gen_Shuffle on the numbers 1 through 52 and represent the hand by the first five numbers.

3.23 Game of Craps

The game of "craps" is played with dice. A simplified version of the rules is described below.

On the first roll of the dice:
> if a 2, 3, or 12 appears the game is over and the player loses $1.
> if a 7 or 11 appears the game is over and the player wins $1.
> If any other number appears, that number is called the "point" and the player continues to roll.

For subsequent rolls of the dice:
> if a 7 appears the game is over and the player loses $1.
> if the point appears the game is over and the player wins $1.
> If any other number appears then the player continues to roll.

Write a simulation of a complete game, which must end in either a win or loss. Note that although in theory the game could go on forever, it is virtually impossible for there to be more than 30 rolls. To be safe, model a maximum of 50 rolls per game. As output cells, keep track of the winnings ($1 or -$1) and the length of the game.

4 ∎∎∎∎∎∎∎∎∎∎∎∎∎∎∎∎∎∎∎∎∎∎∎∎∎∎∎∎∎

Uncertainties That Evolve Over Time

For tribal man space was the uncontrollable mystery.
For technological man it is time that occupies the same role.

MARSHALL MCLUHAN, CANADIAN COMMUNICATIONS THEORIST

As we have seen, Monte Carlo simulation investigates the possible outcomes of a single event by generating numerous possible inputs at random and recording the distribution of outputs. This idea can be extended to systems that evolve over time subject to a continual barrage of uncertain inputs.

- Municipal planners must estimate the disruption to traffic flow caused by toll booths or construction projects.

- Engineers must predict the performance of telecommunications networks given uncertain levels of equipment failure and message traffic.

- The Federal Aviation Agency must implement air traffic control systems that prevent excessive congestion and lengthy holding patterns given uncertain aircraft arrival.

- Marketing managers must estimate the manner in which their market share will evolve over time.

Discrete-event simulation and Markov chains are two approaches to modeling systems that evolve over time.

■ ■ ■ OVERVIEW

Introduction

This section contains a short introduction to discrete-event simulation and instructions for installing and running QUEUE.xla and Q_NET.xla, which model simple queues and queuing networks in Excel.

Simulation Through Time: Discrete-Event Simulation

This section introduces the concept of discrete-event simulation. First, the spread of a forest fire is modeled as a fixed-time-increment simulation. Then queues (waiting lines) and queuing networks are modeled as event incremented simulations. Examples include cars waiting at a toll booth, customers waiting for service at a bank, and air traffic control. The Extend™ discrete simulation package is introduced, and it is shown how to link it to spreadsheet models.

Markov Chains

Certain evolving systems can be modeled effectively as Markov chains, which are also discussed in this chapter and implemented in MARKOV.xls.

INTRODUCTION

Systems That Evolve Over Time

Many systems involve the interactions of discrete random events such as cars arriving at a toll booth or customers showing up at a bank. These systems evolve over time, with traffic jams or lines at the tellers arising and then dissipating. Although large-scale discrete-event simulation is beyond the capability of spreadsheets, a spreadsheet is sufficient to illuminate some important aspects of this technique. Simple queues and queuing networks can be simulated with QUEUE.xla and Q_NET.xla, add-ins for modeling simple queues and small queuing networks, respectively.

Devoted discrete event simulation packages such as Extend™ offer great advantages over the spreadsheet in both ease of use and speed of simulation. Furthermore, these systems may be integrated with spreadsheets to get the best of both worlds.

Markov chains are a powerful way to model evolving populations. These can be populations of customers moving between products, patients moving between states of health, or equipment moving between various states of repair or disrepair. MARKOV.xls is a scalable worksheet used to model several examples.

QUEUE.xla and Q_NET.xla

QUEUE.xla is used with QUEUE.xls to model a simple queue. Q_NET.xla is used with Q_NET.xls to model a queuing network. *QUEUE.xla and Q_NET.xla should not both be loaded at the same time.* Both QUEUE.xla and Q_NET.xla require Excel 5.0 or higher.

Running QUEUE.xla and Q_NET.xla. Launch Excel and open QUEUE.xla and QUEUE.xls or Q_NET.xla and Q_NET.xls from the File menu. QUEUE.xls and Q_NET.xls can be modified and saved under any desired file name. *Important:* Make sure your worksheet's calculation mode is set to automatic under **Tools Options** before running these add-ins.

Auto Load Option. If you want QUEUE.xla or Q_NET.xla to load every time you launch Excel

1. Select **Add-ins** from the **Tools** menu in Excel.

2. Select QUEUE.xla or Q_NET.xla from the list of add-ins and click **OK**. You can later go back and deselect either of them from the Add-in menu to prevent Excel from loading them automatically. Do not load them both at once as they will not run correctly.

SIMULATION THROUGH TIME: DISCRETE-EVENT SIMULATION

It is quite simple to predict the behavior of a single automobile arriving at a traffic light on an empty road, but very difficult to predict the overall traffic flow in a large city at rush hour. By creating a computer model of a large number of cars sharing the same roads, however, we can learn about the dynamics of the larger system. Simulation such as this involves a sequence of discrete random events through time and is known as **discrete-event simulation.** See Law and Kelton (1991) for a thorough treatment of this subject.

Although spreadsheets were not designed for discrete-event simulation, a technique we refer to as the *paste special method* can be used to model a wide variety of situations. Imagine a workbook with two sheets, one called **NOW** and the other called **NEXT TIME.** The **NOW** sheet contains a model of the world at the current time and contains numbers only, no formulas. The **NEXT TIME** sheet contains only formulas, describing how the current state of the world will change by the next time increment. The following example shows a fixed increment simulation of a clock that ticks to a new minute between **NOW** and **NEXT TIME.** Note that the time in **NEXT TIME** is the time in **NOW** plus 1.

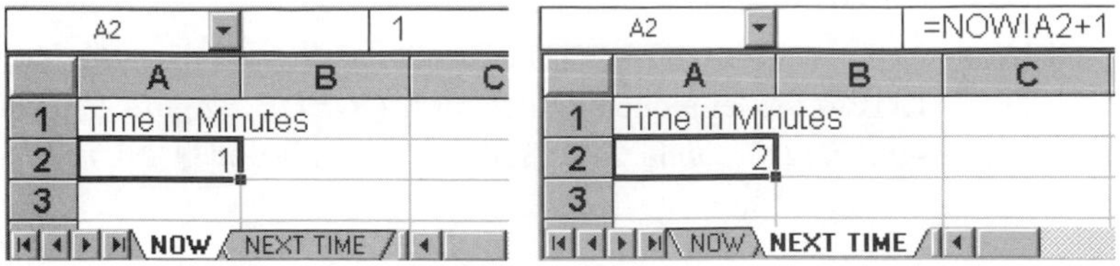

The iterative step to make this clock tick is to copy the contents of **NEXT TIME**, and paste the values only (not formulas) into **NOW** using the **Edit Paste Special Values** command. At this point, **NEXT TIME** will display the state of the world at the following next time, or 3 in this case.

A Fixed-Time-Incremented Simulation of a Forest Fire

The file FIRE.xls contains a fixed-time-increment simulation of a forest fire based on the general approach just described. This file uses a macro to automate the **Paste Special** step. *Important:* Make sure your worksheet's calculation mode is set to automatic under **Tools Options** before attempting to run this model.

The forest is modeled as a grid of squares, one-quarter mile per side. Each square can either contain fire (1), or contain no fire (0). The sheet has been formatted so that 0's appear as blanks and 1's appear as number signs (#). The fire spreads according to two rules:

1. If a square contains fire now, then it will contain fire next time.

2. If a square does not contain fire now, then the probability that it will contain fire next time is proportional to both the number of neighboring squares containing fire and the overall fire danger.

Retrieve FIRE.xls, shown in the following figure.

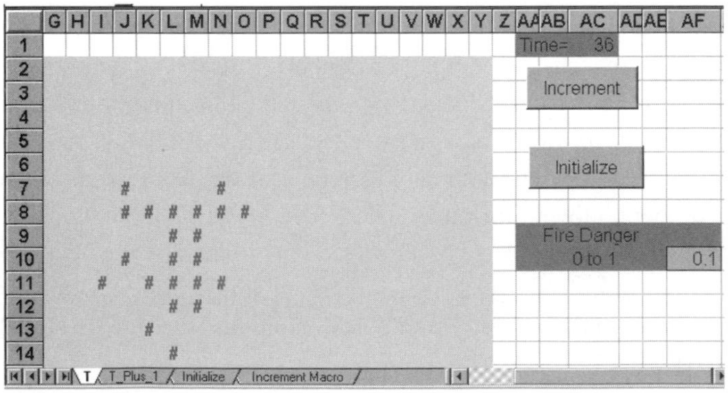

■ **FUNDAMENTALS 4-1**

How Time Is Advanced in Discrete-Event Simulation

Time is generally advanced or *incremented* in one of the following two ways in discrete-event simulation:

- ■ *Fixed-Time Increments.* Time in the simulation advances minute by minute, hour by hour, or by some other fixed increment. Various events either occur or do not occur within each time increment, based on both the system's current state and random variables.

- ■ *Event-Incremented Time.* Time in the simulation advances to the next event of interest. The next event and its time of occurrence are based on both the system's current state and random variables. In practice, most discrete-event simulations are of this type.

There are four sheets in FIRE.xls. **T** displays the state of the forest at the current time and contains only numbers. The fire danger is entered in cell AF10 of this sheet. **T_Plus_1** displays the state of the forest one hour from now and contains formulas that impose the rules of fire spread. For example, the formula that defines the state of cell D3 in sheet **T_Plus_1** is

=IF(T!D3=1,1,IF(Danger*SUM(T!C2:E4)/8>RAND(),1,0))

The **Initialize** sheet contains the initial state of the forest. **Increment Macro** contains the Visual Basic code used to initialize and increment the simulation.

EXERCISE

4.1 EXPLAINING THE FORMULA FOR THE SPREAD OF FIRE

a. Explain how the formula in **T_Plus_1** models the fire spreading rules.

b. How would you model a wind blowing from the west that made it more likely for the fire to spread to the east?

Now experiment with the model:

c. Click **Initialize**.

d. Type 1 into squares where fire has started.

e. Click **Increment** to simulate fire spread. The higher the fire danger, the faster the spread.

This same basic approach could be extended to model the following:

■ The movement of some new popular product into a market.

■ The spread of a disease through a population.

■ The progress of a military engagement.

Cellular Automata

In 1970 Martin Gardner (Gardner2) wrote an article in Scientific American about a fascinating game developed by John Conway, a British mathematician. The "Game of Life" as it was called, swept the scientific community, as people tried to come up with initial population configurations that continued to grow, as opposed to remaining steady or going extinct (see Exercise 4.3). This game was based on cellular automata; arrays of simple computing entities that can be in any one of a few states, and whose states evolve through time based on the states of their neighbors. Spreadsheets are an ideal environment in which to experiment with cellular automata, and indeed this is exactly how we modeled the evolution of the forest fire above. One of the world's leading experts on the subject is Stephen Wolfram, whose recent book; *A New Kind of Science* (Wolfram), applies a similar approach to many aspects of science.

EXERCISE
4.2 **SELF-REPRODUCING PATTERNS**

PART A

One of the most remarkable examples of cellular automata is also one of the simplest. Consider cells in a square grid that can take on only the values of 0 and 1, and obey the following rules:

1) We define the "Neighbors" of a cell to be the four squares immediately above, below, to the left, and to the right.

2) A cell will equal 0 at time T + 1 if it has either 0 or 2 neighboring cells that were equal to 1 at time T. A cell will equal 1 at time T + 1 if it has either 1 or 3 neighboring cells that were equal to 1 at time T.

Modify FIRE.xls to propagate "1"s according to the rules above and, amazingly, you will discover that ANY initial pattern will reproduce! For example, the illustration below shows several stages in the evolution of a simple human figure.

Generation

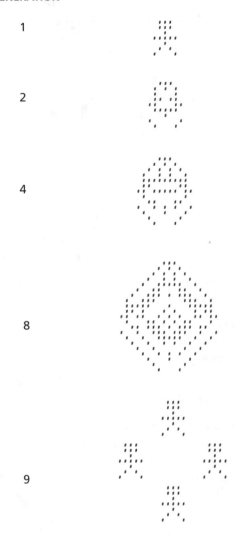

1	
2	
4	
8	
9	

HINTS:

a) Expand the size of the **T** and **T_Plus_1** ranges in FIRE.xls, then zoom the view to 60% so you can see more of the picture. Strange things happen when the pattern runs off the edge. Try it and see.

A simple way to express rule 2 above in the spreadsheets is to use the MOD formula shown below for cell C3 of the T_Plus_1 sheet.

=MOD(T!B3+T!C2+T!D3+T!C4,2)

This formula takes the sum of the neighbors modulo 2, which is 0 for an even number and 1 for an odd number.

PART B

But wait, there's more. It turns out that this will work not only with 2 states, but with any prime number of states, where the transition rule is the sum of the neighbors modulo that prime. Using the Conditional Format command in Excel, create a three-colored version of part A. Remember that BLANK counts towards your colors.

EXERCISE
4.3   THE GAME OF LIFE

Create the Game of Life, which is defined as follows:

1) The "Neighbors" of a cell are the eight cells surrounding it, as in the moves that could be made by a King in chess.

2) If a cell is alive (equals 1) at time T, it will die of loneliness at T+1 if it has one or fewer neighbors at time T. It will die of overcrowding at T+1 if it has four or more neighbors at time T.

3) If there is no life at a cell (equals 0) at time T, a birth will occur at T + 1 if there are exactly three neighbors at time T.

As of the Scientific American article, no one had found an initial configuration of cells that would grow indefinitely. Subsequently a "mother" configuration was discovered that continually bred multi-celled "children" that quickly moved away from home. The reader is urged to look at (Gardner 2) or search the Internet for articles on the Game of Life.

Hint: Because the rules are more complicated than those of the previous example, it would makes sense to write a user-defined function for the cells on sheet **T_plus_1** that govern the birth and death events.

Queuing Models

A process often modeled with discrete-event simulation is a queue of people, jobs, or machines waiting for some sort of service. The number of arrivals at a queue can often be modeled by a *Poisson* distribution.

The Poisson Distribution

The following is a loose rendition of the derivation of the Poisson distribution[1]. Poisson, an early 19th century French mathematician, was studying data concerning the number of soldiers killed per month by horse kick in the Prussian army. Suppose that there were three Horse Kick Deaths (HKD's) per month on average, or equivalently 10% chance of a death each day on average. Then one might model the number killed on a particular day as the flip of an unfair coin that comes up Heads 90% of the time and Tails (because that's the end of the horse you received) 10% of the time. Thus the number of HKD's per month are binomially distributed with **n**=30 and **p**=0.10, right? Close, but no cigar you say, because we have ignored the possibility that two soldiers could get killed on the same day. No problem Poisson says, we will divide the month into 60 half-days. Now the probability of an HKD on a single half-day is 5%, so HKD's per month are still binomially distributed with an average of 3 per month, but now with **n**=60 and **p**=0.05. But two soldiers could receive fatal kicks on the same half-day you complain. No problem Poisson says again, we will model quarter days by upping **n** to 120 and reducing **p** to 0.025. We could go on doubling **n** and halving **p** forever, getting continually more accurate estimates of the distribution of HKD's per month until we dropped from exhaustion. If you have taken a course in calculus, you have heard this process referred to as "taking a limit." The file POISSON.xls allows you to interactively compare the binomial distribution to the theoretical Poisson distribution by moving a slide bar to control the number **n**. Note how quickly the two distributions converge as **n** is increased. For additional discussion of the Poisson distribution, see Law and Kelton (1991), or any book on probability or statistics.

Modeling Cars at a Toll Booth

Now instead of the arrivals of horses hooves on Prussian soldiers, we will consider the arrivals of cars at a toll booth. Suppose in this case, the historical data indicates that the number of cars arriving per minute is Poisson distributed, with a mean of 3.67, and the maximum number of cars that can be serviced per minute is also Poisson distributed, with a mean of 5.

Because the average number that can be served is higher than the average number of arrivals, we would not expect a tremendous traffic jam. But this doesn't mean that there might not occasionally be some cars waiting in line. How many should we expect to be waiting, and how long might they wait on average? We will discuss this from a theoretical perspective, then run a time-incremented simulation.

There is extensive theory on the subject of queues, such as that provided by Hillier and Lieberman (1990). Here we cover only the most fundamental aspects of the theory (see Fundamentals Box 4-2).

---

[1] Reprinted, with permission from Savage (2001) Copyright © INFORMS, 2001.

■ FUNDAMENTALS 4-2

M/M/1 Queues

- Simple queues like the one at the toll booth, in which both arrival rate and maximum service rate are Poisson distributed, are known as M/M/1 queues. Mathematicians have developed a good theoretical understanding of the behavior of these simple queues. The arrival and service rates of a queue are often denoted by λ (lambda) and μ (mu), respectively. The ratio λ/μ is known as the **utilization factor,** ρ (rho). In the current example, $\rho = 3.67/5 = 0.73$.

- The theoretical **average length** of an M/M/1 queue is given by this formula:

  $$L_q = \rho^2/(1 - \rho).$$

  If the arrival rate exceeds the service rate, we would expect big trouble at the toll booth. But notice that according to the formula the average queue length becomes infinite even if the arrival rate just equals the service rate, that is, $\rho = 1$.

- The **average waiting time** someone spends in line is given by this formula:

  $$W_q = L_q/\lambda.$$

3.67 cars arrive every minute on average. Equivalently, the average time between cars is 0.273 minutes.

Up to 5 cars may be serviced per minute on average. Equivalently, the average time to service a car is 0.2 minutes.

EXERCISE

4.4 THE AVERAGE NUMBER OF CARS WAITING AT A TOLL BOOTH

How many cars will be in line at the toll booth on average, according to theory?

Classifying Queues

Queues come in all shapes and sizes. They are typically classified according to three properties:

■ The distribution of arrivals

■ The distribution of service times

■ The number of parallel servers

The toll booth example is known as an M/M/1 queue because both the interarrival times and service times are exponentially distributed (see the following discussion of exponential distribution). This in turn implies that the amount of time you would expect to wait for a car to arrive at the toll booth is independent of how long you have waited without seeing a car. Such a process is known as memoryless or Markovian. That explains the two M's, one for the arrivals and one for the service times. The 1 indicates that there is a single server (the toll booth in this example). So, for example, a queue with distribution A of arrivals and distribution B of service times with N servers would be an A/B/N queue. The theory of queues covers many special cases beyond the M/M/1 queue. In complex circumstances, however, the theory gets overwhelmed and discrete-event simulation can provide the best indication of how such a system will behave.

Fixed- versus Event-Incremented Time

As discussed earlier, a fixed-time-increment simulation models the *number* of events occurring *within a given time* increment. This is a *discrete* random variable (that is, 0, 1, 2, and so on), often Poisson distributed, as in the toll booth example.

An event-incremented simulation, on the other hand, models the *time between* events. This is a *continuous* random variable that is *exponentially* distributed if the number of events per time period is Poisson distributed. The relationship between Poisson and exponential distributions is described in Fundamentals Box 4-3.

Therefore a fixed-increment simulation of the toll booth would model the number of cars arriving per minute as a Poisson random variable with $\lambda=3.67$. An event- incremented simulation of the toll booth models car interarrival time as an exponential random variable with $\alpha=1/3.67 = .273$ minutes.

It is useful to compare the graphs of these two distributions. A Poisson distribution with an average arrival rate of 3.67 is shown on the left in the following figure. The corresponding exponential distribution with an average interarrival time of $1/3.67=0.272$ is on the right.

Poisson distribution, average arrivals/minute, I = 3.67

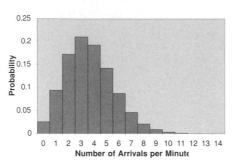

Exponential distribution, average time between arrivals in minutes a = 0.272

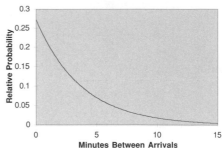

■ FUNDAMENTALS 4-3

Relation Between Poisson and Exponential Distributions

If the number of events occurring in a fixed increment of time is a ***Poisson*** random variable, with a mean of λ per time period, then the amount of time occurring between events is an ***Exponential*** random variable, with a mean of $1/\lambda$ time units, and vice versa. $1/\lambda$ is often referred to as α (alpha) in this context.

TUTORIAL: SIMULATING AN EVENT INCREMENTED QUEUE

To run an event incremented simulation of a queue, we will use QUEUE.xls. This file does not require XLSim.xla but does require that we open QUEUE.xla. Proceed as follows:

1 Open QUEUE.xla. This contains the programs that run the simulation using the **Paste Special** method introduced earlier. It adds a **Queue** menu to Excel when loaded.

2 Open QUEUE.xls. Shown below, QUEUE.xls contains the model of the queue. This file can be modified and saved under other file names.

	A	B	C	D	E	F	G
1				Max Run Time		20.00	
2				Mean Inter Arvl Tm		0.273	
3	Initialize			Mean Svc Time		0.200	
4							
5	Step	Time		Queue Statistics:			
6	Run	1.69			Queue Length		2
7					Number Served		5
8	☐ Make Graph				Total Wait Time		0.28
9	☐ Update Screen				Avg Wait Time		0.06
10					Avg Queue Length		0.17
11	Queue Length				Avg. through-put		2.96
12					Max Queue Length		2
13				Status Indicators:			
14					Server Busy		1
15	0 5 10 15				Arrival		1
16					Departure		0
17							
18				Next Event Times:			
19					Service		1.689214766
20					System Arrival		1.686866213

◄◄ ◄ ► ►► \ **Current State** / Next State / Initial / Rest ◄

3   Specify parameters. Enter total time to simulate, mean interarrival time, and mean service time in cells F1:F3.

4   Initialize counters. Click on the Initialize button or choose **Initialize** from the **Queue** menu to set all counters to the initial state stored on the **Initial** tab of the workbook.

5   Single step the simulation. Click on the **Step** button, use the **Single Step** command, or press **Alt-S** to move the simulation to the next event.

6   Run the simulation. To run the simulation for a specified simulated time, enter the desired stopping time in cell F1, click the **Make Graph** and **Update Screen** boxes, then click on the **Run** button or choose **Run Simulation** from the **Queue** menu. Statistics for the run will appear on the **Current State** tab. A graph of the queue length over time will appear on the **Results** tab as shown below.

Queue Length over Time

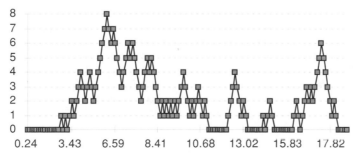

7

The graph will vary a great deal from run to run. Also, since we started the queue length at zero (not its average), it will generally take several events for the queue to reach more representative behavior. This is known as the *startup* or *transient effect*.

Quick run the simulation. **Quick Run** runs faster, but does not produce the graph. This is the model used by the Run button when the **Make Graph** box is not checked. Removing the check from the **Update Screen** box will also greatly enhance runtime. To halt the simulation while it is running, hold down the **Ctrl** and **Break** keys simultaneously.

8

Quit. This removes QUEUE.xla from memory and **Queue** from Excel's menu bar.

EXERCISE
4.5   SIMULATING A QUEUE

a. Run a simulation of one hour of simulated time with a graph of the queue length.

b. Reinitialize and perform this experiment for various lengths of time. Compare these simulated averages with the theoretical average calculated in Exercise 4.4. You might find that it takes a very long time before the average queue length converges to its theoretical value.

Queuing Networks

It is rare that a queue exists in isolation as in the toll booth example. More often a process consists of a number of queues connected in some way. Such situations are known as queuing networks and can be modeled with Q_NET.xls.

Parallel Queues. As an example, suppose the automated toll booth begins to have mechanical problems running at a service rate of 5 cars per minute. It is determined that the maximum rate at which it can consistently provide service is only half the original rate, or 2.5 cars per minute.

In an effort to provide the same level of service, the highway department contemplates putting in two toll lanes. Each lane will have a booth with a maximum service rate of 2.5 cars per minute, or average service time of 0.4 minutes. Assume that incoming cars choose a lane at random with equal probability. This situation is pictured below.

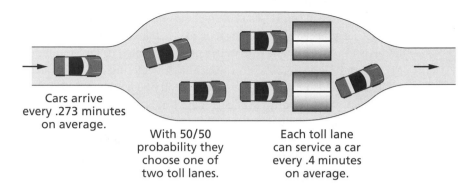

Cars arrive every .273 minutes on average.

With 50/50 probability they choose one of two toll lanes.

Each toll lane can service a car every .4 minutes on average.

Because each toll booth receives, on average, one-half the traffic of the single toll booth and can service one-half the number of cars per minute, we might expect the performance of this system to be similar to the single toll booth.

Q_NET.xls and Q_NET.xla. Q_NET.xls (with Q_NET.xla) works in the same general manner as QUEUE.xls (with QUEUE.xla), with a *current, next,* and *initial* sheet. Instead of a single column of queue statistics, however, there is one column for each of the two stations in the network.

A transition matrix controls the flow between the stations. In the example shown, a system arrival (Station 0) has a probability of 1/2 of going to station 1 or 2. Anything leaving station 1 or 2 has a 100% chance of going to the exit (station 3). New stations can be added or deleted as desired. The **Run** button is on the **Current** sheet, as in QUEUE.xls. The results sheet displays a graph of average throughput of the system over time.

Open Q_NET.xls and Q_NET.xla, shown in the following figure. The worksheet models a general queuing network. Its original configuration represents two parallel queues.

	A	B	C	D	E	F	G	H	I	J	K	L
1	Q_NET.XLS											
2												
3												
4							*****************************					
5		**Add Station**				*	Transition Matrix	*				
6						*****************************						
7												
8		**Delete Station**					Sys. Arvl	Stations:			Exit	
9					From/To		0	1	2	3		
10			System Arrival				0	0.50	0.50	0.00		
11			Stations:				1	0.00	0.00	1.00		
12							2	0.00	0.00	1.00		
13												
14												
15					Mean Times							
16							Sys. Arvl	Service Times by Station:				
17							0.273	0.4	0.4			

Transition Matrix / Current / Next Time / Initial

The **Transition Matrix** sheet of Q_NET.xls displays the average system interarrival time in cell H17 and average service times for the two queues in cells I17 and J17. This sheet also has a transition matrix that defines the flow of traffic through the network. For example, the values of 0.5 cells I10 and J10 indicate that a car arriving at the system has a 50% probability of entering either toll lane. The value of 1.0 in cell K11 indicates that a car leaving toll booth 1 has a 100% chance of exiting the system. *Note:* The rows of this matrix must sum to 1. Probability check sum formulas appear in column M.

The commands for Q_NET are the same as those for QUEUE except for commands to add or delete stations from the network. Also, the graph produced by Q_NET is that of the average throughput of the system as a whole (the number served/total elapsed time), rather than the length of a single queue.

When adding or deleting stations, you must edit both the transition matrix and expected arrival and service times. The rows of probabilities in the transition matrix must sum to 1, but other than that there are no restrictions. In fact, the probabilities in the matrix can be calculated as formulas that depend on the current state of the system. In this way, quite general queuing networks can be simulated.

**EXERCISE
4.6**

Simulating Parallel Queues

a. Run a simulation of 20 minutes without asking for the graph. Compare the results with those from Exercise 4.5. In particular, what are the average queue lengths and waiting times?

b. What is the theoretical value of **r** for each of the two parallel queues?

c. Based on this value of **r**, what is the theoretical average queue length at each of the toll booths?

d. What is the expected waiting time?

e. What would happen to overall system performance if N toll booths, each with 1/Nth of the original service rate, had been placed in parallel?

f. Repeat Exercise 4.4 and Exercise 4.5 for the case of two parallel toll booths, each of which can serve cars at the original service time of 0.2 minutes.

If you successfully completed the last exercises, you should have discovered that the average performance of a single, high-service-rate queue is far superior to two parallel queues chosen at random by customers, where each queue has one-half of the original service rate. In reality, it is unlikely that customers would choose the queues at random. Instead, they would choose the shorter of the two queues.

EXERCISE
4.7 ## A MORE REALISTIC SIMULATION OF PARALLEL QUEUES

Again, model the two toll booth situations in which the cars' expected interarrival time is 0.273 minutes, and each toll booth has an expected service time of .4 minutes. This time, however, the cars will choose the shorter of the two queues. Compare the results with those from Exercise 4.5. *Hint:* The probabilities in the transition matrix must now be formulas based on the current states of the queues. Make sure that the rows always sum to 1.

Serial Queues

Queues commonly feed into each other. The next exercise provides an example of a system of serial queues.

EXERCISE
4.8 ## MODELING AN ASSEMBLY LINE

In assembly, a component commonly runs through a sequence of machines, each of which performs a required step in the production process. In the system shown in the following figure, unfinished components enter station 1 at an average of 9 per minute. Stations 1 through 3 can each process the components, at an average of 10 per minute, completing the process.

a. Model this situation with Q_NET and run a 60-minute simulation with a graph of system throughput. You will need to add a third station, then fill in the transition matrix to correspond to the system shown in the following figure. Don't forget that the rows must sum to 1.

b. Suppose that station 3 also performs quality inspection. Suppose further that 10% of the products passing station 3 must be returned to station 1, and 10% to station 2. Model this situation and run a 60-minute simulation.

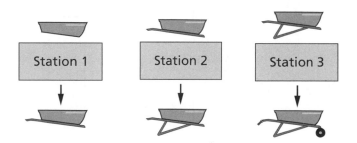

Multiple Queues, Multiple Servers

Another type of queuing system common in banks and airline ticket counters consists of more than one server, each with its own queue as shown in the following figure. This is similar to the two toll booths.

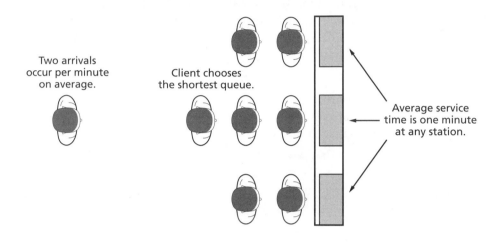

Single Queue, Multiple Servers

A single queue can feed more than one server, as shown in the following figure.

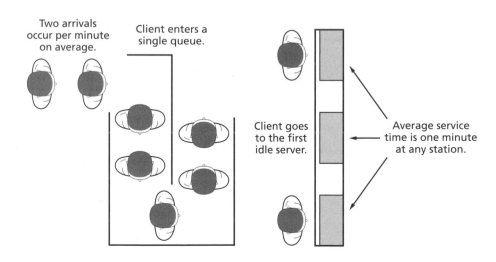

EXERCISE
4.9   **SERVICE AT A BANK**

Consider a bank in which two clients arrive per minute on average. Three tellers perform service, which lasts an average of one minute.

Model this bank's service using each of the two previous queuing systems. Compare the total waiting time from each case. *Hint:* For the single queue case, create a new station that corresponds to leaving the queue and walking to the available teller. The service time for this station should be zero, because as soon as someone leaves the queue, it is possible for the next person to leave if another teller is free. For the multiple queue case, assume that people will choose the shortest of the lines.

It is interesting to note that most banks and ticket counters used to use the multiple queue, multiple server approach. Now they mostly use single queues and multiple servers.

EXERCISE
4.10   **AIR TRAFFIC CONTROL**

Consider an example in air traffic control in which planes arrive at an airport control zone and either land or enter a holding pattern as follows:

(a) Planes enter the system with exponential interarrival times, 1 1/4 minutes apart on average.

(b) If the landing pattern is full, the planes enter a holding pattern. They are cleared to the landing pattern on a first-come-first-serve basis. Once cleared, the time required for a plane to reach the landing pattern is uniformly distributed between zero and two minutes.

(c) Planes are allowed to enter the landing pattern no less than one minute apart. Once in the landing pattern they all fly at precisely the same speed, eliminating any uncertainty in the remaining time spent in the system.

Simulate this situation using Q_NET. *Hint:* Model the landing pattern as a station with a fixed service time of 1 minute. Model the transition between the holding pattern and the landing pattern as a station with a service time uniformly distributed between 0 and 2 minutes. You will need to modify the next service time formula for those stations. The transition matrix will require formulas that depend on the current state of the system.

The Extend™ Discrete Event Simulation Software

As we have seen, simple instructional discrete event simulations can be developed in a spreadsheet. However, for most real world applications, devoted software offers a great advantage in both ease of use and speed of simulation. One such program is Extend (a small version of which is included on your CD). The following tutorial goes through the steps of creating an Extend simulation of the M/M/1 toll booth example done earlier. The Extend user guide in the Extend Documentation directory contains a thorough description of the Extend modeling environment and it may be helpful to look over Chapter 1 before proceeding to the following tutorial.

TUTORIAL: A SIMPLE QUEUE MODELED IN EXTEND

1 Open Extend and select **New Model** from the **File** menu. Then from the **Library** menu, select **Open Library** then open the file Discrete Event.lix. This adds DISCRETE EVENT.LIX to the **Library** menu.

2 Now from the **Library** command select the newly added **Discrete Event Library** and insert the **Executive** block into the model.

3 This block is necessary for all discrete event simulations and it must be placed on the far left side of the screen. As with all blocks, online help can be found by opening the block (double click on it) and clicking the **Help** button in the lower left corner.

4 Insert the **Generator** block from the **Generators** section of the **Discrete Event Library**.

5

This block is used to generate new arrivals to the queue according to the distribution you select. Open the block and select an Exponential distribution with parameter of 0.273.

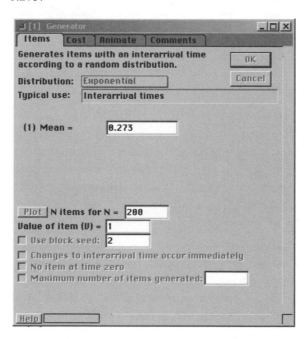

6

Insert a **Queue, FIFO** (first-in-first-out) from the **Queues** section of the **Discrete Event library**. Drag a connection line between the generator block and the queue as shown.

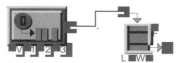

7

The queue block represents the number of cars waiting in line before the toll booth. *Note:* a description of the connector tabs on a module may be found by clicking to open the module, then clicking help and scrolling down to Connectors. The connectors for the FIFO queue are shown below.

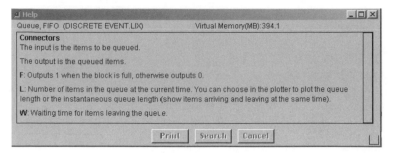

8 Insert an **Activity, Delay** block from the **Activities** menu of the **Discrete Event library**. This block represents the delay experienced by the customer at the toll booth itself. Drag a connection line between the output of the queue block and the input of the **Activity, Delay** block. If the delay time were a constant, we could enter it as a parameter inside the block; but since we want to simulate a system with an exponentially distributed service time, we must generate a random number and use it as an input to this block. This is done with the Input Random Number block.

9 Insert the **Input Random Number** block from the **Input/Outputs** menu of the **Generic library** (*Note:* you will need to open **Generic.lix** first using the **Open Library** command). Connect the output of this block to the **"D" Delay** time connector on the **Activity, Delay** block. Open the **Random Number** block and set the distribution to Exponential and the mean parameter to 0.2.

10 Finally, insert the **Exit** block from the **Routing** menu of the **Discrete Event library** and connect it to the **Activity, Delay** block.

The complete model should look something like this:

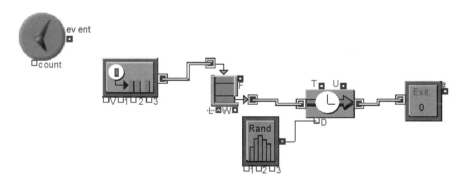

11 It is now ready to run. From the **Run** menu select **Simulation setup** and set the global time units to Minutes. Decide how long you want the simulation to run (try 20 minutes at first). Click OK. From the **Run** menu make sure the **Show Animation**

item has a check mark next to it. This feature is useful in debugging your models, but it slows down execution time considerably. Turn it off once you know the model is working correctly.

12 From the **Run** menu select **Run Simulation** <Ctrl> <R>. You can control the speed of the animation from the toolbar at the bottom of the screen.

After the simulation is over, open the **Queue, FIFO** block and click on the **Results** tab. This provides many useful queue statistics, based on the entire simulation run.

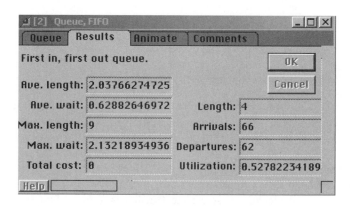

13 Save your model as **MM1 queue.mox**.

You can also try experimenting with the **Plotter, Discrete Event** block from the **Plotter library** which can be used to plot queue statistics over the course of a run. Connect the **"L" Length** tab of the **FIFO Queue** block to one of the inputs of the **Plotter block** as shown.

The next time you run the simulation, you will generate a plot of the queue length over time, as was done using QUEUE.xls.

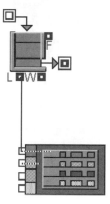

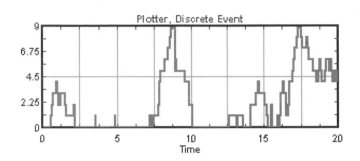

TUTORIAL: SIMULATING MULTIPLE SERVERS (SIMPLE METHOD)

1 Open the MM1 queue model created in the last tutorial.

A very powerful feature of Extend involves the ability to replicate portions of a model that already exist. In this way, large complex models may be rapidly assembled from smaller sub models. We will use this approach to simulating multiple servers.

2 Select the three rightmost blocks in the model (**Input Random Number, Activity Delay**, and **Exit**) and their connecting lines by dragging a box around them. Right-click on the selected blocks and select the **Duplicate** option. Drag the duplicated blocks below the original blocks.

3 Draw a connecting line from the queue to the new **Activity Delay** block. The model should look something like this.

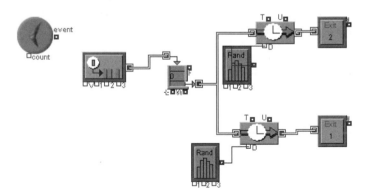

4 You can turn the animation on and run the model to see that it is working. As soon as one of the activity blocks finishes a job it takes another job from the queue – if the queue is not empty.

5 Save this model as MM2.mox.

TUTORIAL: SIMULATING MULTIPLE SERVERS (A MORE GENERAL APPROACH)

1 Start by opening the original MM1 queue model saved earlier.

2 Delete the **Activity Delay** block. Then from the **Discrete Event library,** open **Activities,** and select the **Activity Multiple** block.

3 Draw connecting lines from the queue into the block and out into the **Exit** block. Also, connect the **Input Random Number** block to the **"D" Delay** time connector.

4 Open the **Activity Multiple** block and set the "Maximum Number in Activity" parameter to be the number of servers you want to simulate, in this case 2.

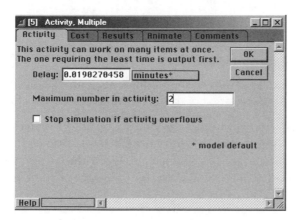

By using this block it is easy to simulate an arbitrary number of servers without cluttering up your model. Your model should look something like this.

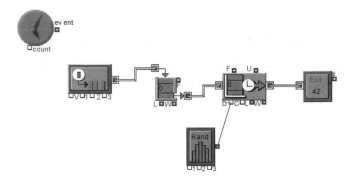

A big advantage of this second formulation of the multiserver queue is that you can parameterize the number of servers. For example, a bank might use a model like this to evaluate the effect of hiring various numbers of tellers at a particular branch.

Save this model as MMN.mox

Exercise
4.11 **Parameterized Simulation Using Extend**

Run a parameterized simulation of the multiserver model using from 1 to 6 servers. Keep track of the utilization of the servers for each of the six experiments.

Hints: Use the **Sensitize Parameters** option by right-clicking the **"Maximum number in activity"** box in the **Activity Multiple** block. Also you will need to store your results in an output file by selecting **File Output** From the **Generic library, Input/Outputs** menu. See the Extend Help system and user guide for assistance.

Combining Excel Models with Extend

Extend allows Excel worksheets and other external components, known as objects, to be inserted into your model. The following tutorial will link an Excel worksheet into the Extend workspace to control a queuing system.

Suppose a bank wishes to explore the policy of adding more tellers as the line of waiting customers grows. The table below shows how many tellers will be made available as the line length varies.

Number Waiting	Number of Tellers
0	1
3	2
5	3
7	4

This is a situation for which queuing theory has no simple answer, so simulation provides the only practical solution. The above table is stored in an Excel worksheet called **TELLERSTAFFING.xls** that will be linked into Extend. Each time the length of the queue changes the number of tellers will be specified according to the table in the worksheet. This approach allows for an Extend model to be experimented with by a manager who has only Excel experience.

TUTORIAL: EMBEDDING AN EXCEL MODEL IN EXTEND

1
Open MMN.mox as saved in the previous tutorial. From the **Edit** menu select **Insert Object...**

2
Select the **Create from File** option and locate the Excel file **TELLERSTAFFING.xls** and click **OK** to insert the Excel file into the Extend model.[2]

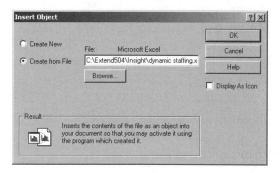

3
Your model should now look something like the figure below. Notice that the maximum number of tellers available is 4, regardless of number of people waiting. This has been implemented in this worksheet by insuring that 5 tellers are not brought on until the line reaches a huge number, 10,000. This worksheet will be linked to Extend so that the number of tellers will be driven by the table. Also, Extend will be linked back to the spreadsheet so that the cells labeled Current Queue and Current Tellers will display these quantities as they change in the simulation.

---

[2]*Note:* this file has an embedded macro to ensure smooth operation with earlier versions of Extend. You may view the macro using the VBA editor in Excel.

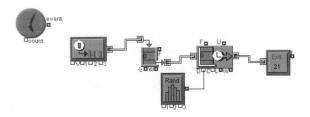

More tellers are added as the line grows longer:		
Number Waiting	Number of Tellers	
0	1	
3	2	
5	3	
7	4	
10000	5	
Current Queue	Current Tellers	
0	1	

4 Double-click on the Excel window to make the object active which enables you to edit the cells. Click anywhere within the Extend window to leave the Excel interface. Save the model as MMV.mox before continuing.

In order to compute the number of tellers based on the queue length, a Conversion Table will be used. This block will receive the length of the queue on the left and produce the number of tellers on the right.

5 From the **Generic library, Math** select the conversion table block and place it below the **Input Random Number** block. Connect the queue length (L) connector of the queue to the input connector on the Conversion table. Connect the output of the Conversion Table to the capacity (C) connector of the **Activity Multiple**. Now, when the length of the queue changes the number of tellers will change as well.

Your model should now look like this:

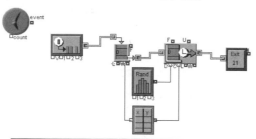

More tellers are added as the line grows longer:		
Number Waiting	Number of Tellers	
0	1	
3	2	
5	3	
7	4	
10000	5	
Current Queue	Current Tellers	
0	1	

6 Link the table from Excel to Extend by double-clicking on the embedded Excel workbook and selecting the 5 rows and 2 columns that contain the conversion values from the **Number Waiting** to the **Number of Tellers**. Do not include any text in the table, select only the numbers. Then right-click on the selected area and choose **Copy** or use the <Ctrl><C> key combination.

7 Next, click on the Extend worksheet to move back into Extend. Double-click on the icon of the Conversion table block to open the dialog box.

8 Select the first five rows and two columns in the conversion table block. Right-click on the selected area and choose **Paste Link**. Now, when the values in the Excel spreadsheet are changed, the Conversion Table in Extend will be changed automatically. Test this by leaving the dialog box open, and going back to the Excel model by double-clicking. Change some of the numbers in Excel and watch them change in the Conversion Table dialog box. Be sure to change them back before leaving the Excel sheet.

The queue length can be displayed in the Excel Workbook by linking the queue length dialog item to the workbook.

9 Double-click on the icon of the queue to open the dialog. Click on the **Results** tab, select the **Length** dialog item, then copy it using the <Ctrl><C> key combination.

10 Double-click on the Excel workbook to make it active. Right-click on the cell which is to contain the current queue length and select **Paste Special**, select **Text** and select the **Paste Link** option, then click OK.

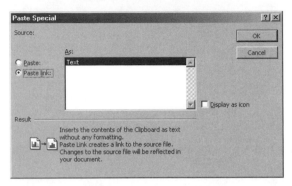

Every time the length of the queue changes, the number will be automatically passed to the Excel worksheet.

11 Perform a similar link from the Maximum Number in Activity field, of the **Activity** tab, of the **Multiple Activity** block, to the Current Tellers cell of the spreadsheet.

Your model should now look like this.

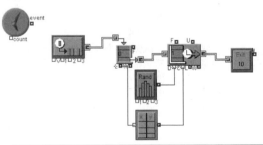

More tellers are added as the line grows longer:		
Number Waiting	Number of Tellers	
0	1	
3	2	
5	3	
7	4	
10000	5	
Current Queue	Current Tellers	
0	1	

12

Be sure to save the model again after you have set up the links. To see the customers moving though the bank, turn on animation by selecting **Animation** from the Extend **Run** menu. Run the simulation by selecting **Run Simulation** from the **Run** menu. As the queue length changes, the number of tellers will change accordingly.

13

Experiment with the model. What happens if the average time between customer arrivals (in the **Generator** block) is decreased, or if the service time is increased?

MARKOV CHAINS

Certain evolving systems can be modeled in a particularly elegant manner. Consider a population of individuals, each of which can change state as time progresses. For example, the individuals might represent consumers whose states correspond to the brand of detergent they are currently using. Or they might correspond to machines whose states represent various levels of operating efficiency. Time is modeled in fixed increments. In going from time T to time T+1, the individuals transition between states with certain probabilities. Such a system is known as a Markov chain. For a more complete discussion of Markov chains, see Luenberger (1979).

An Example: Market Share

Markov chains have been used to model the dynamics of competitive markets. Consider, for example, a population of software developers, where the state of a given developer is defined by the programming language in which he or she is currently developing code. Here, Markov chains can be used to predict the market share of the various languages over time.

New generations of programming languages commonly replace older ones. Generally, the newer languages are better in most respects than their predecessors. But often the older languages remain superior for certain tasks.

Suppose that in a particular application area virtually all developers are currently using language A when two new competing languages, B and C, are introduced. Language B has similar syntax to A, but is more powerful. Language C is more powerful still and shares some properties with B, but is a complete departure from A. Suppose the probability that a developer using language A will stay with A over the next three months is 65%. The probabilities that the developer will move to either B or C during this period are 30% and 5%, respectively. Of developers who move to B, 75% stay with this environment, 10% return to A, and 15% move on to C. Of those who use C, 90% stay with this language and 10% move to B.

■ **FUNDAMENTALS 4-4**

Markov Chains

Markov chains model evolving systems such as populations of individuals, each of which can move from state to state. The probability that an individual moves from a given state to another given state is known as the *transition probability* between those states. If the transition probabilities do not change over time, the Markov chain is said to be *stationary.*

Before continuing, try to guess what the market shares of these three programming languages will look like over time.

The transition probabilities for software developers moving between programming languages can be displayed in an array known as a transition matrix, shown in the following table:

To Language	From Language		
	A	**B**	**C**
A	65%	10%	0%
B	30%	75%	10%
C	5%	15%	90%

Notice that the columns sum to 100%, implying that all developers will be using one of the three languages.

MARKOV.xls

Open MARKOV.xls, shown in the following figure:

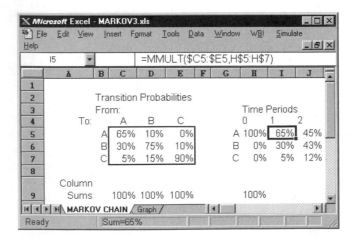

Notice that the transition probabilities are in the upper left corner, and that the formulas in row 9 are used to check that the columns sum to 100%. Column H contains the percentage of developers across the three languages in the initial time period, and must also sum to 100%.

Given the numbers using each language at time 0, what are the numbers at time 1? The percentage using language A at time 1 is the sum of those who stayed with A from time 0, plus those who moved to A from B, plus those who moved to A from C. This is

65%*A(0)+10%*B(0)+0%*C(0).

Similarly, the percentage using B is

30%*A(0)+75%*B(0)+10%*C(0)

and the percentage using C is

5%*A(0)+15%*B(0)+90%*C(0).

A convenient way to calculate this is with the MMULT formula as shown in the formula bar in the screen shot of MARKOV.xls. See the Excel help system for a full explanation of MMULT. As implemented here, MMULT is equivalent to a SUMPRODUCT formula in which the first range is a row and the second range is a column. With careful use of absolute $ references, a single instance of this formula has been copied down and across to calculate the percentage of programmers in each state for 36 periods.

Notice that by two time periods after introduction, language B has captured 43% of the market, and A has dropped to 45% from its initial 100%. Language C, on the other hand, has only managed to capture 12% of the market. If we were myopically tracking this market activity, it would be tempting to predict that B was the big winner and that C was a loser. However, the Markov model clearly shows otherwise. To get an idea of the dynamics of this situation, click on the **Graph** tab to view the changes in market share for each of the three languages over time. You should see the following figure.

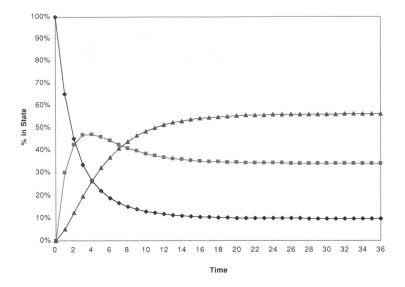

Notice that language C eventually ends up with 56% of the market, followed by B with 34%, and A with only 10%. These market shares are known as the *equilibrium percentages* or *equilibrium distribution* of the Markov chain.

A Remarkable Property of Markov Chains

As a thought experiment, imagine that at time 0 language B had the entire market instead of A. Model this by setting A(0) (cell H5) to 0 and B(0) (cell H6) to 100%. The results are graphed in the following figure.

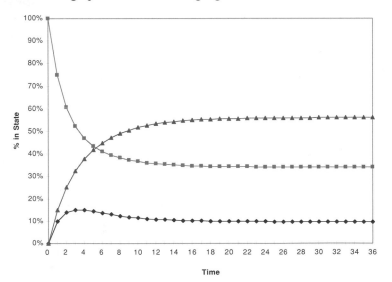

■ **FUNDAMENTALS 4-5**

Markov Chain Equilibrium

- A Markov chain is said to be ***irreducible*** if it is possible to move between any two states eventually.

- This will be the case unless there is a set of states from which it is not possible to escape. Such a set is known as an ***absorbing*** class of states.

- If a Markov chain is irreducible, then its long-term or ***equilibrium*** behavior does not depend on the initial percentages across states.

The market displays a very different dynamic for the first 10 periods, but the shares later settle down to exactly the same equilibrium as before. Try any initial market share for this transition matrix (remember column H must sum to 100%), and the market share will always reach the same equilibrium!

This remarkable property implies that it might be more important to understand the transition between states, than to understand the current distribution of the population across states.

Solving for Markov Chain Equilibria

Beyond copying the formulas of the Markov model until the numbers have converged, there are two other ways ways to determine the equilibrium distribution. The first method, which uses the Excel Solver, is the subject of Exercise 4.12. For those with an understanding of matrix algebra, we present a second method at the end of this chapter based on the Excel matrix inverse function, =MINV.

EXERCISE
4.12   SOLVING FOR MARKOV CHAIN EQUILIBRIA

Enter the transition matrix below and place all programmers in state A at time 0.

To Language	From Language		
	A	B	C
A	99%	10%	0%
B	1%	75%	1%
C	0%	15%	99%

Although theoretically there should be an equilibrium, you will see that it has not been reached by the 36th period. An analytical method for finding the equilibrium percentages is discussed in Appendix D. This exercise makes use of the Excel Solver to accomplish the same goal.

Note that the definition of equilibrium is that the percentages do not change from period to period. Therefore if we could find values of A, B and C summing to 1 at time period zero that gave the same results at time period one, then we would know we had found the equilibrium percentages.

Use the Excel Solver to change the values of A(0), B(0), and C(0) until they equal A(1), B(1), and C(1) respectively. Don't forget that your percentages at time 0 must be non-negative and must sum to 100%. See Chapter 7 on optimization to learn more about the Solver.

TUTORIAL: MODELING MACHINE REPLACEMENT

Imagine a manufacturing environment in which a number of identical machines are used to process material. The quality of the machines deteriorates from month to month as follows. In the first month after replacement, 90% of the machines are still OK, but 10% of them are worn. Of the machines that are OK in a given month, 60% are still OK in the next month, 30% are worn, and 10% fail. Of the worn machines, 60% are still worn by the next month, and 40% fail. Whenever a machine fails, it is replaced by a new one. This situation is reflected in the transition matrix shown below.

To Condition	From Condition			
	New	**OK**	**Worn**	**Fail**
New	0%	0%	0%	100%
OK	90%	60%	0%	0%
Worn	10%	30%	60%	0%
Fail	0%	10%	40%	0%

Proceed as follows to model the machine replacement scenario.

1 Open MARKOV.xls, and save it as MACHINE.xls.

2 We need four states to model this situation, so insert a row and column in the transition matrix. The formulas to the right of the transition matrix will display ##### or #VALUE. This is all right. *Note:* Do not insert the new rows and columns at the first row and column of the current matrix.

3 Fill in the transition matrix and its labels.

4 Specify 100% new machines at time 0.

5

Copy the MMULT formula in cell J5 down to J8 to complete period 1.

6

Copy J5:J8 to the desired number of future periods. The number of time periods should be sufficient to ensure convergence to the equilibrium distributions. For this example, 20 periods will be adequate.

7

Using the **Chart Wizard**, create a new graph of the percentages over time as shown below.

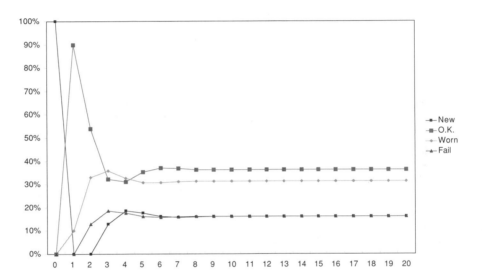

Clearly, equilibrium has been reached well before month 20. In this transition matrix it is possible to move from any state to any other state eventually (perhaps first passing through the Fail and New state). Therefore the equilibrium is independent of the initial distribution and is shown in this table.

New	16%
OK	36%
Worn	31%
Fail	16%

Each month, just over 16% of the machines fail and must be replaced with new ones.

Modifying the Transition Matrix to Evaluate Replacement Strategy

Suppose that when a machine fails, it spoils $2,000 worth of materials. Also suppose that a new machine costs $1,000. Then the equilibrium cost per machine per month is

$1000* Equilibrium % New Machines +

$2000 * Equilibrium % Failed Machines = $484.85

Set up this formula in the worksheet and experiment with different replacement policies.

EXERCISE 4.13 Machine Replacement

Try to find a better strategy than waiting until the machines fail to replace them. For this alternative strategy determine the following:

a. The new transition matrix.

b. The equilibrium distribution.

c. The equilibrium cost per machine per month.

EXERCISE 4.14 Health Care Screening

In this exercise, we examine the results of two different health management policies: screening or not screening a population for a particular treatable but potentially fatal disease (PFD). Here are the key facts about PFD:

■ It is not contagious, but occurs in any member of the population at large with a 10% chance in any year.

■ For those who are not screened, there is only a 1% chance that PFD will be detected early and a 9% chance that it will be detected late. For those who are screened, 9% are detected early and 1% late.

■ It is much more treatable if detected early than if detected late. Of those detected late, only 10% will be cured by the following year and 90% will be deceased. Of those detected early, 90% will be cured by the following year and only 10% will be deceased.

■ Those who have been cured of PFD have a 20% chance of getting it again in any year. But because they are regularly screened, it is always detected early.

■ It goes without saying that those who die from PFD in a given year will remain deceased the following year.

This is represented by the following transition matrix:

To Condition	From Condition					
	Unscreened	Screened	Early Detect	Late Detect	Cured	Deceased
Unscreened	90%	0%	0%	0%	0%	0%
Screened	0%	90%	0%	0%	0%	0%
Early Detect	1%	9%	0%	0%	20%	0%
Late Detect	9%	1%	0%	0%	0%	0%
Cured	0%	0%	90%	10%	80%	0%
Deceased	0%	0%	10%	90%	0%	100%

Note that because Deceased represents a state from which you cannot leave, the matrix is not irreducible. Thus, the behavior of this system will be somewhat different from those discussed earlier. Also, instead of merely following a given population until they all died off, one could allow for births into the population as well. This could be accomplished by renaming the Deceased state to Out of Population. Transitions *from* this state would represent births while transitions *into* it would represent deaths.

a. Without constructing the Markov chain, predict the equilibrium state of this system if you start with 100% of the population unscreened and wait long enough.

b. Create a Markov chain and graph covering 26 years into the future.

c. If you start with 100% of the population in the unscreened state at time 0, what percentage is deceased by period 26?

d. What percentage is deceased by period 26 if the population that has not had PFD is screened every year?

Finding Markov Chain Equilibria With =MINV

The following discussion involves matrix algebra. For those with no knowledge of this subject, I suggest that you dive in anyway. If the going gets rough, there is no shame associated with skipping to the conclusion of this chapter.

Start with the transition matrix of Exercise 4.12.

To Language	From Language		
	A	B	C
A	99%	10%	0%
B	1%	75%	1%
C	0%	15%	99%

We will denote the percentages of programmers using each of the languages by x_a, x_b and x_c respectively, and all three numbers together as X (a column vector). Noting that the definition of equilibrium means that things don't change from period to period, we will have reached equilibrium only when we find values for x_a, x_b and x_c which sum to 100% and which satisfy the following three equations.

$.99*x_a + .1*x_b + 0* \ x_c = x_a$

$.1*x_a + .75*x_b + .1* \ x_c = x_b$

$0*x_a + .15*x_b + .99 * x_c = x_c$

The three equations above can be written in matrix terminology as

$A*X=X$,

where A is the transition matrix, X is the column vector of equilibrium percentages, and "*" represents matrix multiplication (recall the MMULT formulas of which MARKOV.xls is constructed). Subtracting X from both sides yields

$A*X-X = 0$ which may be written as $(A-I)*X = 0$,

where I, known as the ***Identity Matrix*** has 1's on the diagonals and 0's elsewhere. Thus, equivalent to the equations above, we can write:

$(.99-1)*x_a + .1*x_b + 0* \ x_c = 0$
$.1*x_a + (.75-1)*x_b + .1* \ x_c = 0$
$0*x_a + .15*x_b + (.99-1) * x_c = 0$

or

$(-.01)*x_a + .1*x_b + 0* \ x_c = 0$
$.1*x_a + (-.25)*x_b + .1* \ x_c = 0$
$0*x_a + .15*x_b + (-.01) * x_c = 0$

Now you might think that you could solve these three equations in three unknowns for x_a, x_b and x_c and be done. But the equations are not independent because the sum of each column of coefficients is zero (in the original matrix A they summed to 1, but now we have subtracted 1 from each column). This means that we can express any of the three equations as the negative sum of the other two.

We still have the condition that the equilibrium percentages must sum to 1, however, and that gives us one more equation. Dropping the first of the three equations and adding this new one results in three independent equations in three unknowns, as follows:

$$.1 * x_a + (-.25) * x_b + .1 * x_c = 0$$

$$0 * x_a + .15 * x_b + (-.01) * x_c = 0$$

$$1 * x_a + 1 * x_b + 1 * x_c = 1$$

Defining the matrix of coefficients of the new system of equations to be *A*, and the column vector of two zeros and a one to be B, we must solve the system below for X.

$$A * X = B$$

Multiplying both sides by the inverse of *A*, we get

$$A^{-1} * A * X = A^{-1} * B \text{ or simply } X = A^{-1} * B$$

This is accomplished in the file MARKOVminv.xls, using Excel's MINVERSE function. Open the file and experiment with it to satisfy yourself of the above.

Conclusion

We have seen that complex evolving systems can be modeled using discrete-event simulation. Powerful graphical simulation software exists that can actually show the movement of people, airplanes, or other items while the process is underway. For certain evolving systems, Markov chains can provide a powerful theoretical understanding of long-term behavior.

END OF CHAPTER EXERCISES

4.15   CAPACITY PLANNING

A bank is planning to open a new branch at which they expect customer arrivals to be Poisson distributed with a mean of λ, estimated to be 80 per hour. The standard error of the arrival rate estimate is 10 per hour, that is they are 95% certain that the true arrival rate will be between 60 per hour and 100 per hour. The bank decides to build the facility with a capacity of 100 customers per hour, giving it an expected utilization factor r, of .8. Recalling that the formula for the expected length of a queue is $\rho^2/(1-\rho)$, the bank estimates an average of 3.2 people waiting in line, well below the 5 they consider undesirable. Critique this analysis.

4.16   CALL CENTER MANAGEMENT

A telephone company runs a large call center handling on average 20,000 calls per day. Half of these involve the sales of new company services, the other half involve repair service. The current staff of 1,000 is trained to handle both types of transaction, which have the same distribution of service times. The firm believes it would be more efficient to break the call center into two separate centers, each with 500 staff handling just a single type of transaction. Do you agree with this strategy? Explain your position.

Create simulations of the following using Extend

4.17 Simulations with Extend

  a. The assembly line of problem 4.8

  b. The bank service lines of problem 4.9

  c. The air traffic landing pattern of problem 4.10

4.18 Accounts Receivable

A firm bills its customers on a monthly basis. Of those customers who have been billed, 80% will pay in a given month, 5% will be sent a 2nd notice, and the remaining 15% will simply remain in the billed category. Of those who receive a 2nd notice, 50% will pay, and the remaining customers are written off as bad debt. Create a Markov chain to determine the value of $1 in the billed category. You do not need to model the time value of money (NPV). Use the following four states: Billed, 2nd Notice, Paid, Bad Debt. Once customers reach either the Paid or Bad Debt state, they stay there.

4.19 Customer Relationship Management

A credit card company is competing in a market of 10 million potential customers. It views its customers as falling into one of three states:

Acquired. That is, they have received their credit cards within the past quarter (three month period).

Retained. A customer who has had an account for over three months is more profitable and less likely to abandon the company than one who has just been acquired. Furthermore they may be become a "Developed" customer.

Developed. A developed customer is more profitable and less likely to abandon the company than a retained customer.

Every quarter, 2% of the population of 10 Million potential customers are acquired as new customers. Of these, 75% will be retained, while 25% will drop their account and return to the population at large by the following quarter. Of the Retained customers, 25% will become Developed customers, 15% will return to the population at large, and 60% will stay in the Retained category. Developed customers are very loyal, with only 5% dropping their accounts, and the rest staying where they are.

Each category of customer has an associated revenue per quarter. A retained customer brings in $25 on average, while a developed customer brings in $125. Because of the costs of acquiring new customers, there is a $100 charge associated with this category. There is no revenue associated with members of the population at large.

Create a Markov model of this situation (don't forget to include the population at large as a 4th state) and answer the follow questions:

a. What percent of market share does the firm have in equilibrium? Note: this Markov chain converges slowly. It is suggested that you use either the Solver or MINV method of finding the equilibrium distribution.

b. Given that the total population is 10 million, what is the firm's quarterly revenue at equilibrium?

c. All other things held equal, what percent of the population at large would need to be recruited each quarter to give the firm 25% of the market?

d. The firm is considering two marketing efforts, each of which will cost $150 million per quarter. The "New Acquisition" plan is aimed at bringing in more new customers, and is estimated to increase the percent of the population acquired each quarter from 2% to 3%. The "Retention" plan is aimed at increasing customer satisfaction in an effort to increase retention. The second plan is estimated to increase the retention of Acquired customers from 75% to 90%. Although it would not increase the movement of Retained customers into Developed customers, it would increase their retention from 60% to 70%. Developed customer retention would go from 95% to 97%. Which plan would you support? Don't forget that the columns of the transition matrix must sum to 100%.

5 ▪▪▪▪▪▪▪▪▪▪▪▪▪▪▪▪▪▪▪▪▪▪▪▪▪▪▪▪▪▪▪▪

Forecasting

Tomorrow is an old deceiver, and his cheat never grows stale.

SAMUEL JOHNSON, ENGLISH AUTHOR

Modern forecasting falls into two broad categories: causal forecasting and time series analysis.

Causal forecasting predicts how an uncertain quantity is related to other quantities. This type of forecasting might be used by

- A retail outlet to determine the extent to which business is increased through advertising.

- A pharmaceutical lab estimating the influence of dosage on the effectiveness of a new pain killer.

Time series analysis predicts future values of an uncertain quantity based on past values of the same quantity. Time series analysis might be used by

- A telecommunications firm to predict future demand for service based on several years of past data.

- An integrated circuit manufacturer to estimate next year's sales so it can expand its plant to meet required production.

Regardless of the technique used, forecasts are generally not exact. It is important, therefore, not to ignore the estimates of errors also produced by most types of forecasts.

■ ■ ■ OVERVIEW

Introduction
This section contains a short introduction to causal forecasting and time series analysis. It also includes instructions for using the regression routines that come with Excel and XLForecast, a time series analysis add-in.

Tutorials: Regression and Time Series Analysis
This section's tutorials cover regression to estimate sales based on advertising level, and time series analysis to predict future business based on past history. The second tutorial shows how forecasting can be tied to Monte Carlo simulation.

The Importance of Errors
Forecasting errors provide valuable insight into the quality of the results. Errors also allow the forecast to be linked to Monte Carlo simulation. Random and nonrandom errors are discussed.

Regression and Exponential Smoothing
Intuitive explanations of regression and exponential smoothing are provided.

INTRODUCTION

Modern forecasting falls into two broad categories. Causal forecasting predicts how an uncertain quantity is related to other quantities. Time series analysis predicts future values of some quantity based on past values of the same quantity. We introduce these topics in this chapter, but for a more extensive presentation, see Gardner (1986, 1992).

Causal Forecasting

The term "causal" implies that these methods determine the extent to which changes in one quantity **cause** changes in another. However, this is a misnomer. Generally, all that is learned from causal forecasting is the extent to which the changes in two or more quantities are statistically linked, and linking alone does not imply causality.

For example, it has been known for decades that there is a strong link between smoking and lung cancer. Does this necessarily mean that smoking causes lung cancer? Without additional medical evidence, you could make either of the following arguments:

- *Argument 1:* More smokers get lung cancer than do nonsmokers. Therefore, smoking must be one of the causes of lung cancer.

- *Argument 2:* People prone to getting lung cancer have discomfort in their lungs that can only be alleviated by inhaling nicotine. Thus, although smoking and lung cancer are indeed linked, it is the propensity for getting lung cancer that causes people to smoke in the first place. That is, cancer causes smoking!

This issue was not conclusively settled until recently when medical researchers were finally able to determine the biochemical process whereby smoking does indeed cause cancer.

Regression is the most commonly used form of causal forecasting. In its simplest form regression fits a straight line to the scatter plot of two quantities that are suspected of being related. This line can be used to predict the value of one of the quantities given the value of the other. For example, as shown in the following figure, we might be able to predict monthly sales based on the amount of advertising.

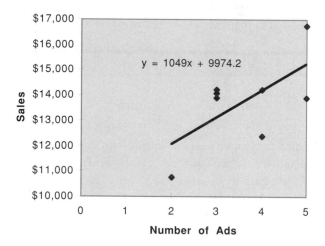

You can get regression results from within Excel using one of three methods. The most thorough of these is contained in the Analysis ToolPak, which will be discussed later.

Time Series Analysis

Time series analysis predicts future values of some quantity based on past values of the same quantity. For example:

Web site hits by day

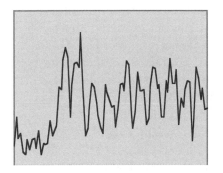

Yen/dollar ratio by week

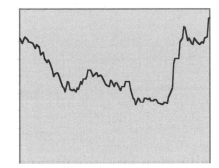

Motorcycle sales by month

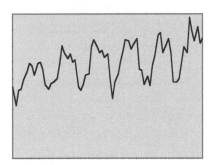

Corporate sales by year

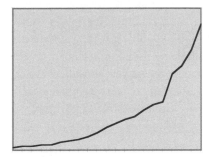

There are many varieties of time series analysis and numerous software packages that provide this capability. Most time series software programs take historical data as input and estimate expected future values as output along with a confidence interval.

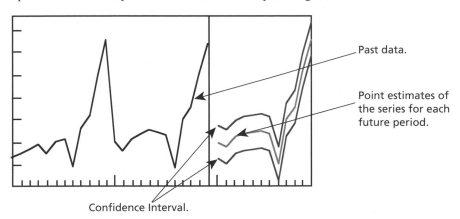

Past data.

Point estimates of the series for each future period.

Confidence Interval.

Management is likely to plug these point estimates of the future into spreadsheet models to predict future business conditions while ignoring the degree of uncertainty displayed by the confidence intervals. This can lead to serious errors because average inputs will not necessarily result in average outputs (The Flaw of Averages). An analogy exists between the future values of the series and the position of the drunk wandering around on a busy highway, described in Chapter 3. The estimates of the future values of the series correspond to the most likely position of the drunk, or the highway's center line. However, we cannot assume that the drunk will remain alive just because his most likely position is the center line where he is safe. Similarly, we cannot assume that plugging in most likely future values of the series will result in the most likely future values of profit, cost, or other measures of business.

Fortunately, there is a convenient solution to this problem. Most forms of time series analysis also produce a set of errors that correspond to the past deviations of the drunk away from the center line. These errors can help estimate the reliability of the forecast, or, better yet, they can be used to run a simulation of the future instead of simply outputting a point estimate. This will be demonstrated in the tutorial.

XLForecast is a time series analysis add-in for Excel 97 and higher that performs exponential smoothing on series with or without trends or seasonality. An option allows you to create a formula that simulates the behavior of the quantity one period into the future. This formula can be used to run a simulation in conjunction with XLSim.

Using Excel's Regression and XLForecast

Regression

You can get regression results from within Excel through three separate methods.

1. *Analysis Tools.* Choose **Data Analysis** from the **Tools** menu. From the Data Analysis dialog box that opens (shown in the following figure), select **Regression**.

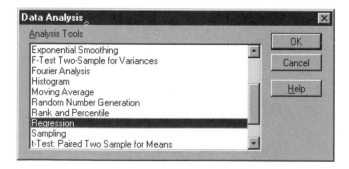

This provides the most detailed output statistics, which in some cases are more than are needed. *Note:* The Analysis Tool Pack must be installed to use this regression routine. Use the Excel **Help** command for details.

2. *Scatterplot.* If there are only two variables, you can create a scatter plot of the data, and click on the graph. Then select **Add Trendline** from the **Chart** menu. This is a quick-and-dirty way to determine the significance of any linear trends in data.

3. *Linest and Trend Functions.* The =Linest() and Trend() functions will instantly calculate regression statistics from "live" data.

Running XLForecast. Launch Excel and open XLForecast.xla from the **File Open** command.

Auto Load Option. If you want XLForecast to load every time you launch Excel, follow these steps:

1. Select **Add-ins** from the Tools menu in Excel.

2. Select **XLForecast** from the list of add-ins and click **OK**.

3. You can later go back and deselect **XLForecast** from the **Add-in** menu to prevent Excel from loading it automatically.

TUTORIALS: REGRESSION AND TIME SERIES ANALYSIS

The basic steps of both causal and time series forecasting are these:

1. Eyeball the data.

2. Choose and run a forecasting technique.

3. Observe the results and possibly go back to step 2.

We will begin by discussing causal forecasting with regression.

Regression: Estimating Sales Based on Advertising Level

Consider a restaurant in a large city that has experimented with newspaper ads on eight occasions over several years. For each experiment, they have kept track of the number of newspaper ads placed, along with that month's sales. Managers have already concluded that whatever effect an ad has is limited to the month in which it ran. Hypothetical data for this situation is contained in the range **Ads_vs_Sales** in the file SERIES.xls[1], which contains numerous sample data sets for experimentation. The

---

[1] I am indebted to Professor Everette S. Gardner Jr. of the University of Houston who provided the historical data for SERIES.xls, as well as advice about the time series programs.

first sheet of SERIES.xls contains an index, shown in the following figure, which lists the range names of the various data sets.

	A	B	C	D	E	F	G
1		Range name					
2	Historical Data			Hypothetical Data			
3		AIRCONDITIONERS			Ads_vs_Sales		
4		BEER			TRANS_VS_PETROL		
5		CALCULATORS			Dish Washers		
6		CHAMPAGNE			Kitchen Ranges		
7		CIGARS			Exercise Equipment		
8		CLOTHING			Bicycles		
9		COMPANY			RAND()		
10		DEMAND			TREND		
11		EMPLOY			CONVEX		
12		FIBERS					
13		FRANCE					
14		FUEL DEMAND					
15		GASOLINE					
16		IBMSALES					

Select the **Ads_vs_Sales** data by pulling down the range name list at the far left of the formula bar as shown. Or, press the F5 key to access the range names.

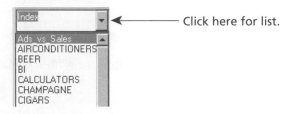 ←———— Click here for list.

Once the **Ads_vs_Sales** series has been selected, copy and paste it into a blank workbook, then close SERIES.xls. See Fundamentals Box 5-1 for definitions of dependent and independent variables.

Eyeball the Data

Statistical techniques are best used with common sense and intuition, and a good way to gain intuition about data is by graphing it. In this example, the dependent variable is sales and the independent variable is number of ads. We can easily imagine other independent variables that might influence sales as well, such as weather, the state of the economy, and so forth.

■ **FUNDAMENTALS 5-1**

Dependent and Independent Variables

The variable you want to predict is known as the ***dependent variable.*** The variable(s) on which the prediction is based is(are) known as the ***independent variable(s).***

TUTORIAL: CREATING A SCATTERPLOT

1 Start by creating an XY scatter plot with **Ads** on the X axis and **Sales** on the Y axis (refer to the Excel Help system for details).

2 Because all sales figures are greater than $10,000, it is helpful to scale the vertical axis of the graph to start at $10,000. To do this, first click on the graph. Then double-click the vertical axis. In the Format Axis dialog box that opens, click the **Scale** tab and type 10000 as the minimum Y value as shown in the following dialog box.

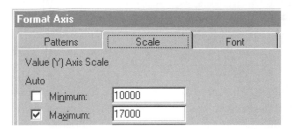

3 The graph should now appear as follows:

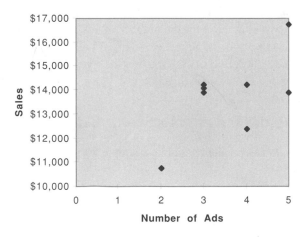

The Inter-Ocular Trauma Test. Over the years many statistical tests have been developed for verifying hypotheses: f tests, t tests, and the like. A biostatistician at the Mayo clinic, Joe Berkson, had his own favorite, mentioned in Chapter 1, which he called the *Inter-Ocular Trauma Test* (that is, it hits you between the eyes). The IOTT as applied to this situation indicates that sales tend to increase with advertising, but can we be more precise?

Choose and Run a Forecasting Technique

The simplest relationship to describe how one thing goes up or down in relation to something else is a straight line. This assumes that when the independent variable x is increased by one unit, the dependent variable y is expected to increase or decrease by a fixed amount a. This is shown in the following figure.

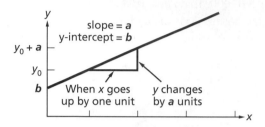

Although few things in life are truly linear, linearity is often a reasonable assumption, especially if the range of x values is small. Assuming a linear relationship exists between sales and advertising level, we now show how linear regression can provide estimates of a and b in the previous figure.

If a straight line relationship seems reasonable visually, then linear regression can be a useful technique. Of course there is still plenty of uncertainty in sales left over, even after we have accounted for the number of ads, so we wouldn't expect a straight line to fit the data perfectly. Nonetheless, linear regression does its best to fit such a line, where "best" is defined as minimizing the sum of squares of the vertical distances by which the line misses the data points.

Tutorial: Performing Regression with a Single Variable

If there is only a single independent variable, a simple way to perform regression in Excel is as follows:

1 Click on the graph. Then select **Add Trendline** from the **Chart menu.**

2 In the Trendline dialog box, select **Linear**, but also note the other types.

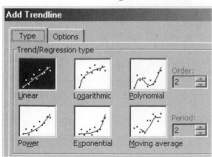

3

From the **Options** tab, check **Display Equation on Chart**. Then click **OK**.

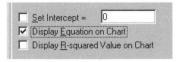

The regression line and equation will appear on the chart as shown below.

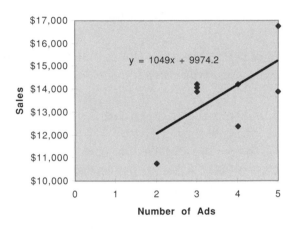

Observe the Results of the Regression

The equation indicates that the predicted sales with no ads is $9,974.20 and that the expected increase in sales per ad is $1,049. Thus, if six ads were placed, a reasonable estimate for sales would be $9,974 + 6 * $1,049 or $16,268. Remember that $16,268 is just an estimate of the mean of the distribution of possible sales. We will discuss the distribution further in the section "The Importance of Errors," later in this chapter.

If there were two independent variables, the data would consist of a cloud of dots in three dimensional space, and instead of a line, linear regression would fit a plane to the data. Similar analogies hold for any number of independent variables, but the picture becomes impossible to visualize. This could not be done within the context of a scatter plot. The regression routines from the *Analysis Tools* are required to perform this task—known as *multivariate linear regression.*

A common mathematical relationship that is not linear is the exponential model. This is used to describe quantities that grow at a roughly constant rate, for example, money earning a fixed percent per year in a savings account.

The exponential model assumes that when the independent variable x is increased by one unit, we expect the dependent variable y to be *multiplied* by a fixed amount, as shown in the following figure. This model applies to many areas in finance.

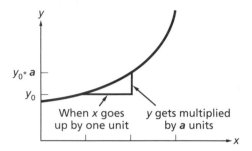

With exponential models, it is convenient to work with the logarithm of the dependent variable because this makes the model linear.

Time Series Analysis: Predicting Future Sales Based on Past History

If you flip a coin repeatedly, it will continually have a 50/50 chance of coming up heads. The number of heads appearing on each toss (either 0 or 1) is known as a stationary random variable. On the other hand, if you draw playing cards from a deck, the chance of getting an ace goes down if you have already drawn three aces, and goes up if you have drawn many cards already without drawing an ace. The number of aces appearing on a single draw from a deck (again 0 or 1) is not a stationary random variable.

■ **FUNDAMENTALS 5-2**

Stationary Random Variable

A random variable whose statistical properties do not change over time is known as a *stationary* random variable.

When you are forecasting future values of a random variable based on past values, it is important to determine whether or not it is stationary.

Two common causes of nonstationarity are *trend* and *seasonality*. Trend means that in the long run, the average value of the random variable is either rising or falling. Seasonality means that the series has repeating highs and lows in the data, caused by seasonal effects.

You should identify these two primary characteristics visually, if possible, before applying XLForecast.

An Example: Champagne Sales

Eight years of monthly sales data will be used to forecast future sales of champagne in thousands of cases. Select the champagne data from SERIES.xls by pulling down the range name list on the formula bar as shown. Or, press the F5 key to access the range names. Once the champagne series has been selected, copy it and paste it into a blank workbook, then close SERIES.xls.

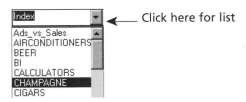 ← Click here for list

Forecasting with XLForecast

TUTORIAL: LOADING AND EYEBALLING THE DATA

Make sure that XLForecast is loaded and the **Forecast** menu is visible before beginning these steps.

1 Select the CHAMPAGNE data in the workbook just created.

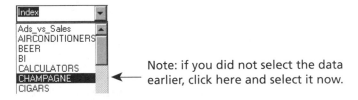
Note: if you did not select the data earlier, click here and select it now.

2 Invoke the **Forecast Run Forecast** command. You will see the following dialog box.

3 Click **OK**.

A new workbook is created that allows you view and manipulate the forecast.

The Graph sheet should look like this initially:

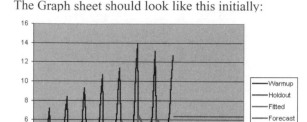

The inter-ocular trauma test, applied to the black line (historical data), reveals two things. First, champagne sales are seasonal with a high peak in December and a smaller one in summer. Second, in the long run there appears to be an upward trend in sales.

EXERCISE

5.1 ACCOUNTING FOR THE TWO PEAKS IN CHAMPAGNE SALES

Given what you know about the consumption of champagne, explain the two peaks that occur in sales each year.

TUTORIAL: SPECIFYING A TRENDED AND SEASONAL FORECAST

Because this series has a trend (rising in this case), select **Trended.** This applies two parameter exponential smoothing to the series as discussed in detail in Appendix B. Because the series displays 12-month *seasonality,* click **Seasonal** and make sure the length of the period is 12. As you make these changes you will see the green line (fitted model) mold itself more closely to the historical data. You will also see the forecast of the future, represented by the blue line, and the **Forecast** tab change to extrapolate the green line. We will discuss the other forecasting parameters in more detail in the next section. Note that the point estimate forecast of the first period into the future (period 97) is about 4,600 cases. We will now discuss how to simulate the distribution of this uncertain number. But first, save this workbook as FCAST.xls for future reference.

TUTORIAL: SIMULATING THE FUTURE BASED ON FORECAST ERRORS

You will find the full distribution of an uncertain number to be more helpful than a point estimate. The distribution of champagne sales in the first period of the forecast can be simulated as follows:

1

Make sure that the current forecast of champagne is the active workbook. Then, open **XLSim.xla** if it is not open already.

2

On the **Simulation** sheet invoke the **Thaw** command from the **Simulate** menu.

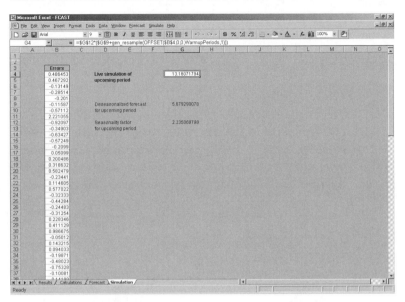

The simulated first future period sales, shown in cell G4, is created by adding one of the randomly chosen past errors to the deseasonalized forecast in G9, then multiplying by the seasonality factor in G12. Press the calculate key a few times to make sure it is working. Cell G4 can now be used as input to any model such as INVNTORY.xls, which was presented in Chapter 3.

**EXERCISE
5.2**

LINKING FORECASTING TO A SIMULATION MODEL

As a major distributor of champagne, you must order inventory for month 97 based on the previous forecast (assume the units of the forecast are thousands of cases). You make a profit of $50 per case sold, but of course you cannot sell more than you inventory, so you do not want to be short. On the other hand, if you over purchase, the storage and capital costs are $12.50 per excess case. How many cases should you order (in multiples of 500) to maximize expected profit? *Hint:* Modify INVNTORY.xls to reflect the new economics. Then link the live simulation to the demand cell as follows: Place the cursor in cell A2 of INVNTORY.xls and press <=>. Move to the **Simulation** sheet of FCAST.xls using the Excel **Window** command. Place the cursor in cell G4. Then press **Enter.**

THE IMPORTANCE OF ERRORS

Forecasting is somewhat like throwing darts. You rarely get a bull's eye, but by observing your errors (also known as residuals) you may be able to improve your technique. Fundamentals Box 5-3 describes the differences between random and systematic errors.

EXERCISE

5.3   FORECASTING FREIGHT

The U.S. freight manager for a foreign airline complained that the home office always gave him terrible forecasts: They were "consistently too high." When he complained about the quality of their forecasts, management in the home office challenged him to provide them with a better forecast. How could the freight manager have improved the home office forecasts?

■ FUNDAMENTALS 5-3

Random versus Systematic Errors

When there is no pattern to the errors, as depicted in the left figure below, the errors are known as **random**. If the errors are truly random, it may be impossible to improve the forecast. Nonetheless, the errors provide a valuable source of information concerning the reliability of the forecast.

If there is a clear pattern to the errors, as depicted in the right figure below, the errors are known as **systematic**. Systematic errors will usually suggest some obvious way to improve the situation.

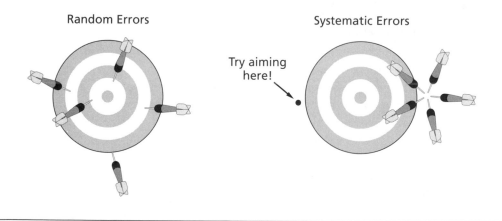

Random Errors   Systematic Errors

Try aiming here!

Errors Generated by Regression

The coefficients found by regression ensure that the sum of squares of the errors has been minimized. We will return to the tutorial example where we analyzed the effect of advertising on sales, to further investigate these errors. This time, however, we will use the regression routines in Excel's **Data Analysis Tools** to investigate the reliability of the results.

TUTORIAL: RUNNING REGRESSION FROM THE DATA ANALYSIS TOOLS

1 Copy the Ads_vs_Sales data in SERIES.xls to a blank workbook.

2 From the worksheet containing your copy of the Ads_vs_Sales data, invoke the **Tools Data Analysis** command, as shown below.

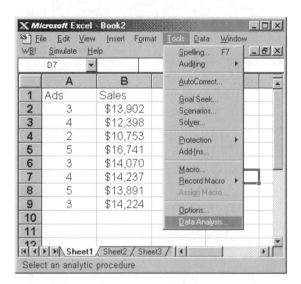

3 Select **Regression** from the **Analysis Tools** menu.

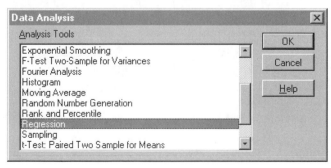

4

Fill in the dialog box as shown below. Then click **OK** to initiate the regression calculation.

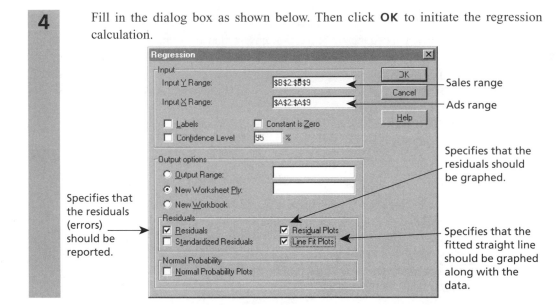

Sales range — Input Y Range: $B$2:$B$9

Ads range — Input X Range: $A$2:$A$9

Specifies that the residuals (errors) should be reported.

Specifies that the residuals should be graphed.

Specifies that the fitted straight line should be graphed along with the data.

Interpret the Results

The regression routine outputs more results than are needed in many situations. We will discuss a few of the more important results.

Residual Plot. It is a good idea to view the residual plot, shown in the left of the following figures, in order to spot systematic errors. In this case, the errors appear to be random. The three points in a straight line above the X Variable 1 at 3 do not represent systematic errors, but merely indicate that on three occasions, exactly three ads were run.

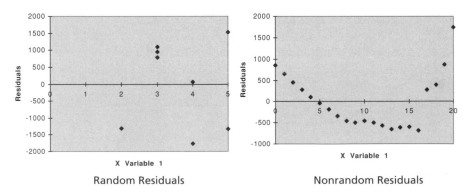

Random Residuals   Nonrandom Residuals

Had the errors displayed any obvious systematic (nonrandom) pattern, such as shown in the figure on the right, this would indicate that there was not a linear relationship between sales and ads; and it would not make sense to use the linear regression. Because the errors do appear random, however, the next step is to look at the regression outputs. We will cover only the most fundamental regression outputs. For a complete explanation, see a text on statistics.

Regression Statistics. The regression statistics appear as shown in the following figure and brief descriptions.

Regression Statistics	
Multiple R	0.652413114
R Square	0.425642871
Adjusted R Square	0.329916683
Standard Error	1396.063433
Observations	8

- ***Multiple R:*** This is the correlation between the sales and ad data (see the discussion of correlation in Chapter 3).

- ***R Square:*** The square of the correlation. The R^2 measures the percentage of the variance of sales explained by the variance in ads.

- ***Adjusted R Square:*** The R^2 is usually adjusted to reflect the number of data points. This is often used as a measure of the ultimate predictive power of the regression, with a value of 1 signifying perfect prediction and 0 signifying none.

- ***Standard Error:*** An estimate of the standard deviation of the errors.

- ***Observations:*** The number of data points.

Coefficients. The coefficients for the linear equation, Y = Slope * X Variable 1 + Intercept, are shown in the following figure, with descriptions following. Had the regression been run on more than one type of ad—say, radio, newspaper and so on— there would have been a corresponding X coefficient for each one.

	Coefficients
Intercept	9974.218447
X Variable 1	1049.028216

- ***Intercept:*** The Y intercept, which shows predicted sales with zero ads.

- ***X Variable 1:*** Slope, which is the expected increase in sales per ad.

The Reliability of the Regression Results

The following picture is a reminder that for any value of the independent variable, the regression line is just a point estimate for the mean of the dependent variable. We must not forget that the true value of the dependent variable is distributed about this line. The standard error is an estimate of the standard deviation of this distribution as shown below for the example of sales versus ads.

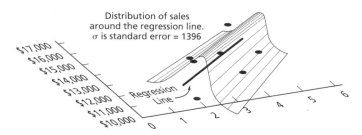

Recall from the tutorial that the estimate of sales with six ads was $16,268. However, we almost certainly would not get exactly this amount if we actually took out six ads. The standard error of 1396 indicates that to be 95% confident, we must accept a range of $2,792 (two standard errors) to either side of this figure—a range between $19,060 and $13,476. This is a far cry from being certain that sales will be $16,268.

Standard errors associated with each coefficient can also provide additional insight. For example, it seems very likely that sales increase with ads, as the expected rate is $1,049 per ad. What is the chance sales might actually decrease with the number of ads? The standard error of the slope (X Variable 1 coefficient) in this case is about 500. For the actual slope to be negative, it would have to be more than two standard errors below the estimate of $1,049. The chance of this is less than 2.5%, so we can be very sure that advertising does indeed increase sales.

EXERCISE
5.4   A SIMULATION BASED ON A REGRESSION

Suppose we plan to run four ads.

a.   Use the slope and intercept to calculate the expected sales given four ads.

b.   Load XLSim.xla and use gen_Resample with the residuals of the regression to simulate the uncertainty in sales.

c.   We can often reasonably assume that the residuals are normally distributed. In a separate cell, simulate the uncertainty in sales using gen_Normal(0,S) where S is the standard error determined by the regression.

d.   Run a simulation of both cells and compare the results.

e.   What are the advantages of each approach?

Errors Generated by Time Series

Forecasting errors are the gauge by which the quality of forecasting techniques is measured. Usually the mean of the square of the errors is used for this purpose. We will now discuss some of the parameters that can be adjusted to improve forecasts. Open, the file FCAST.xls (the champagne forecast saved from the tutorial).

Minimizing the Mean Squared Error

Under **Forecast Statistics** on the **Graph** sheet locate MSE(Warmup). This is the mean of the squared errors between the points on the fitted model (green line) and the past data (black line). We will discuss the MSE(Holdout) shortly.

Un-check and re-check the **Seasonal** box to see how it effects the MSE. Now do the same with the **Trended** box.

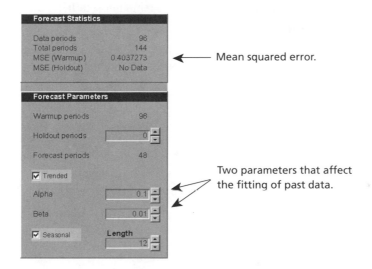

Alpha and Beta are two additional parameters discussed in more detail later in this chapter and also in Appendix B. They too affect the fit of the model, and therefore the MSE. They are set to values that provide reasonable forecasts for most trended time series. However, for any particular series, the MSE can generally be reduced further by adjusting Alpha and Beta. This can be done by directly entering new values into cells M20 and M22 (values between 0 and 1) or using the scroll buttons. In addition, the Solver built into Excel can adjust these parameters to come up with a "best fit" to the historical data. *Note:* this is generally not a "convex" problem (see Chapter 8), and therefore it may be necessary to start the Solver out at various points to insure that you have found the true minimum value of MSE.

EXERCISE

5.5   Minimizing Mean Squared Error in Time Series Analysis

Use the built-in Solver in Excel to change alpha and beta to minimize the mean squared error (MSE). *Note:* Alpha and Beta must be constrained to be between 0 and 1.

Predicting the Past

No one would ever apply an experimental drug to a human patient without first testing it in a controlled laboratory experiment. The same thing holds for applying forecasts. The controlled experiment in this case is forecasting the past. By using early periods of past data to predict later periods of past data, we can get a feeling for the method's accuracy. A period called the *holdout period* is set aside at the end of the historical data as a surrogate for the future. The remaining (earlier) period is known as the *warmup period.*

Tutorial: Experimenting with the Holdout Period

1

To forecast the last three years of data from the first five years, type 36 into the Holdout periods cell (M14) on the Graph sheet.

The number of warmup periods now equals 60. This means that the forecast is now based on only the first 60 months of data. To find out how this forecast compared with the next three years of actual sales, look at the Forecast graph as shown below. Also note the value of the MSE for the holdout period.

Fitted
(model)

Warmup
(data)

Forecast
(model)

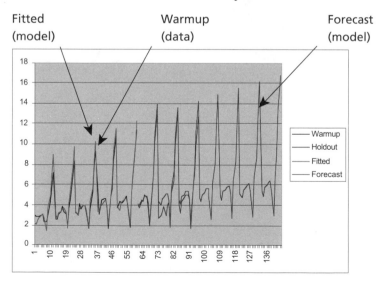

Modeling the Error in Future Months

In the time series tutorial, we generated a live simulation of the first period into the future based on the past errors. Industrial time series analysis packages generally include information about the uncertainty in periods further into the future.

For example, many time series packages provide confidence intervals as shown in the following figure. In this case, we can be 95% confident that the actual series will lie within the range shown in any particular future month. If we assume the errors are normally distributed, then the difference between the expected results and the 95% percent intervals will be 2σ.

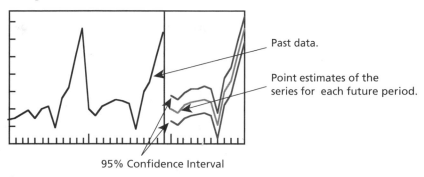

Past data.

Point estimates of the series for each future period.

95% Confidence Interval

To forecast the future confidence intervals accurately is beyond the scope of this work. The approach used in the next exercise will serve as a useful introduction, however.

EXERCISE

5.6 SIMULATING FUTURE PERIODS OF A TIME SERIES BASED ON CONFIDENCE INTERVALS

The following table contains a forecast, and upper and lower 95% confidence intervals for 12 periods. Assuming that the errors are independent and normally distributed, create a simulation for each of the months.

Month	Lower	Forecast	Upper
1	1.25	4.05	6.84
2	0.76	3.70	6.63
3	1.26	4.34	7.43
4	1.27	4.50	7.74
5	1.40	4.80	8.20
6	1.31	4.88	8.45
7	0.48	4.23	7.98
8	-1.83	2.10	6.04
9	1.28	5.42	9.55
10	2.66	7.00	11.34
11	5.84	10.39	14.95
12	8.31	13.09	17.88

Autocorrelation

Autocorrelation is a property of time series that is related to seasonality. It represents the degree to which the elements of the series are dependent on previous elements. The Autocorrelation function shows the degree to which the series is correlated with shifted versions of itself. See AUTOCORRELATION.xls for an interactive explanation of this phenomenon. There are times when the residuals of a regression or some other type of forecast look random to the naked eye, but are nonetheless autocorrelated, implying a hidden structure. ARIMA models are a family of forecasting techniques designed to remove the autocorrelation from the residuals of the forecast.

The Champagne series along with its autocorrelation functions is shown below.

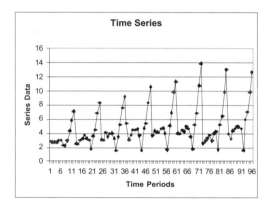

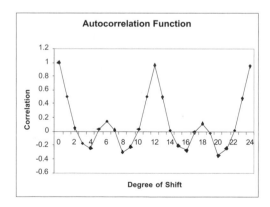

EXERCISE
5.7

AUTOCORRELATION

a. Open AUTOCORRELATION.xls and observe the scatter plot for various values of shift, S.

b. What do you think the autocorrelation function would look like if the Champagne series were replaced by random numbers generated by =RAND()? Try to sketch it for yourself, then perform an experiment to find out if you were correct, by replacing the series in AUTOCORRELATION.xls with =RAND().

Conclusions

Remember, nearly all forecasting techniques provide an estimate of the error of the forecast along with a point estimate of the mean. In many cases, throwing out the errors and keeping the mean is not like throwing out the baby with the bathwater, but is closer to throwing out the baby and keeping the bathwater.

EXPLANATION OF REGRESSION AND EXPONENTIAL SMOOTHING

Regression

The basic idea of linear regression is to find a straight line that "best" fits the data. The "best" fit is defined as the line that minimizes the sum of the squares of the differences, or errors *e*, between the model and the data. The parameters that linear regression can adjust in trying to fit the line to the data are the line's slope *a* and its *y*-intercept *b*. This is shown in the following figure. Note that $\bar{x}$ and $\bar{y}$ refer to the mean of the *x* and *y* values respectively.

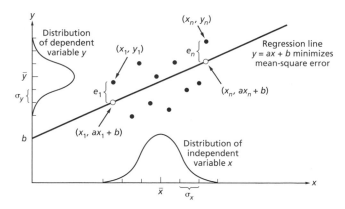

The formulas shown in Fundamentals Box 5-4 refer to the previous figure. They relate the slope and intercept of the regression line to the concepts of covariance and correlation introduced in Chapter 3.

■ **FUNDAMENTALS 5-4**

The Formulas of Linear Regression

The slope **a** and y-intercept **b** are found through the following formulas:

Covariance = $\qquad \sigma_{xy} = \dfrac{1}{n} \sum\limits_{i=1}^{n} (x_i - \bar{x})(y_i - \bar{y})$

Correlation = $\qquad r = \dfrac{\sigma_{xy}}{\sigma_x \sigma_y}$

Slope of line = $\qquad a = \dfrac{\sigma_{xy}}{\sigma_x^2}$

y-intercept = $\qquad b = \bar{y} - a\bar{x}$

Exponential Smoothing

To explore exponential smoothing, a common form of time series analysis, we will start with the game of basketball. We will forecast the movement of an offensive player running down the court with the ball.

Forecasting the Offensive Player's Position

Our mathematical model of a basketball player makes an important simplifying assumption. The player's motion **down** the court is assumed to be constant, only his position relative to the center line, or **across** the court, is uncertain. The time series consists of the player's off-center distances (OCD) at regular time intervals of 2 seconds. Four time periods of this time series are shown in the following figure, with the position of the player marked by **O**.

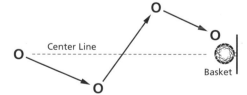

Now consider a defensive player, **D**, who must defend against **O**. At each time interval, **D** tries to forecast **O**'s off-center distance (OCD) at the next time interval. We will examine three simple defensive strategies for **D**, each in the context of **O**'s path as depicted in the previous figure.

First Defensive Strategy: Avoid the "Fake Out." To avoid being faked out by his opponent, **D** pays no attention whatsoever to **O**'s current position. According to this strategy, **D** simply repeats his own current **OCD**.

Suppose, for example, that defense knows that the average position of all players over the game's history has been the court's center line. Then **D** might simply stay on the center-line regardless of what **O** does.

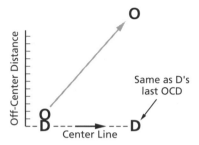

This unadaptive strategy allows **O** a leisurely shot from the side, as shown in the following figure.

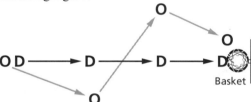

Second Defensive Strategy: Monkey See Monkey Do. This is the extreme opposite of Avoiding the Fake-Out. **D** tries to do exactly what **O** does. According to this strategy, **D**'s OCD next time will be the same as **O**'s OCD this time, as shown in the following figure.

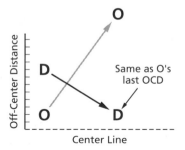

If defense adopts this strategy, **O** can throw **D** off his intended course, or "fake him out," by devious feinting as shown in the following figure.

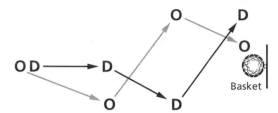

Third Defensive Strategy: Split the Difference.This adaptive approach is a compromise between the previous two. According to this strategy, defense observes the difference between his last prediction of **O**'s OCD, (**D**'s current OCD) and **O**'s current OCD. **D**'s next off-center distance will split this difference halfway.

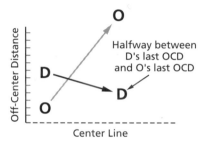

In summary, the first strategy is so tied to past history that it cannot react to current events, and the second strategy takes no account of past history whatever. The third strategy is a compromise between these two extremes.

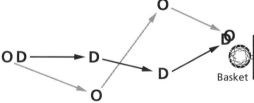

This strategy has two notable characteristics. First, **D**'s current position is based on 50% of his last position, which is based on 50% of his position before that, and so on. Thus **D**'s past history decays exponentially. Secondly, **D**'s trajectory is smoother than **O**'s.

This third strategy is an example of the important family of forecasting techniques known, not surprisingly, as *exponential smoothing*. Specifically, this example demonstrates *single parameter exponential* smoothing with a *parameter* of .5. The parameter value .5 refers to the fact that at each step, **D** moves half way from his previous guess toward the offense's actual position. Technically speaking, strategies one and two are also extreme cases of exponential smoothing, with parameter values that equal 0 and 1, respectively.

One Parameter Exponential Smoothing

Exponential smoothing is a family of moving weighted average techniques that considers all past observations of a time series, putting less and less weight on the early observations. One parameter exponential smoothing, the simplest of this family of techniques, is applicable to time series whose mean is either **constant** or **slowly changing** over time. The three basketball defenses described earlier are special cases of one parameter exponential smoothing. We discuss two parameter exponential smoothing in Appendix B.

The Formulas for One Parameter Exponential Smoothing. Given a time series $Y(t)$, a series of forecasts, $F(t)$, are made that adapt to $Y(t)$ over time. $Y(t)$ and $F(t)$ correspond to the off-center distances at time t of O and D, respectively, in the basketball analogy. As a new observation $Y(t)$ arrives in time period t, a forecast $F(t+1)$ is made for the observation $Y(t+1)$, which will arrive in time $t+1$. These estimates are computed as follows:

1. A value of $F(1)$ is chosen. This might be $Y(1)$ itself, the average of historical data, or some other reasonable estimate. Even if this first forecast is not very accurate, future estimates will improve because of the adaptive nature of the technique.

2. For each additional time period t, $F(t) = F(t-1) + \alpha E(t-1)$, where $E(t-1) = Y(t-1) - F(T-1)$ is the error of the forecast in the previous period and α, known as the smoothing parameter, is a number between 0 and 1.

   Notice that if $F(t-1)$ is too low, then $E(t-1)$ is positive, and the forecast is raised in the next period. If $F(t-1)$ is too high, then $E(t-1)$ is negative, and the forecast is lowered in the next period. This behavior has been compared to that of a thermostat that monitors the difference between desired and actual temperature, and adjusts an air conditioning system accordingly.

Future Forecasts. If there are **n** time periods of actual data, then the forecast for period **n+1** is

$$F(n+1) = F(n) + \alpha E(n)$$

But how about periods further in the future? The series $Y(t)$ was assumed to have either a constant or slowly changing mean. Hence for all future periods we have

$$F(t) = F(n+1), t > n+1$$

The Effect of Changes in α. The number α is the adjustment that controls how fast or slow the weighting of past observations diminishes.

A value of 0 puts all the weight on past history and corresponds to the Avoid the "Fake Out" strategy. A value of $\alpha = 1$ puts all the weight on the current observation and corresponds to the Monkey See Monkey Do strategy. A value of $\alpha = 0.5$

corresponds to the Split the Difference strategy. In the basketball analogy, as α ranges from 0 to 1, **D**'s next off-center distance changes continuously between **D**'s current OCD and **O**'s current OCD. In practice, typical values of α in time series analysis are smaller than the 0.5 of the basketball example.

For time series with trends, a two parameter version of exponential smoothing is used. XLForecast can perform either one or two parameter smoothing, with or without seasonality. The formulas for two parameter smoothing and seasonality are discussed in Appendix B.

Note that linear regression can also be used to forecast trends. However, exponential smoothing places more weight on recent data and less on older data. It is therefore more adaptive than regression, which places equal weight on all past data points.

END OF CHAPTER EXERCISES

5.8   FORECASTING EXPONENTIAL GROWTH

Apply XLForecast to the Exponential_Growth data in SERIES.xls. Select **Trended** and use the Excel Solver to minimize the warmup MSE by adjusting Alpha and Beta.

5.9   EXAMINING SEASONALITY

Examine the REPAIR data in SERIES.xls. Estimate the seasonality two ways:

a.   Apply a trended forecast in XLForecast, and adjust the seasonality so as to minimize the MSE.

b.   Paste the REPAIR data into AUTOCORRELATION.xls.
     Do the two methods agree? What do you believe the time seasonality is in this data?

5.10   EXAMINING ERRORS

Return to the forecast of the CHAMPAGNE data in SERIES.xls, which was created with trending and 12 month seasonality. The Simulation sheet contains a column of deseasonalized errors, that is, the difference between the deseasonalized data and the fitted points. Do these errors look random when graphed? How about the autocorrelation of the errors?

6 ∎∎∎∎∎∎∎∎∎∎∎∎∎∎∎∎∎∎∎∎∎∎∎∎∎∎∎∎

Decision Trees

Simple it's not, I'm afraid you will find,
for a mind-maker-upper to make up his mind.

DR. SEUSS

We must often decide between a few alternative actions in the face of uncertainty. For example:

- A pharmaceutical manufacturer must decide whether or not to pursue development of an experimental drug that might or might not be effective and, even if effective, might not be approved for use.

- A petroleum exploration firm must decide either to drill for oil on a particular site or abandon the site without knowing how expensive it will be to drill or whether oil is present.

- A toy manufacturer must decide between a large or small production run of a new toy, without being certain about either production costs or the price that the toy will ultimately sell for.

- A legal team must decide whether or not to settle a case out of court, given the uncertainty of a trial outcome.

- Military strategists, uncertain about the capabilities of potential adversaries, must decide in advance between two or three responses to hostile action.

Decision trees can sharpen and formalize the decision-making process in situations such as these. They can both aid us in making up our minds and bring into focus future events that should change our minds.

■ ■ ■ **OVERVIEW**

Introduction

This section introduces the use of decision trees in making yes/no decisions in the face of uncertainty. Also presented are instructions for installing and running XLTree, a decision tree add-in for Excel.

Tutorial: Building a Decision Tree

Use of decision trees is introduced through the example of a pharmaceutical manufacturer deciding whether or not to pursue development of an experimental drug whose effectiveness, as well as approval for use, are in question.

Decision Analysis: Basic Concepts

Through examples, this section presents basic decision analytic concepts: utility, probability, expected value, decision trees, sensitivity analysis, value of information, and state variables.

INTRODUCTION

An Example: Ice Cream and Parking Tickets

Suppose that while driving home from an errand you pass an ice cream parlor and suddenly develop the urge for a cone. You must decide whether to pull over and buy an ice cream cone for $1, or go straight home where a sink full of dirty dishes is waiting for you. This decision can be represented by the following diagram:

The choice between eating ice cream and doing dishes generally does not require advanced analysis, but now you notice that the only place to park your car is an illegal spot on the end of the block. The uncertainty of getting a $20 parking ticket has just transported you to the realm of decision analysis, which addresses sequences of decisions interspersed with uncertainties. In this case we have just one decision (whether or not to stop) and one uncertainty (whether or not we will get a ticket).

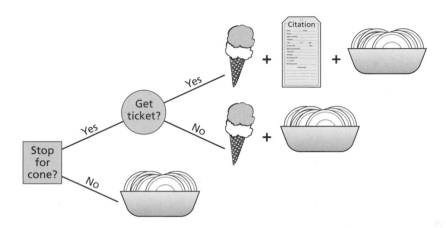

The figure displaying this situation looks like a tree on its side, hence the term *decision tree*. Decision trees are tools for sharpening and formalizing the decision-making process. They can both aid us in making up our minds and help us focus on future events that might change our minds. As with most analytical techniques, the insight derived from developing a model with the tool is an important part of the process.

EXERCISE
6.1

UMBRELLA PROBLEM

Suppose you have traveled to London and have forgotten your umbrella. The probability that it will rain is 40%. If you get caught in the rain, you will do $75 worth of damage to your suit. The cost of an umbrella is $25. Draw the decision tree for this situation.

EXERCISE
6.2

FASTEST ROUTE

Suppose that you need to travel from your job to your home located 60 miles away. You can travel by four-lane expressway or surface road, which you estimate will take 60 minutes or 90 minutes, respectively. However, you think that three of the expressway's four lanes might be closed because of road work, in which case travel by expressway would take 120 minutes. Draw a tree that represents this decision situation.

Good Decisions versus Good Outcomes

In all decision making it is important to appreciate that good decisions can lead to bad outcomes and vice versa. For example, you can carefully look both ways before crossing the street, then get killed by a plane that crashes into the intersection. On the other hand, you can cross the street blindfolded and survive unscathed. Yet, before the fact, no one would dispute that looking both ways is a better decision than using a blindfold. Thus, with decision analysis there are no guarantees. The process is analogous to carefully studying the traffic pattern on the street and then deciding how to cross.

XLTree

XLTree.xla is an add-in for Microsoft Excel 97 and higher. It is easy to install and learn, and works in either Windows or Macintosh environments.

Running XLTree. Launch Excel and load XLTree.xla from the **File Open** command.

Auto Load Option. If you want XLTree to load every time you launch Excel, follow these steps:

1. Select **Add-ins** from the **Tools** menu in Excel.

2. Select XLTree from the list of add-ins and click **OK**.

3. You can later go back and deselect XLTree from the **Add-in** menu to prevent Excel from loading it automatically.

TUTORIAL: BUILDING A DECISION TREE

Experimental Drug Development

The development of a new drug poses many risks. The following simplified example focuses on two primary risks: Will the drug be effective, and, if so, will it be approved for use in humans?

Imagine that you work for a pharmaceutical company that has been investigating cures for *Some Horrible Disease* (SHD). If a cure could be developed, it would be a boon to humankind and yield a profit of $200 million. Initial research indicates a 25% chance that a particular compound X will be effective against SHD. However, it will require an additional $10 million in research and development to know for sure. Furthermore, even if the resulting compound is proven effective, another $10 million in testing will be required to get it approved for use in humans. It is estimated that there is a 40% chance that the testing will reveal serious side effects and approval will be denied.

As SHD's project director, you are concerned with two primary issues. First, should you pursue the commercial development of compound X? Second, if you do pursue development, what value should you place on the project when comparing it with competing projects?

Building a Decision Tree with XLTree

The basic steps of building a decision tree are as follows:

1. Starting the tree and optionally specifying state variables.

2. Adding decision and uncertainty forks.

3. Entering utility values at the leaves of the tree.

4. Performing sensitivity analysis.

5. Creating a presentation graphic of the tree if desired.

Once XLTree is loaded and the Tree menu and Tree Editing toolbar appear as shown below, proceed with the tutorial. *Note:* If you make a mistake in adding a decision or uncertainty fork, you can remove it with the Remove Subtree command. See Appendix C, "Software Command Reference," for details.

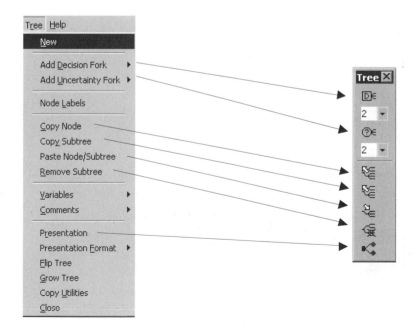

Tutorial: Starting the Tree

1 Select **New** from the **Tree** menu to open the dialog box shown below.

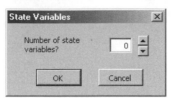

2 Leave the number of state variables at 0, as this simple example will not use them (state variables are discussed later in this chapter). Click **OK** to proceed.

A new workbook is created that contains the root of the tree as shown in the figure below. Note that there are hidden columns in this worksheet that can be viewed with the **Variables, Show** command (discussed in Appendix C, "Software Command Reference").

	F	G	H
1			
2	*		
3			
4			

Tutorial: Adding Decision and Uncertainty Forks

1 Add a two-branch Decision Fork by invoking **Tree**, **Add Decision Fork, 2 Branches**, or by using the toolbar button. The sheet should now look like this:

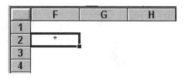

Note that the formula in cell F2 is simply the maximum of cells J2 and J3. This cell is formatted as bold blue, denoting that this is a decision fork.

2 Type the two alternatives, "Develop" and "Abandon," as shown.

	F	G	H	J
1				
2	0	Develop		*
3		Abandon		*
4				

3

To see how the decision fork works, imagine that there were no risks in developing the drug. Then the value of developing the drug would be $200 million, and the value of abandoning would be $0. Type these values (in millions) into the corresponding cells containing asterisks, then place the cursor in cell F2.

F2	▼		=MAX(J2:J3)	
	F	**G**	**H**	**J**
1				
2	200	Develop	==>	200
3		Abandon		0
4				

As you can see, given the choice of the values in cells J2 and J3, the decision fork took the maximum, 200. Also, notice that an arrow points along that branch of the best decision.

4

Of course you cannot be sure of getting that $200 million if you proceed with development, so we will add an uncertainty fork at cell J2. Normally this would have been done without first typing a number into the cell containing the asterisk. Replace the value 200 with an asterisk (*) and, with the cursor in cell J2, invoke **Tree, Add Uncertainty Fork, 2 Branches**, or use the toolbar button. The sheet should appear as shown below.

J2	▼		=SUMPRODUCT(L2:L3,N2:N3)			
	F	**G**	**H**	**J**	**K**	**L**	**N**
1							
2	0	Develop	==>	0	Outcome 1	Prob.	*
3					Outcome 2	1	*
4							
5		Abandon	==>	0			
6							

Note that cell J2 now contains a SUMPRODUCT formula that will be discussed in detail later. This cell is formatted as italicized red, denoting that it is an uncertainty fork.

5

Type the two outcomes "Effective" and "Ineffective" in cells K2 and K3, and the probability that the compound is effective, .25, in cell L2. Note that cell L3 contains 1 minus the probability in cell L2, or .75.

L3	▼		=1-SUM(L2:L2)			
	F	**G**	**H**	**J**	**K**	**L**	**N**
1							
2	0	Develop	==>	0	Effective	0.25	*
3					Ineffective	0.75	*
4							
5		Abandon	==>	0			
6							

6

Next, add the uncertainty of approval. With the cursor in cell N2, invoke **Tree, Add Uncertainty Fork, 2 Branches**. Then type the outcomes in cells O2 and O3 and the probability of approval, 0.6, in cell P2.

	F	G	H	J	K	L	N	O	P	R
1										
2	0	Develop	==>	0	Effective	0.25	0	Approved	0.6	*
3								Not Approved	0.4	*
4										
5					Ineffective	0.75		*		
6										
7		Abandon	==>	0						
8										

TUTORIAL: ENTERING UTILITY VALUES AT THE LEAVES OF THE TREE

1

Each end node or leaf of the tree corresponds to a different state of the world. In this case, each state of the world has an associated monetary value. Fill these into the leaves of the tree as follows.

Cell	State of the World	Value
J7	The project was abandoned. Nothing is ventured, lost or gained.	0
N5	The initial $10 million is invested but the compound proves ineffective.	-10
R3	The compound is effective after the first $10 million investment, but the drug does not get approved after the additional $10 million in testing.	-20
R2	The compound is effective and the drug is approved. Company receives $200 million in net profit	200

Evaluating the Decision Tree

Once the leaves have been filled in, the tree evaluates automatically and should appear as shown in the following figure.

	F	G	H	J	K	L	N	O	P	R
1										
2	20.5	Develop	==>	20.5	Effective	0.25	112	Approved	0.6	200
3								Not Approved	0.4	-20
4										
5					Ineffective	0.75	-10			
6										
7		Abandon		0						
8										

Node N2 contains the expected value given that the compound is effective, calculated as follows:

Probability that drug is approved given that it is effective (0.6)	x	Value if approved (200)	+	Probability that drug is not approved given that it is effective (0.4)	x	Value if drug not approved given effective (–20)

This is calculated as =SUMPRODUCT (P2:P3,R2:R3) and results in an expected value of *112*.

Node J2 contains the expected value given that the drug is developed, calculated as follows:

Probability that compound is effective given development (0.25)	x	Expected value if effective (112)	+	Probability that drug is ineffective given development (0.75)	x	Value if drug is ineffective given development (-10)

This is calculated as =SUMPRODUCT (L2:L5,N2:N5) and results in an expected value of *20.5*.

Node F2 contains the expected value of the entire project, calculated as follows:

Maximum of	Expected value given development (20.5)	and	Expected value given no development (0)

This is calculated as =MAX(J2:J7) and results in an expected value of *20.5*.

Notice that the arrow indicates that the best choice is to develop the drug, but—far from $200 million—the expected value is only $20.5 million. If you must choose between this and some other potential cure for SHD, you should compare both their relative expected values and their associated risks.

Performing Sensitivity Analysis

In practice it is seldom possible to know the inputs to a decision tree with great accuracy. However, by performing sensitivity analysis on the uncertain inputs, you can increase your confidence in the decision suggested by the tree. Furthermore, the decision tree can help you see future events that should make you change your mind. Sensitivity analysis can be quite involved or very simple, as demonstrated in the following exercise.

**EXERCISE
6.3**

THE PROBABILITY OF EFFECTIVENESS

The probability that the experimental compound will be effective is not easy to determine and opinions vary widely from person to person. Suppose the opinions that count in this case are the chief SHD researcher (who estimates a probability of 35%), the chairman of the board (15%), and you (25%). Return to the model and experiment with the probability that the drug is effective, located in cell L2, to determine how small a probability still leads to the choice to develop the drug. Does this finding make it easier to sell the project?

Tree Presentation

After building and evaluating a decision tree you may wish to prepare a graphical presentation using the presentation tools.

TUTORIAL: GRAPHICAL TREE PRESENTATION

1   **Node Labels**. Short comments can be attached to a node using the **Tree, Node Labels** command. For example, with the cursor in the first decision node (cell F2) select **Tree, Node Labels**. The Node Properties dialog box should appear:

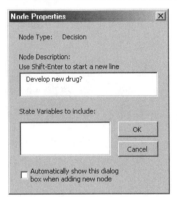

In the Node Description section enter a short phrase describing the decision node (e.g. "Develop new drug?"). Since we did not store any state variables with this tree, you may ignore the state variable field. For further discussion of the Node Labels box refer to Appendix C: Software Command Reference.

2   Comments may also be added to the uncertainty nodes (cells J2, N2) and the leaf nodes (J7, N5, R2, R3) to help clarify the decision-making process modeled by the tree. In cell J2 add: "Does Drug Work?", and in cell N2 add: "Is Drug Approved?"

3   The **Presentation Format** worksheet places many aspects of the tree's appearance under your control. Click on the **Presentation Format** tab and specify that the **Decision Descriptions** and **Uncertainty Descriptions** be above the nodes. Experiment with the formatting options to create trees of different appearance. For a further description of the formatting features refer to Appendix C.

4   From the **Tree** menu, select **Presentation** (or use the toolbar button) and a graphical version of the tree will be created in a new sheet labeled **Presentation**—using the formatting styles set in the **Presentation Format** worksheet. *Note:* Subsequent changes to the **Presentation Format** worksheet will not appear until the **Tree Presentation** command is re-run. Also be sure to examine the **Global Option** parameters at the bottom of the **Presentation Format** worksheet to control the size of the nodes and relative spacing of elements in the tree. Your tree should appear like the following figure.

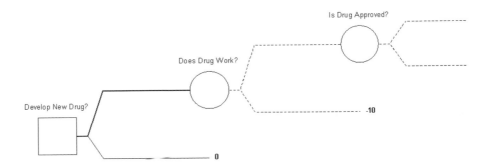

DECISION ANALYSIS: BASIC CONCEPTS

Now that decision trees have been discussed, we return to the example involving ice cream and parking tickets. Such everyday questions can reveal a lot about the way we make more important decisions. The basic concepts are the following:

- *Utility.* The concept of utility helps us compare things that are as different as apples and oranges, or as ice cream and parking tickets.

- *Probability.* We must analyze what we mean by the chance or probability of uncertain events before we can make a reasonable decision. In this example, the uncertain event of concern is whether or not we get a parking ticket.

- *Expected Value.* Expected value defines what would happen "on average" if we were to imagine repeating the situation numerous times.

- *Decision Trees.* Decision trees are a tools for sharpening and formalizing the decision-making process. They are constructed from forks representing decision alternatives and uncertain outcomes.

- *Sensitivity Analysis.* Often the inputs to a decision tree are not known with certainty. Sensitivity analysis can increase your confidence in the decision making process by revealing input ranges over which particular decisions are optimal.

- *Conditional Probability.* The probability that it will rain is generally less than the probability that it will rain given that you have just heard thunder. We use the term *conditional probability* to refer to the probability that one event will occur, given that we know that another event has occurred.

- *Value of Information.* An important benefit of decision analysis is that it can quantify the value of obtaining additional information, even if that information is not completely dependable.

- *State Variables.* State variables are a convenient way of describing the various states of the world in which decision makers may find themselves. State variables allow you to develop complex utility functions that depend on numerous inputs.

- *Mustering the Courage of Your Convictions.* Just because you or your organization have determined a rational course of action in the light of uncertainty does not mean it will be expedient to carry it out.

For a more thorough discussion on these topics, see Winston, Christian, and Broadie (1997) or a good textbook on decision analysis.

Utility

Recall the dilemma raised in the introduction, which led to the following figure. This example allows us to think about things we can relate to on a day-to-day basis. Yet even here it is not so easy to compare outcomes involving ice cream, dirty dishes, and parking tickets. One approach is to ask, for each outcome, what amount of cash would be of equal value to you.

For example, would you rather have one dollar than the ice cream? Probably not. The ice cream costs a dollar, and we assume that you are more than willing to pay that for it. How about two or three dollars? Of course, it depends on your personal tastes and even on the time of day, but suppose at this moment you would be indifferent to receiving either $5 in cash or the ice cream. Then one would say that your *utility* for a single ice cream cone at this moment is the same as your utility for $5, and your *net utility* is $4 because the cone costs $1. Note that utility is not the equivalent of money. It is unlikely that you would be indifferent to receiving either $500 in cash or 100 ice cream cones.

Also, two people's utility for the same thing need not be the same. For example, if you are allergic to milk, you may have very low utility for ice cream under any conditions.

The parking ticket would appear to have a utility of –$20, but this is not necessarily the case. Suppose you have many unpaid tickets and fear the consequences of another one. You might find that you would be as upset getting another ticket as you would be paying $30. Thus, the ticket would have a utility to you of –$30.

As for the dishes, you will have to do them sooner or later anyway. Therefore, for the decision at hand, it doesn't matter what utility you place on doing them. For convenience, we will use a utility of $0.

It is not necessary that money be used to evaluate the various items. The important thing is to place *relative* values on them. So for example we could have measured everything in terms of free ice creams (FICs). In this case, paying $1 for ice cream would be worth 4/5 of a FIC, a ticket would be worth –6 FICs, and dishes would still be zero. The full theory of utility also accounts for such factors as your willingness to take risks in decision making. As a reminder, the net utilities we will use for this example are shown in the following figure.

Item			
Net Utility	$4	–$30	$0

EXERCISE

6.4   UTILITY FOR ICE CREAM

What are your own utilities for each of the possible outcomes in the ice cream problem?

EXERCISE

6.5   UTILITY FOR THE UMBRELLA

What are your utilities for each of the possible outcomes in the umbrella problem?

EXERCISE

6.6   UTILITY FOR FASTEST ROUTE

What are your utilities for each of the possible outcomes in the fastest route problem? Remember that because XLTree maximizes utility, you will need to use something such as the negative of the time wasted on the road.

■ FUNDAMENTALS 6-1

Probability

- Consider an uncertain event that can have multiple *outcomes.* For example, the event of rolling a die might have the outcomes 1,2,3,4,5, or 6. The *probability* of an outcome means the likelihood that the outcome will occur.

- The probability of any particular outcome is between 0 and 1. For example, the probability that the number 3 will occur when you roll a die is 1/6.

- The complete set of outcomes along with their associated probabilities is known as the *distribution* or *histogram* of outcomes as discussed in Chapter 2, *The Building Blocks of Uncertainty.*

- The sum of the probabilities of *all* outcomes is 1. That is, the chance that you will roll some number on the die is 1.

- The probability that an outcome *will not occur* is 1 minus the probability that it does occur. Thus, the probability of not rolling a 3 is $1 - 1/6 = 5/6$.

- If two outcomes are *mutually exclusive*, then the probability that *either* will occur is the *sum* of their probabilities. The probability of rolling a 3 or a 4 is 2/6 or 1/3.

- If two outcomes are *independent,* then the probability that they *both* occur is the *product* of their probabilities. The probability of rolling a 3 on the first of two dice and a 4 on the second is 1/6 times 1/6 or 1/36.

Probability

We cannot make a sensible decision concerning the ice cream problem without assessing the likelihood or probability of getting a ticket. What do we really mean by probability? Although a full definition of probability is beyond the scope of this work, an intuitive explanation is provided in Fundamentals Box 6-1. Fundamentals Box 6-2 provides an alternative subjective definition.

Imagine that you had stopped at this same place for ice cream 1,000 times in the past and got 100 tickets. Then you would assess the probability of a ticket as being 10%. The greater the number of times you have stopped in the past, the more accurate the estimate. The probability of no ticket is $100\% - 10\% = 90\%$.

But let's get real! You've never even been in this part of town before, let alone parked here 1,000 times. As in most situations involving uncertainty, you must estimate the probability of getting a ticket based on your personal beliefs.

■ **FUNDAMENTALS 6-2**

Subjective Definition of Probability

The probability of an event is an estimate based on your personal beliefs. To assess your estimate of the probability of event A, imagine two games of chance. In the first game, you win $100 if event A occurs. In the second game, you win $100 if you get YES on the probability wheel (discussed in the text). Now adjust the probability on the wheel by clicking the arrows until you are indifferent as to which game you play. The number on the wheel is your subjective probability that A will occur.

The probability wheel is a device that helps people assess the probability of a given outcome based on their personal beliefs. A decision analyst named Carl Spetzler developed this concept in the mid 1960s while helping oil executives assess uncertain investments. Although originally constructed of clear plastic and colored paper, we will use a software version accessible by loading SPINNER.xls and selecting **Probability Wheel** from the Settings screen.

Click the **Spin** button a few times and you should see that the outcome is **YES** about 50% of the time. Next, adjust the probability to 25% by clicking the down arrow and repeat the experiment. Now you should get **YES** about 25% of the time.

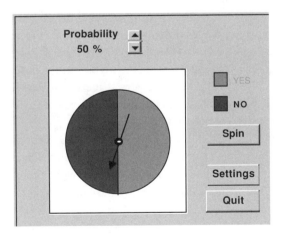

As an example of subjective probability, suppose that event A is "you get a ticket," and suppose you are indifferent to playing the two games when the wheel is set to 10%. This means you believe there is a 10% probability of getting a ticket.

This doesn't mean you are right. This just means that this is what you think. But what you think is what is important when you are the decision maker.

EXERCISE
6.7 COURSE GRADE

If you are using this book in a graded course, you will receive an A, B, C, D, or F. What is the probability that you will receive an A?

EXERCISE
6.8 THUMB TACKS

A classroom exercise used to demonstrate the concept of personal probability involves tossing a thumb tack in the air. It will either land head up or point up (which we will call tails). Unlike a coin which, is symmetric and therefore has equal probably of heads or tails, the tack is quite asymmetric.

a. Use the probability wheel to assess your probability that a tossed thumb tack will come up heads without experimenting with a real thumb tack.

b. Perform an experiment with a real thumb tack to improve your estimate of the probability.

Expected Value

Decision analysts use several criteria for making decisions under uncertainty. A common one is known as *expected value.* If you can specify utilities for all the outcomes in your problem and can also estimate the probabilities of the uncertain outcomes, then the expected value criterion can be used. Intuitively, you can view the expected value of a situation as the average outcome if you could repeat the situation many times. As we saw in Chapter 2, even situations that can't be repeated can often be modeled using Monte Carlo simulation. In this case, the expected value would be estimated by the average on the Simulation Statistics sheet.

Once you have assessed the utilities and probabilities of all uncertain outcomes, you can calculate the expected value of a situation. The expected value is calculated by summing the utility of each possible outcome multiplied by the probability of that outcome's occurrence. Fundamentals Box 6-3 shows the formulas used for expected value.

■ **FUNDAMENTALS 6-3**

Expected Value

Expected Value = (Probability of outcome 1)(Utility of outcome 1)

+ (Probability of outcome 2)(Utility of outcome 2)

$$\vdots \qquad \vdots$$

$$\vdots \qquad \vdots$$

+ (Probability of outcome k)(Utility of outcome k)

or more compactly $\quad EV = \sum_{i=1}^{k} P_i U_i$

where P_i and U_i are the ith probability and utility, respectively, with a total of k mutually exclusive outcomes.

EXERCISE
6.9   EXPECTED VALUES

a. Suppose you are betting on a coin and will win $1 if you throw heads and lose $1 if you throw tails. What is the expected value?

b. What is the expected value of each of the options in the umbrella problem?

c. What is the expected utility of each of the two routes in the fastest route problem of Exercise 6.2? Use 0.2 as the probability that three lanes of the expressway are closed. Use the negative of time of travel as a measure of utility. For example, the utility for traveling 60 minutes by expressway is −60, and so on.

Decision Forks

Observe that the diagram on page 194 resembles a tree turned on its side. By adding utilities and probabilities to the figure, we create what is known as a decision tree which can be used to determine the alternative that maximizes expected utility.

Decisions are modeled by forks with one branch for each alternative facing the decision maker at a given stage. The utility value of the associated alternative goes into each branch, whereupon the decision node displays the utility of the best alternative.

■ **FUNDAMENTALS 6-4**

Decision Trees

Decision trees, like real trees, are made of forked branches that in turn lead to additional forked branches. The base of each fork is known as a **node.** The base of the first fork is known as the **root.** Branches that do not lead to additional forks are known as **leaves.**

There are two kinds of forks. **Decision forks** represent the alternatives the decision maker will have at various stages. **Uncertainty forks** represent the uncertainties the decision maker will face at various stages.

An analogy may be helpful in gaining insight into the nature of decision forks. Imagine that the fork is made of pipe with a valve on each branch. Water of different temperatures flows into each branch where the temperature represents the utility, that is, the hotter the better. You get to decide how to open the valves. You want hot water, so you open the valve on the hottest branch and close all others. A schematic diagram of a two alternative decision fork is shown in the following figure.

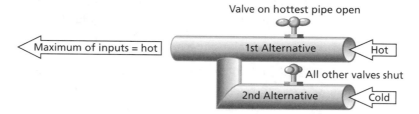

When a decision fork is created using XLTree, the node contains a formula of the form MAX (Utilities of all inputs), which in effect automatically opens the valve to the hottest branch.

Uncertainty Forks

Uncertainties are modeled by forks with one branch for each possible outcome of an uncertainty facing the decision maker at a given stage. For each possible outcome, its utility value as well as its probability of occurrence go into a branch. The uncertainty node then displays the expected (or average) utility of all outcomes.

Again using the hot water analogy, the valve of the uncertainty fork corresponding to the outcome that actually occurs will be open, with all others being shut. But you don't know which one will be open in advance, so you don't know what temperature the water coming out will be. You can determine the expected temperature, however, by opening each valve in proportion to the probability of the associated outcomes. A schematic diagram of a two-outcome uncertainty fork is shown below.

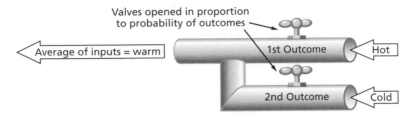

When an uncertainty fork is created using XLTree, the node contains a formula of the form SUMPRODUCT (Probabilities of Inputs, Utilities of Inputs), which calculates the expected utility.

The following figure shows the decision tree for the ice cream example. Usually decision nodes are drawn as squares, and uncertainty nodes as circles. Notice that the decision is to stop for ice cream, and that the utility of the root is $1. This means that if you were offered $1 to go straight home and wash the dishes, you would be indifferent to the two alternatives.

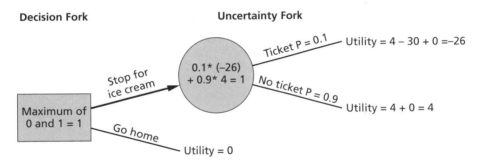

EXERCISE
6.10 **THE ICE CREAM EXAMPLE DECISION TREE**

Use XLTree to create the decision trees for the following:

a. The ice cream example. No state variables are needed, so leave the number set to 0 when you make the new tree. If you have difficulty, go through the tutorial in the last section. Save the workbook as ICECREAM when you are done.

b. The umbrella problem. Save your completed workbook as LONDON.

c. The fastest route problem. Save your completed workbook as FASTEST.

Sensitivity Analysis

Often the inputs to a decision tree are not known with certainty. For example, you usually can't accurately estimate the probability of getting a ticket. Sensitivity analysis can increase your confidence in the decision-making process by revealing input ranges over which particular decisions are optimal.

In the next exercise, we experiment with our estimates of probabilities.

EXERCISE

6.11   Experimenting with Probability Estimates

a. Retrieve the ICECREAM model created earlier and incrementally increase the probability of getting a ticket until you are just indifferent to stopping for the cone or going home. Record the result.

b. Retrieve the LONDON model and adjust the probability of rain until you are indifferent to whether or not you buy the umbrella.

c. Retrieve the FASTEST model and adjust the probability that the three expressway lanes are closed until you are indifferent to taking the expressway or surface street. What is this probability? What is the expected value of the two routes at this probability?

Tutorial: Using a Graphical Approach to Sensitivity Analysis

It is often useful to determine how the expected utility depends on some particular aspect of the situation. Here we will plot expected utility versus the probability of getting a ticket for the ice cream example by using a data table.

1   Retrieve ICECREAM, move to cell G8 (any empty cell below the tree will do) and enter 0, then .01 in the same column as pictured below.

	F	G	H	J	K	L	N
1							
2	1	Stop	==>	1	Ticket	0.1	-26
3					No Ticket	0.9	4
4							
5		Go Home		0			
6							
7							
8		0					
9		0.01					

2   Select the two cells just entered (as shown in Step 1), click on the small black square in the lower right corner, and drag downward until the series reaches 0.2 as pictured below.

	G	H
7		
8	0	
9	0.01	
10	0.02	
11	0.03	
12	0.04	
13	0.05	
14	0.06	
15	0.07	
16	0.08	
17	0.09	
18	0.1	
19	0.11	
20	0.12	
21	0.13	
22	0.14	
23	0.15	
24	0.16	
25	0.17	
26	0.18	
27	0.19	
28	0.2	

3 In cell H7 (one up and one to the right of the cell containing 0) enter "=F2" to make "overall utility" drive the table.

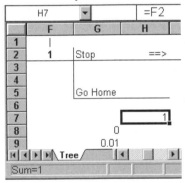

4 Select cells G7 through H28 (don't forget to start in row 7), then invoke the **Data Table** command. The Table dialog box shown below will appear. This is a column table for which the "input" is the probability of a ticket (L2).

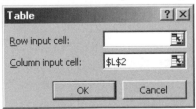

5 With the cursor in the **Column Input Cell** field, select cell L2, which contains the probability of getting a ticket.

6

Click **OK**. This has the effect of sequentially plugging each value from G8 through G28 into cell L2, and recording the resulting value of overall utility in the corresponding row of column H. You should see the following table.

	G	H
7		1
8	0	4
9	0.01	3.7
10	0.02	3.4
11	0.03	3.1
12	0.04	2.8

7

To graph this relationship, select cells G8:H28 (this time you are starting in row 8), click on the Chart Wizard icon, and select an XY(Scatter) chart.

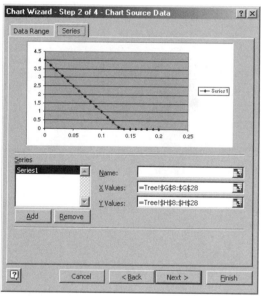

This graph's X axis represents a range of probabilities of getting a ticket, and its Y axis represents the utility of the overall situation. The next exercise involves the interpretation of this graph.

EXERCISE
6.12

THE PROBABILITY OF GETTING A TICKET, REVISITED

a. Why is the value 4 when the probability of a ticket is 0?

b. The graph consists of a bent line. Why does it bend, and what do the two straight segments correspond to?

Conditional Probability

The probability that it will rain is generally less than the probability that it will rain given that you have just heard thunder. We use the term conditional probability to refer to the probability that one event will occur, given that another event has occurred. If the occurrence of event B does not affect the probability of event A, then events A and B are said to be **independent.** And if most people are confused by the concept of probability, they are confounded by conditional probability. Consider the story of a Mr. X who was convicted of selling marijuana. The judge, having observed that 95% of heroin addicts start on marijuana declared: "You are in effect a heroin pusher" and gave the fellow a thirty year sentence. It was fortunate for Mr. X that he didn't deliver milk, because 100% of heroin addicts start on milk! The fallacy here is that the judge was assuming that the conditional probability of heroin use given the use of marijuana was higher than the unconditional probability of heroin use. This may or may not be the case, but in any event, it cannot by inferred merely from the judge's initial observation.

Example: Medical Testing

Imagine Some Rare Horrible Disease (SRHD) with which only one percent of the population is infected (that is, they are SRHD positive, or SRHD+ for short). Suppose there is an accurate test for the infection. For those who are SRHD+, the test will be positive 98% of time (a true positive) and be negative only 2% of the time (a false negative). For those who are SRHD negative (SRHD-), the test will be negative 98% of time (a true negative) and be positive 2% of the time (a false positive).

Now imagine someone drawn at random from the population who tests positive for SRHD. What is the chance that they are actually infected? Test your intuition by choosing among the possible answers below.

The probability that someone drawn at random is SRHD+ given that they test positive is:

a.   99%
b.   98%
c.   50%
d.   33%

We will frame this problem in terms of the chance that a randomly thrown dart will hit a particular target. Consider a geometric model, in which the entire population is represented by a square with a shaded strip denoting the 1% that is SRHD+.

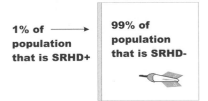

It should be evident that the probability of randomly drawing an SRHD+ individual from the population is the same as the chance that a dart thrown randomly into the square will hit the shaded strip.

With this analogy in mind we will now consider the probability of testing positive. Remember that the proportion of the population that is SRHD+ is shaded. The proportion of the population that would test positive is marked with a pattern. Note the population has now been partitioned into four categories as listed below.

False Negative	The 2% of the SRHD+ individuals who would test negative.
True Positive	The 98% of the SRHD+ individuals who would test positive.
False Positive	The 2% of the SRHD- individuals who would test positive.
True Negative	The 98% of the SRHD- individuals who would test negative.

This is reflected in the figure below.

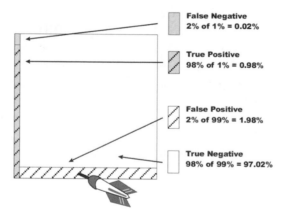

False Negative
2% of 1% = 0.02%

True Positive
98% of 1% = 0.98%

False Positive
2% of 99% = 1.98%

True Negative
98% of 99% = 97.02%

Notice that the percentage of the population that would test positive (the entire patterned area) is 0.98% + 1.98% = 2.96%.
Now lets return to the original question:

What is the chance that someone picked at random who *tests* positive for SRHD is truly positive? This is just the chance that a randomly thrown dart hits an area that is *shaded and patterned* (SRHD+ and Positive), given that it has hit an area that is *patterned* (Positive). But from the geometry this is just the area of the shaded and patterned region divided by the total *patterned* area or 0.98%/2.96% = 33%.

Thus two thirds of people who test positive are in fact not infected because the chance of a false positive is twice the chance of a true positive. This is why universal screening for rare diseases can result in unnecessary anguish and is often bad policy.

Bayes' Theorem

When dealing with conditional probability a small dose of analytical medicine can cure a serious case of misconception. The medicine in this case is known as Bayes' Theorem, named after Rev. Thomas Bayes, an 18th century minister and mathematician. The previous result may be re-stated in a form closer to Bayes' important theorem as follows:

The probability of being positive given a positive test = the probability of having a positive test and being positive divided by the probability of having a positive test.

Or abbreviating,

P(SRHD+ given TEST+) = P(TEST+ and SRHD+)/P(TEST+)

■ FUNDAMENTALS 6-5

Bayes' Theorem

The general statement of Bayes' Theorem is: P(B|A) = P(A and B)/P(A) where A and B are events, and | stands for "given".

Tree Flipping

In the example above, we were presented with the probability of getting a positive or negative test result given the infection status of the subject. Recalling that a tree is a graphical representation of how an uncertain future can unfold, we could represent the information as follows.

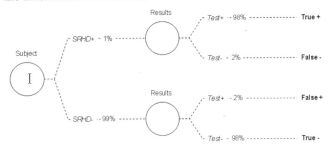

But what we really wanted to know was the probability of a positive or negative infection status of the subject given the results of the test. This in effect flips the order of the nodes in the tree as shown below.

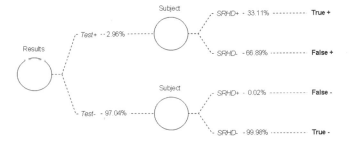

Of course all the probabilities must be recomputed for the flipped tree, much as we did with the dart throwing analogy described earlier. From this tree we can easily read the probability of 33.11% of the subject actually being positive, given that they tested positive. As you will see in the next section, XLTree can flip a tree and perform the revised probability calculation.

The Value of Information

In almost any decision-making situation, it is possible to obtain additional pertinent information at some cost. An important benefit of decision analysis is that it can quantify the value of such information.

Returning to the ice cream example, suppose you have a friend on the police force with information on the whereabouts of the ticket patrol. Imagine that you can call your friend from your cellular phone as you arrive at the ice cream parlor. What would this information be worth to you?

The Value of Perfect Information

Let us first assume that your friend knows the ticket patrol's exact location and will relay this to you correctly. This is known as *perfect information.* Now, unlike the uncertain case, you get to learn if you will get a ticket *before* you decide instead of *after.*

One of two things can happen. First, there is 90% chance that you will get the "all clear" from your friend, in which case you will go in and get your $4 worth of utility from the ice cream. Second, there is a 10% chance that you will be warned of the ticket patrol, in which case you will go straight home and get 0 utility from washing the dishes. Thus, the expected utility is 90%*$4+10%*$0= $3.60.

Now suppose your friend implies that a donation to the Policeman's Benevolent Association would be appreciated before he gives you his information. The maximum amount you should be willing to pay (cost of the call plus the donation) is the difference between the expected utility with perfect information ($3.60) and that without any information ($1.00). So in this case the *value of perfect information* is $2.60.

Since in the above analysis we learned whether or not we would get a ticket before we made our decision to stop or not, we were in effect interchanging the order of the decision and uncertainty nodes. This can be done automatically using the XLTree **Flip Tree** command as follows:

Flipping the Ice Cream Tree

In the following tutorial we will reverse the order of the levels of the Ice Cream Tree. Retrieve ICECREAM.xls, created earlier, before proceeding.

TUTORIAL: FLIPPING THE ICE CREAM TREE

1 Add Node labels to the Decision Node (F2) and Uncertainty Node (J2) of the ICECREAM tree in case you have not done so, since it will facilitate keeping track of the levels when flipping the tree. In the following example we have used "Decision" and "Uncertainty" as the node labels.

2 Flipping a tree makes sense only for *symmetric* trees, that is, those for which the branching is the same throughout each level of the tree. In your version of ICECREAM, you probably did not keep track of the fact that the Meter Maid could show up even if you went home. Assuming your tree looks like the one below, replace the 0 on the branch where you go home with an "*".

	F	G	H	J	K	L	N
1							
2	1	Stop for cone	==>	1	Get ticket	0.1	-26
3					No ticket	0.9	4
4							
5		Don't stop		*			
6							

Place an asterick in this cell to allow a branch to be added.

3 Now use the **Tree Grow Tree** command and your tree should like this.

	F	G	H	J	K	L	N
1							
2	1	Stop for cone	==>	1	Get ticket	0.1	-26
3					No ticket	0.9	4
4							
5		Don't stop	==>	1	Get ticket	0.1	-26
6					No ticket	0.9	4
7							

4 Notice that the same utility values have been copied down to leaves of the lower Meter Maid fork which has been added to the tree. Replace these utilities with 0s, because even if the Meter Maid patrols the ice cream parlor, there is no way you will get a ticket if you go home. Now your tree should look like this.

	F	G	H	J	K	L	N
1							
2	1	Stop for cone	==>	1	Get ticket	0.1	-26
3					No ticket	0.9	4
4							
5		Don't stop		0	Get ticket	0.1	0
6					No ticket	0.9	0
7							

Grow Tree is a very powerful command that will extend a partially completed tree. In this way you can build large trees quickly by starting with just the first few rows of your spreadsheet. *Note:* The earlier version of the tree is saved on a sheet named _Old Tree_ in case the "grown" tree is not what you expected. In that case, simply delete the new Tree sheet, then rename the _Old Tree_ sheet Tree.

5

Next, perform the **Tree Flip Tree** command and interchange the order of the decision and uncertainty nodes by selecting the "Uncertainty" label and clicking the **Raise** button.

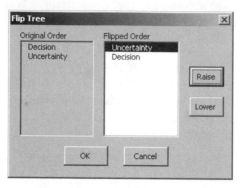

The flipped tree should appear as below:

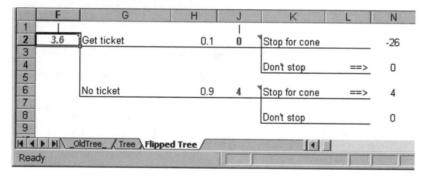

Note: The **Flip Tree** command creates a new sheet called **Flipped Tree** with formulas that refer to the Tree sheet. On a larger tree there might have been several ways to change the levels of the nodes. If you wish to keep more than one flipped version of a tree, rename the **Flipped Tree** sheet each time or it will be overwritten.

6

Notice that the overall value of this tree is $3.60, confirming that this situation is worth $2.60 more than before you had the information about the Meter Maid. Be sure to save this file for later use.

EXERCISE
6.13 Friend's Information

What would the value of your friend's perfect information be if the probability of getting a ticket was 5% instead of 10%? *Note:* Do not change data in the Flipped Tree. It calculates its values based on the data in the Tree sheet.

EXERCISE
6.14 A New Test for SRHD

Suppose a new, cheaper test for SRHD correctly identifies 98% of those who are positive as in the earlier test. However, for those who are negative, it gives correct results only 96% of the time. What is the probability that someone picked at random who tests positive is actually infected?

EXERCISE
6.15 Expressway Hotline

To help you decide which route to take, you call the expressway hotline to obtain an accurate report of expressway roadwork. You believe that there is a 5% chance that the report will say there is roadwork, in which case you will travel by city road. Otherwise, there is a 95% chance that the report will say there is no roadwork and you will travel by expressway.

a. Modify the FASTEST decision tree that you drew earlier to reflect this new situation.

b. What is the expected value of this situation? Remember that your utility is in terms of the negative of travel time rather than in terms of money.

c. What is the most (again measured in time) that this information is worth?

You proceed to call the hotline. When you call, however, all lines are busy, and a recorded message tells you to expect a 30-minute wait before a representative can answer your line.

d. Should you wait?

The Value of Imperfect Information

Returning to the Ice Cream example, suppose that your friend's warnings are not completely accurate. That is, on those occasions when you got a ticket, he had failed to warn you 25% of the time, and furthermore, on those occasions when you did not get a ticket, he falsely warned you 25% of the time.

TUTORIAL: MODELING IMPERFECT INFORMATION

1

Open the symmetric ICE CREAM file that you saved in the last tutorial and replace all leaf nodes with *'s.

	F	G	H	J	K	L	N
1							
2	0	Stop for cone	==>	0	Get ticket	0.1	*
3					No ticket	0.9	*
4							
5		Don't stop	==>	0	Get ticket	0.1	*
6					No ticket	0.9	*
7							

2 Next, in cell N2, add a two branch uncertainty fork to model whether or not you would have received a warning from your friend if you had called him. Remember he is only 75% accurate. Enter a Node Label of "Friend".

	F	G	H	J	K	L	N	O	P	R
1										
2	0	Stop for cone	==>	0	Get ticket	0.1	0	Warning	0.75	*
3								No Warning	0.25	*
4										
5					No ticket	0.9	*			
6										
7		Don't stop	==>	0	Get ticket	0.1	*			
8					No ticket	0.9	*			
9										

3 Now use the **Grow Tree** command to complete the symmetric tree. Change cells P5 and P11 to 25%, because these are the cases in which there would have been no ticket and these are the false alarms. Also fill in utilities of -$26 for the cases in which you stopped and got nailed by the ticket patrol, and $4 for the cases in which you stopped and got away with it. Then put in 0s for the cases in which you went home. Note that the value of the tree is still $1 because nothing in our decision making process has changed.

	F	G	H	J	K	L	N	O	P	R
1										
2	1	Stop for cone	==>	1	Get ticket	0.1	-26	Warning	0.75	-26
3								No Warning	0.25	-26
4										
5					No ticket	0.9	4	Warning	0.25	4
6								No Warning	0.75	4
7										
8		Don't stop		0	Get ticket	0.1	0	Warning	0.75	0
9								No Warning	0.25	0
10										
11					No ticket	0.9	0	Warning	0.25	0
12								No Warning	0.75	0
13										

4 Now let's see what would have happened if you had listened to your friend before you made your decision. Use the **Flip Tree** command to raise the "Friend" node above the decision node.

	F	G	H	J	K	L	N	O	P	R
1										
2	2.05	Warning	0.3	0	Stop for c		-3.5	Get ticket	0.25	-26
3										
4								No ticket	0.75	4
5										
6					Don't stop	==>	0	Get ticket	0.25	0
7										
8								No ticket	0.75	0
9										
10		No Warning	0.7	2.928571	Stop for c	==>	2.92857	Get ticket	0.035714	-26
11										
12								No ticket	0.964286	4
13										
14					Don't stop		0	Get ticket	0.035714	0
15										
16								No ticket	0.964286	0
17										

Notice that there is a 30% chance of receiving a warning from your friend, and even though the information is imperfect, it pays to heed his advice; that is, the tree tells you not to stop for that case. The overall expected value of this tree is $2.05. The difference between this and the original value with no information is $1.05. This is known as the *value of imperfect information*. Your contribution to the Policeman's Benevolent Association should not be as great as it was with perfect information.

EXERCISE 6.16

SUPPOSE YOUR FRIEND'S ERRORS ARE ALWAYS SYMMETRIC

That is, the probability of a missed warning is the same as that of a false alarm. How inaccurate would your friend have to be before you should ignore his advice altogether and stop for the cone even with the warning? *Hint:* set up a single cell which represents the probability that your friend will make an error of either type, and link all the probabilities in the tree that are related to your friend to this one cell.

State Variables

Use of state variables is a way of quantifying the various states of the world in which decision makers may find themselves. When there are numerous things to keep track of in a decision problem, it is convenient to set up state variables within the tree.

We will discuss the problem faced by a wildcatter deciding whether or not to drill for oil at a particular site. Although the example below is greatly simplified for demonstration purposes, it shows how state variables can increase the power and flexibility of decision trees.

Imagine that a wildcatter owns a lease that grants him the rights to any oil discovered at a particular site. This lease can be sold for a guaranteed $150,000. On the other hand, if the wildcatter endures the multiple risks of drilling for oil, much greater rewards might be in store. The first state variable, L, is the amount of money received for the lease. This is $150,000 if the lease is sold, and $0 otherwise.

The first risk is the uncertainty in the actual cost of the drilling operation. There is a 70% chance that the cost will be high ($2,000,000) and a 30% chance that it will be low ($200,000). The state variable (C) is thus $2,000,000 with probability 70% or $200,000 with probability 30%.

There is the even bigger risk involving the quantity (Q) of oil found. There is only a 5% chance of a real gusher (1,000,000 barrels) and a 95% chance of 50,000 barrels. Finally, the price (P) of oil by the time the well comes in is expected to be $20 per barrel with probability 40% and $15 per barrel with probability 60%.

The utility is calculated as Revenue from Selling Lease – Cost of Drilling + (Quantity of Oil × Price of Oil). This can be rewritten as

$$\text{Utility (Lease, Cost, Qty, Price)} = \text{Lease} - \text{Cost} + \text{Qty} \times \text{Price}$$

Thus, in the event that the lease is sold, Lease=$150,000 and Cost, Quantity, and Price are 0. If the well is drilled, then Lease=0 and Cost, Quantity, and Price are all uncertain, as described. Lease, Cost, Quantity, and Price are known as the problem's *state variables.*

A possible tree for the wildcatter's problem is shown in the following figure. Note that the uncertainties could have been modeled in any order in this situation.

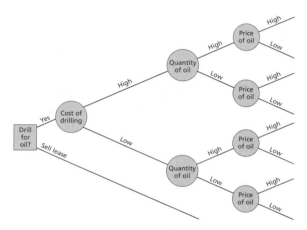

We could solve this problem without state variables, but it would be difficult to keep track of what utility to place at each of the leaves of the tree.

State variables streamline the process by letting you enter values for the lease revenue, cost, quantity, and price as the tree is constructed. When the tree is completed, a single formula for the utility of the top leaf is entered and copied down to the remaining leaves, at which point the tree is evaluated automatically.

TUTORIAL: USING STATE VARIABLES TO DRILL FOR OIL

We will now create a new tree and name the state variables for the wildcatter's problem. Proceed as follows:

1

First, specify the state variables: Invoke the **Tree New** command, specifying four state variables. The root of the tree will be created with places for these four variables.

	B	C	D	E	F	G	H	I	J
1	I			Var 1	Var 2	Var 3	Var 4	JP	
2	*	Root	1						1	*
3									

2

Type "Lease," "Cost," "Qty," and "Price" into the cells containing Var 1 through Var 4.

	B	C	D	E	F	G	H	I	J
1	I			Lease	Cost	Qty	Price	JP	
2	*	Root	1						1	*
3									

The cell labeled JP is involved in calculating the joint probabilities of the outcomes, as described later.

3 Specify the root decision: Move the cursor to the root (J2) and add a two-branch decision fork. Label the two alternatives: "Drill" and "Sell Lease."

4 Move the cursor to M3, the value of L if the lease is sold, and enter 150 (all numbers will be in 1,000's in this model). Because the value of the lease will be 0 if you drill, leave cell M2 as it is.

	J	K	L	M	N	O	P	Q	R
1				Lease	Cost	Qty	Price	JP	
2	0	Drill		0	0	0	0	1	*
3		Sell Lease		150	0	0	0	1	*
4									

5 Specify the drilling cost uncertainty: Move the cursor to the "*" in cell R2 (the utility at the end of the Drill branch) and insert a two-outcome uncertainty fork. Name the outcomes "Hi Cost" and "Low Cost," respectively.

6 Enter a probability of 0.7 in cell T2 for the chance of a high drilling cost. Note that T3 becomes 0.3. Enter 2000 and 200 (remember all numbers are in 1,000's) for the high and low values of cost in cells V2 and V3.

7 Move the cursor to the "*" in cell R5 (the utility at the end of the Sell Lease branch) and insert a one-branch (null) decision fork. This keeps all the leaves of the tree in the same column.

	Q	R	S	T	U	V	W	X	Y	Z
1	JP				Lease	Cost	Qty	Price	JP	
2		1	0	Hi Cost	0.7	0	2000	0	0	0.7	*
3				Lo Cost	0.3	0	200	0	0	0.3	*
4										
5		1	*		==>	150	0	0	0	1	*

8 Specify the quantity uncertainty: Move the cursor to the "*" in cell Z2 (the utility at the end of the High Drilling Cost branch) and add a two-branch uncertainty fork. Name the outcomes "Hi Qty" and "Low Qty," respectively.

9 Enter a probability of 0.05 in cell AB2 for the chance of a high quantity of oil. Enter "1000" and "50" for the high and low values of Qty, the quantity state variable (cells AE2:AE3).

	Z	AA	AB	AC	AD	AE	AF	AG	AH
1					Lease	Cost	Qty	Price	JP
2	0	Hi Qty	0.05	0	2000	1000	0	0.035	*
3		Lo Qty	0.95	0	2000	50	0	0.665	*
4									
5	*								

10 Move the cursor to the "*" in cell Z5 (the utility at the end of the Low Drilling Cost branch) and add a two-branch uncertainty fork.

11 Because you face exactly the same quantity of uncertainty in either the Hi Cost or Low Cost case, you can simply copy the uncertainty fork in cells AA2:AH3, then use **Edit Paste** to place it over the fork you have just entered in cell Z5. Or, you can simply re-enter the same information.

12 Move the cursor to the "*" in cell Z9 and insert a one-branch decision fork. As before, this keeps all the leaves of the tree in the same column. Before continuing, notice that the state variables always inherit the values of their parent branches.

Lease revenue if you sell out   Hi Costs   Lo Costs

	Y	Z	AA	AB	AC	AD	AE	AF	AG	AH
1	JP				Lease	Cost	Qty	Price	JP	
2	0.7	0	Hi Qty	0.05	0	2000	1000	0	0.035	*
3			Lo Qty	0.95	0	2000	50	0	0.665	*
4										
5	0.3	0	Hi Qty	0.05	0	200	1000	0	0.015	*
6			Lo Qty	0.95	0	200	50	0	0.285	*
7										
8										
9	1	*		==>	150	0	0	0	1	*

13 Specify the price uncertainty: Move the cursor to the "*" in cell AH2 (the utility at the end of the Hi Cost, Hi Qty branch) and insert a two-branch uncertainty fork. Name the first and second outcomes "Hi Price" and "Lo Price," respectively.

14 Enter a probability of 0.4 in cell AJ2 for the chance of a high price of oil. Enter "20" and "15" for the high and low values of Price, the price state variable (cells AN2:AN3).

15 Add two-branch uncertainty forks at cell AH5, then at AH9, and finally at AH12. Copy the uncertainty fork in cells AH2:AP3 to cells AH5, AH9, and AH12. *Note:* We have specified the quantity of oil in thousands of barrels and the price per barrel in dollars. Thus, revenue will be in thousands of dollars, consistent with our cost figures.

16 Move the cursor to the "*" in cell AH17 and insert another one-branch decision fork. There should now be nine "*"s in column AP representing the leaves of the tree.

	AH	AI	AJ	AK	AL	AM	AN	AO	AP
1				Lease	Cost	Qty	Price	JP	
2	0	Hi Price	0.4	0	2000	1000	20	0.014	*
3		Lo Price	0.6	0	2000	1000	15	0.021	*
4									
5	0	Hi Price	0.4	0	2000	50	20	0.266	*
6		Lo Price	0.6	0	2000	50	15	0.399	*
7									
8									
9	0	Hi Price	0.4	0	200	1000	20	0.006	*
10		Lo Price	0.6	0	200	1000	15	0.009	*
11									
12	0	Hi Price	0.4	0	200	50	20	0.114	*
13		Lo Price	0.6	0	200	50	15	0.171	*
14									
15									
16									
17	*		==>	150	0	0	0	1	*

17

Specify the utility of the leaves: Carefully inspect cells AH2:AP17 and compare them with the cells in the previous figure to verify that the correct values of the state variables are associated with each leaf of the tree. Recall that the utility as a function of the state variables is Utility= Lease – Cost + Qty * Price. Place this formula in the top leaf by entering "=AK2 – AL2 + AM2 * AN2" in cell AP2. The result should be 18000 as shown below.

AP2	▼		=AK2-AL2+AM2*AN2				
	AJ	**AK**	**AL**	**AM**	**AN**	**AO**	**AP**
1		Lease	Cost	Qty	Price	JP	
2	0.4	0	2000	1000	20	0.014	18000
3	0.6	0	2000	1000	15	0.021	*

18

With the cursor still in cell AP2, invoke the **Tree Copy Utilities** command. The utility formula will be copied to each of the remaining leaves of the tree.

19

Inspect the tree: Invoke the **Tree Variables Hide** command to hide the columns containing the state variables and joint probabilities. Use the **View Zoom** command if necessary to get the whole tree to fit on the screen. You will see that the decision is to drill, yielding an expected value of $197,500. Notice the arrow pointing down the Drill branch.

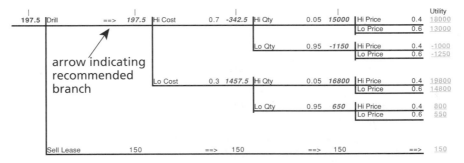

20

We now discuss the joint probabilities. The joint probability columns are labeled JP. Invoke the **Tree Variables Show Variables** command and move the cursor to AO2. The value in this cell indicates that given that you drill, the *joint probability* of simultaneous high values of cost, quantity, and price is 1.4%. Similarly, cell AO3 indicates that the joint probability of a high cost, high quantity, and low price is 2.1%. Cell AO17 indicates that given that you decide to sell the lease instead of drilling, then the probability that you actually do so is 100%. The joint probabilities of all leaves emanating from the same decision branch should sum to 1. Save your model as WILDCAT.xls.

EXERCISE
6.17 EXPERIMENTING WITH THE PROBABILITY OF A GUSHER

At what probability of a gusher would you be indifferent to drilling or selling the lease? Don't forget this probability appears in more than one cell in your model.

EXERCISE
6.18 TOY MANUFACTURING

A toy manufacturer must decide between a large (100,000 unit) or small (50,000 unit) production run of a new toy. The production costs are uncertain, but it is known that there are economies of scale. For 50,000 units, there is believed to be a 50/50 chance that the cost per unit will be either $5 or $4. For 100,000, there is a 50/50 chance that the cost per unit will be either $4 or $3. The demand for the toy is thought to be elastic—that is, to sell a larger quantity, the firm will have to lower the price. The price at which 50,000 units can be moved is estimated to be $10 or $8, with equal probability. At 100,000 units, this drops to $6 and $5, again with equal likelihood. How many toys should the firm produce to maximize expected profit?

TUTORIAL: USING TWO-WAY SENSITIVITY ANALYSIS

Earlier we investigated the sensitivity of the utility of the ice cream scenario relative to the probability of getting a ticket. We will now perform a more complex sensitivity analysis on the drilling decision. The greatest uncertainties in oil exploration generally involve both the probability of making a high quantity discovery and the size of the discovery itself. This time, instead of changing a single parameter (probability of a ticket), we will simultaneously vary both the probability of a high quantity and the high quantity itself by means of a two-way data table. Start with the wildcat model developed earlier, and display the state variables.

1 First, we must make sure that when we change the value of one of the parameters of interest, it changes throughout the tree. In cell AB9, enter the formula "=AB2" for the probability of a high quantity of oil. In cell AE9, enter the formula "=AE2" for the high quantity itself.

2 In a blank section of the worksheet create a two-way data table as follows: (See your spreadsheet manual for details on the two-way data table if necessary.)

3 Create a column of values in cells AS3:AS18 for the high quantity running down the left side of the table from 2000 to 500, decremented by 100.

4 Then, in cells AT2:BI2, create a row of values for the probability of a high quantity from 0 to .15 incremented by 0.01. Now select columns AT through BI and reduce the column width so the entire row fits on a single screen. *Hint:* Reducing the font size with the **Format Cells** command will allow a tighter fit.

5 Next, in cell AS2, enter the formula "=IF(J2=R2,"D",".")". J2 is the root of the tree, and R2 is the expected utility if the well is drilled. So this formula returns a "D" if the combination of the probability of a high quantity and the quantity itself are sufficient to make drilling the optimal decision. Otherwise it returns ".".

6 Next, select cells AS2:BI18 and invoke the **Data Table** command, selecting AB2, the probability of high quantity, as the Row input and AE2, the quantity itself, as the column input.

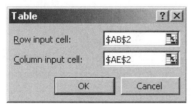

Your table should look like the one below. This shows that as the probability of a gusher drops below .02, no quantity of oil shown is adequate to justify drilling. We also see that once the probability of a gusher reaches .1, any amount of oil greater than 500 justifies drilling.

AS2   =IF(J2=R2,"D",".")

	AS	AT	AU	AV	AW	AX	AY	AZ	BA	BB	BC	BD	BE	BF
1														
2	D	0	0.01	0.02	0.03	0.04	0.05	0.06	0.07	0.08	0.09	0.1	0.11	0.12
3	2000	.	.	.	D	D	D	D	D	D	D	D	D	D
4	1900	.	.	.	D	D	D	D	D	D	D	D	D	D
5	1800	.	.	.	D	D	D	D	D	D	D	D	D	D
6	1700	.	.	.	D	D	D	D	D	D	D	D	D	D
7	1600	.	.	.	D	D	D	D	D	D	D	D	D	D
8	1500	.	.	.	.	D	D	D	D	D	D	D	D	D
9	1400	.	.	.	.	D	D	D	D	D	D	D	D	D
10	1300	.	.	.	.	D	D	D	D	D	D	D	D	D
11	1200	.	.	.	.	D	D	D	D	D	D	D	D	D
12	1100	.	.	.	.	.	D	D	D	D	D	D	D	D
13	1000	.	.	.	.	.	D	D	D	D	D	D	D	D
14	900	.	.	.	.	.	.	D	D	D	D	D	D	D
15	800	.	.	.	.	.	.	D	D	D	D	D	D	D
16	700	.	.	.	.	.	.	.	D	D	D	D	D	D
17	600	.	.	.	.	.	.	.	.	.	D	D	D	D
18	500	.	.	.	.	.	.	.	.	.	.	D	D	D
19														

Mustering the Courage of Your Convictions

Just because you or your organization have determined a rational course of action in the light of uncertainty does not mean it will be expedient to carry it out. In a fascinating book entitled *Weapons and Hope,* Freeman Dyson (1984) relates the following first-hand account of such a difficulty.

As an operations research analyst in the British bomber command during World War II, he determined that the allied pilots, anxious about mid-air collisions, were not flying in tight enough formations. This left them vulnerable to attack by enemy fighters. Dyson worked out the optimal formation pattern to minimize expected losses from all causes. This required the pilots to start having five times as many mid-air collisions! Freeman writes, "The Command followed our advice, and the crews reluctantly obeyed. This decision confirmed the crews' belief that their commander in chief, familiarly known as Bert Harris or Butcher Harris, was as callous toward them as he was toward the Germans."

END OF CHAPTER EXERCISES

6.19   VALUE OF A WEATHER FORECAST

You must decide whether or not to buy a $25 umbrella, given a 40% chance of rain and consequent $75 damage to an unprotected suit. What is the dollar value of a precise weather forecast?

6.20   SETTLE OR LITIGATE

A firm is suing a competitor over copyright infringement. Just before the trial, the other side indicates a willingness to negotiate a settlement. The firm must now decide whether to settle the case or go to court. If they go to court, they will incur an additional $100,000 in legal expenses, but believe that they have a 50% chance of winning $2 million. There is also a 40% chance of losing, in which case they must pay the other firm's legal costs of $200,000. With probability 10% there will be a draw, in which case neither side is liable. Create a decision tree to determine the amount of settlement that would make the firm indifferent to the two courses of action, from an expected value perspective.

6.21   CHOOSE A MARKETING CAMPAIGN

A financial institution is considering inserting marketing material along with its monthly statements to its customers. They must decide between three options:

■ Including materials promoting other services within the institution.

■ Including materials that promote external products or services in return for an advertising commission.

■ Staying with the status quo.

The cost of the marketing insert is $150 per thousand, but there is uncertainty about the success of either the internal or external promotion. For simplicity, management has come up with two revenue scenarios for each of the promotions.

The following table shows the revenue per thousand brochures by promotion and scenario.

Scenario	Internal Promotion	External Promotion
High	$200	$250
Low	$100	$125

Although the likelihood of the various scenarios has not yet been assessed, management wishes to frame the problem as a tree to aid in the decision making process.

a. Create a decision tree for this problem using temporary probabilities for the occurrences of the scenarios.

b. Create a two way data table which explores probabilities of a High scenario for both promotions, ranging from 0 to 1 in increments of 0.1. For each element of the table, display the optimal decision for that combination of probabilities, with an "I" standing for the internal promotion, an "X", for the external promotion, and a "." for remaining with the status quo. This will provide management with a roadmap to assist with the decision.

6.22 PROTECTIVE ARMOR FOR FIGHTER AIRCRAFT

During WWIIs, the Allies observed that the bullet holes on returning fighter planes were not uniformly distributed. That is, there were more bullet holes some places than others. The obvious suggestion was made to armor plate those locations with high densities of bullet holes, because these were the places that were being hit. Obvious maybe, but dead wrong. Explain using a Dart target, like the one used in the SHRD example, why one should actually armor plate those locations where there were no bullet holes.

6.23 ASSESSING THREATS OF TERRORISM

In a certain unstable part of the world, terrorist car bomb attacks have occurred with regularity. On any given day it is estimated that there is one chance in 1000 of an attack. Intelligence agents are sometimes able to warn of such attacks, but these warning are not very accurate. It has been observed that warnings were received for only 60% of the attacks. Furthermore, false alarms are received 25% of the time when there has not been an attack. Use tree flipping to determine the probability of an attack given that a warning has been received. How much more likely is an attack given a warning than an attack without a warning?

7 ■■■■■■■■■■■■■■■■■■■■■■■■■■■■■■

Overview of Optimization

For want of a nail, the shoe was lost, For want of a shoe, a horse was lost,
For want of a horse, a rider was lost, For want of a rider, a battle was lost,
For want of a battle, the kingdom was lost, And all for the want of a horseshoe nail!

MOTHER GOOSE

Human endeavor has always involved activities that compete for scarce resources. Imagine yourself as a medieval king, preparing to battle an adversary. You take inventory of your horses, men, swords, shields, armor, horseshoes, and nails, and head over to the local arms merchant with your war chest. You must coordinate your purchases to maximize the likelihood of a successful military campaign. If you could postpone the conflict for 1,000 years, you would have access to mathematical optimization, which would provide the best allocation of your men, materials, and funds. Further, it would illuminate the true value of scarce resources such as horseshoe nails in the coming conflict.

The following are some modern resource allocation problems:

- A boat manufacturer with limited raw materials must specify production quantities for several types of small craft to maximize profit.

- A municipality must schedule its police force for maximum effectiveness while meeting work rules such as shift length, number of work breaks, and overtime hours.

- Managers of a pension fund want to invest their assets to achieve 8% growth while minimizing risk.

- A steel mill must determine how to ship its product to meet demand at minimum cost.

■ ■ ■ **OVERVIEW**

Introduction

This section contains a short introduction to optimization followed by brief descriptions of two widely used spreadsheet optimization packages, the Excel Solver and What's*Best!* All optimization examples in this book have been included in formats for each of these packages.

A Tutorial: Maximum Profit

A boat manufacturer with limited raw materials must specify production quantities for several types of small craft to maximize profit.

Basic Examples

Additional linear optimization examples are introduced in product mix, blending, scheduling, transportation, and network flow models.

INTRODUCTION

Optimization means determining the best way to accomplish an objective given the limited resources under your control. The field of mathematical optimization has produced several powerful techniques for dealing with a wide class of problems in such areas as manufacturing, transportation, scheduling, and finance. A simple ABC checklist can help you optimize a given situation.

The ABC's of Optimization

A. *What can you adjust?* That is, what is under your direct managerial control? This may include such things as the number of widgets to manufacture, the number of people to hire for the 9 o'clock shift, or the amount of money to invest in a given security.

B. *What do you mean by best?* This constitutes the desired objective. Is the best solution the one that maximizes profit, minimizes cost, or maximizes the chance that you keep your job? The answer to this question depends on management's preferences.

You cannot optimize more than one objective at one time. You might hear people say that they want to both maximize profit and minimize cost simultaneously. But these objectives are mutually exclusive—bankruptcy minimizes cost but does nothing for profit, and making a profit requires an investment.

C.   What constraints must be obeyed? In taking managerial steps to optimize your objectives, certain things are simply impossible. These are known as constraints and can be of several kinds. Some involve limited resources. That is, any plan you devise must stay within your budget and not use more raw materials than you have at your disposal. Constraints can also involve meeting performance criteria. For example, you must have at least three people on duty during the 9 o'clock shift, or your portfolio must be composed of at least 20% AAA bonds.

Classes of Optimization Problems and Algorithms

Optimization is analogous to a hill-climbing activity in which the goal is to arrive at the highest point in some geographical area. This corresponds to maximizing altitude, but there are also situations analogous to finding the lowest point, or minimizing altitude. The computer algorithm plays the role of a traveler continually seeking out higher (or lower) ground. Using this rough analogy, the table below describes three classes of optimization problems in terms of terrain. Also listed are the appropriate algorithms, described in terms of transportation modes.

Problem Type	Terrain Mode	Algorithm	Transportation
Linear	Single paved road direct to the summit, which is clearly indicated by a summit marker so you know when you have arrived.	Linear Program (LP)	Automobile
Linear Integer	Thousands of branching dead-end roads, one of which reaches the summit. End of each road has an altitude marker and some information about other roads, but there is no summit marker.	Integer Program (IP)	Automobile, but sometimes the trip is so long you run out of gas before reaching the summit
Smooth Non-linear	Smooth hills without roads. Each hilltop has an altitude marker but there is no summit marker so you must compare all hilltops.	Non-linear Program (NLP)	Horseback
None of the above	Jagged mountains. No paths. Many places to get stuck.	Heuristics	By foot, ropes and pulleys when needed. Forget the summit, just go for maximum altitude.

Linear Problems

In order for a problem to be linear, all the formulas defining the model must be linear. These problems are susceptible to very powerful linear programming (LP) solution techniques. As discussed later, linearity is a serious restriction. However, many problems in manufacturing, transportation, scheduling, finance, and other areas have been formulated to be solved with linear programming. Some of these problems involve hundreds of thousands of variables. All of the examples in Chapter 7 are in this category.

Linear Integer

If some of the answers to a linear problem must be restricted to integer variables, integer programming algorithms must be applied. Although this greatly slows down the solution time for large numbers of integer variables, this is still a very powerful technique.

Nonlinear

If any of the formulas are not linear, the problem is known as nonlinear. If the formulas define continuous (smoothly changing) relationships between variables, nonlinear programming (NLP) algorithms may be used. These techniques typically handle fewer variables than linear programming techniques and can require good initial guesses at a solution for dependable results. Nonlinear problems often arise in the fields of engineering and finance, and are more difficult to solve than linear ones. NLP may be applied to linear problems as well, but like riding a horse on a paved road, it is not efficient. The distinction between linear and nonlinear problems will be discussed further in the next chapter.

None of the above

Problems that do not fall into the above categories include discontinuous formulas (also known as non-smooth), and combinatorial problems, which involve combinations or permutations of variables. The Traveling Salesman problem discussed in Chapter 8 is a famous combinatorial problem. For most of these problems, there is no guarantee of finding the optimal answer. Instead, "heuristic" algorithms incrementally generate improvements until the analyst gets tired of waiting and settles for the best solution so far. Although these algorithms are often much slower than the ones discussed previously, they may be applied to virtually any sort of problem. Similarly, although traveling by foot is the slowest mode of transportation, there is no way to climb a ladder with either a horse or a car.

Spreadsheet Optimization Software

There are two primary spreadsheet optimization packages:

- ***The Excel Solver.*** The Excel Solver ships with Excel. Be sure to select it for inclusion during installation. It is then added to Excel under **Tools Add-Ins,** whereupon a **Solver** item is added to the **Tools** menu. A Premium version of the

Solver (a small copy of which is included with Insight.xla) provides enhanced capabilities. For example, the Evolutionary algorithm of the Premium Solver is applied to the Traveling Salesman problem in Chapter 8.

■ **What's*Best!*.** Also included with Insight.xla is a small version of What's*Best!*. This package, introduced in 1985, was the first widely marketed spreadsheet optimization software (Savage, 1985). Recent improvements in What's*Best!* include the automatic conversion of certain non-smooth formulas such as IF statements and logical conditions into integer programs. When What's*Best!* is installed, a WB! menu item appears in Excel along with tool bar as discussed below.

Most optimization examples in this book have been included in formats to run with each of these packages. A brief comparison appears in the following table.

	The Excel Solver	**What's*Best!***
Model Specifications	Input through a dialog box. Can be stored to or retrieved from a range in the worksheet.	Stored directly into the worksheet model as formulas and cell properties.
Formula Interpretation	Interprets formulas through differencing. All Excel formulas recognized.*	Interprets formulas algebraically.
Linear versus Nonlinear solutions	Type of model must be specified in Options dialog box.	Type of model automatically detected.
Advantages	Universally available, allowing small models to be shared widely throughout organizations.	Because models can be merged without losing optimization specifications, large integrated models can be created from smaller sub-models. See SUPPLYW.xls and SUPPLYUW.xls.
	Can interpret even user defined functions in Excel allowing for great flexibility.	Models can be built across multiple worksheets within a workbook.
	The Premium Solver includes Evolutionary heuristic algorithms for non-smooth and combinatorial problems.	Now supports SUMIF statement. See NEWFLOWW.xls.
		Automatic linear versus nonlinear solutions are provided.
		Linearization feature converts some important discontinuous Excel formulas such as IF, ABS and MAX for solution using fast IP algorithms.
Upgrades	Available through Frontline Systems at www.frontsys.com.	Available through LINDO Systems, Inc., at www.lindo.com.

*Note: although discontinuous functions such as IF statements will not result in error messages, they do not yield reliable results with the standard Solver. Such formulas require either the Evolutionary algorithm of the Premium Solver or the Linearization feature of What's*Best!*

TUTORIAL: MAXIMUM PROFIT

How Many Boats to Produce?

We start with a common type of a linear programming problem known as a product mix model. A manufacturer of fiberglass boats must produce during the winter in preparation for the spring selling season. The manufacturer wants to maximize its profit given its limited raw materials. The product line is shown in the following figure in order of decreasing profit per unit.

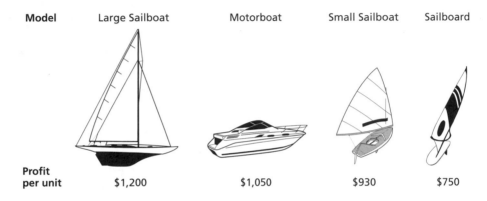

Model	Large Sailboat	Motorboat	Small Sailboat	Sailboard
Profit per unit	$1,200	$1,050	$930	$750

Although numerous raw materials are required to manufacture the boats, only five items are in short supply and might limit production. These are sailcloth for the sails on all but the motor boat, glass fiber for all the boats' hulls, epoxy resin for molding the glass fiber, aluminum for masts and other trim, and engines for the motor boat only.

The raw materials required for each boat and the units on hand are summarized in the following table. For example, a large sailboat requires 4 units of sailcloth of which 700 units are on hand.

| Raw materials | On hand (units) | Requirements by Product | | | |
		Large Sailboat	Motorboat	Small Sailboat	Sailboard
Sailcloth	700	4	0	3	1
Glass fiber	1,380	8	4	3	2
Epoxy resin	1,280	3	3	3	2
Aluminum	1,100	4	2	2	2
Engines	120	0	1	0	0

The Workbook: BOATS.xls

Load BOATS.xls and inspect the model. This is an expansion of the BOAT model discussed in the first chapter.

- **The Profit Calculation.** The total profit is the production quantity of large sailboats times the profit per unit of large sailboats plus the production quantity of motorboats times profit per unit of motorboats, and so on for the remaining boat types.

- **The SUMPRODUCT formula.** Total profit can be conveniently calculated using the SUMPRODUCT formula. The SUMPRODUCT is an important building block for optimization models and was discussed in Chapter 1, "Analytical Modeling in Spreadsheets."

	A6		=SUMPRODUCT(C2:F2,C3:F3)			
	A	B	C	D	E	F
1			Large Sailboat	Motor Boat	Small Sailboat	Sailboard
2	Production Quantity		0	0	0	0
3	Profit Per Unit		$1,200	$1,050	$930	$750
4						
5	Total Profit					
6	$0					

- **Raw Material Utilization.** Each raw material's usage is also calculated using SUMPRODUCT formulas in which the first argument uses absolute referencing (denoted by $ signs). This ensures that when the formulas are copied, they continue to refer to the production quantities in cells C2:F2.

	G10		=SUMPRODUCT(C$2:F$2,C10:F10)						
	A	B	C	D	E	F	G	H	I
8			Large Sailboat	Motor Boat	Small Sailboat	Sailboard			
9	Raw Materials			Requirements by product			Usage		On Hand
10	Sailcloth		4	0	3	1	0		700
11	Glass Fiber		8	4	3	2	0		1,380
12	Epoxy Resin		3	3	3	2	0		1,280
13	Aluminum		4	2	2	2	0		1,100
14	Engines		0	1	0	0	0		120

- **Maximizing Profit by Hand.** Try experimenting with the values in cells C2:F2 to maximize profit without having any of the usage formulas exceed the amounts on hand. The large sailboat has the highest profit margin, so a logical place to start is to produce as many of these as you can until you run out of a raw material. You will see that if you produce 172 large sailboats, yielding a total profit of $206,400 you will use all but 4 units of glass fiber which is not enough for an additional sailboat. The next most profitable product is the motorboat. You can produce only one of these for a total profit of $207,450 before completely exhausting the supply of glass fiber. Because every boat uses glass fiber, you are now out of production. Before we optimize this model, see if you can do better through experimentation. Be sure to write down your highest profit figure.

The ABC's of Optimization

We will now apply the ABC's discussed earlier.

A. ***What can you adjust?*** In this case, it is the quantity of each boat to produce. Such controls are known as the ***decision variables*** of the model. They are referred to as **changing cells** in the Excel Solver and as ***adjustable cells*** in What's*Best!*.

B. ***What do you mean by best?*** We will start by maximizing profit as the optimization's **objective.** This is known as the **target cell** in the Excel Solver and the **best cell** in What's*Best!*.

C. ***What constraints must be obeyed?*** This model has two types of constraints:
*   The production quantities must not be negative. Negative production would mean buying boats, disassembling them, and storing the raw materials in inventory, which we won't allow.
*   The total usage of each raw material must not exceed the quantity on hand.

TUTORIAL OPTIMIZING BOATS.XLS

The following steps show how to use the Excel Solver or What's*Best!* to find production figures that maximize profit from the resources on hand. Be sure that your optimization package is installed and that BOATS.xls is loaded.

SPECIFYING CHANGING OR ADJUSTABLE CELLS

Excel Solver

1. Invoke **Tools Solver** to open the solver dialog box.

2. With the cursor in the **Changing Cells** field of the dialog box, select cells C2:F2.

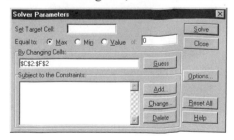

What's*Best!*

1. Highlight the adjustable cells C2:F2 in the worksheet, then invoke the **WB! Adjustable** command.

2. Click **OK**. The text of the adjustable cells is colored blue. You can also use the adjustable cell icon on the toolbar as shown on the left below. The icon on the right removes the adjustable property.

Specifying Objective

Excel Solver

1. With the cursor in the Target Cell field of the dialog box, select the "Total Profit" cell, A6.

2. Be sure the radio button is set to **Max.**

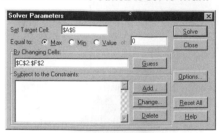

What'sBest!

1. With the cursor in the "Total Profit" cell of the worksheet, A6, invoke the **WB! Best** command.

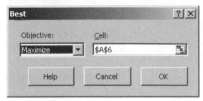

2. Be sure the drop down box is set to **Maximize.** Click **OK.** The background of the best cell is colored blue. You can also use the Maximize icon on the toolbar as shown on the left below. The Minimize icon is shown on the right.

Specifying Constraints

Usage constraints ensure that raw materials used do not exceed those on hand.

Excel Solver

1. Click the **Add Constraint** button.

2. With the cursor in the left constraint field, highlight "usage" cells G10:G14.

3. With the cursor in the right constraint field select the "on hand" cells.

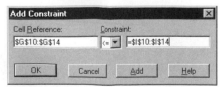

4. Make sure constraint type is <=.

5. Click **Add** to add the next set of constraints.

What'sBest!

1. Select the range H10:H14 separating the "Usage" and "On Hand" columns. Then invoke the **WB! Constraints** command.

2. Make sure constraint type is <=.

3. Because of the way this model was intentionally laid out, the left, right, and constraint fields default to the correct ranges. Click **OK.**

Constraints don't have to be laid out in any particular format on the worksheet except for convenience. However, if the cells are arranged with a blank column or row in between, then the use of the Constraint

(continued on the next page)

What's*Best!* *(continued from previous page)*

icons shown below make it easy to add constraints.

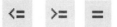

The constraint formulas should appear as shown below. Notice that constraint formulas and their associated ranges can be either rows or columns.

	H10	▼		=WB(G10,"<=",I10)	
	G	**H**	**I**	**J**	**K**
9	Usage		On Hand		
10	0	<=	700		
11	0	<=	1,380		
12	0	<=	1,280		
13	0	<=	1,100		
14	0	<=	120		

NONNEGATIVITY CONSTRAINTS

Excel Solver

If you are using Excel 97 or later, check the Assume Non-Negative box in the Options dialog box. In earlier versions of Excel, these constraints must be specified explicitly as follows.

1. With the cursor in the left field of a new constraint dialog, select the "changing" cells C2:F2.

2. Type 0 (zero) in the right constraint field as shown below.

3. Change the constraint type to >=.

4. Click **OK.** The Solver dialog box should now appear as shown below:

What's*Best!*

Nonnegativity constraints are not needed for adjustable cells. These default to nonnegative. If you want adjustable cells to be able to go negative, they must be designated as **Free** in the **Adjustable Cell** dialog box.

OPTIMIZING

Excel Solver

1. Although you could click the **Solve** button at this point, you will get better results on this example if you first click the **Options** button and check **Assume Linear Model.**

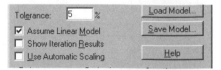

This will be explained in the next section.

2. Now click **Solve.**

3. In a few seconds you should see the Solver Results dialog box.

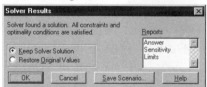

4. Click **OK** to save the results.

5. Save your optimized version of BOATS.xls as BOATSOPT.xls.

What's*Best!*

1. Invoke the **WB! Solve** command. Or, you can use the Solve icon as shown below.

2. A screen will display the status of the optimization.

3. Save your optimized version of BOATS.xls as BOATSOPT.xls.

The Results

The optimization results are shown in the following figure.

	A	B	C	D	E	F
1			Large Sailboat	Motor Boat	Small Sailboat	Sailboard
2	Production Quantity		0	100	80	370
3	Profit Per Unit		$1,200	$1,050	$930	$750
4						
5	Total Profit					
6	$456,900					

Notice that:

■ Total Profit is $456,900—more than twice as great as the $207,450 that resulted from starting with the highest profit large sailboat and working down.

■ The optimal production has *no* large sailboats!

Also notice that all the production figures are integers (whole numbers). This will not generally be the case, as discussed later.

Interacting with the Model: What's Best If

Once an optimization model has been created, you can explore it from various points of view.

Hierarchical Objectives

The previous optimized production plan leaves 20 remaining engines unused. Suppose these remaining engines become obsolete after the current production run. You might consider maximizing the usage of engines instead of profit.

Try this with either the Excel Solver or What's*Best!*:

1. Specify that cell G14 be maximized.

2. Re-optimize the model.

Engine usage will now be maximized without regard to the former objective of maximizing total profit. The resulting production of 120 motor boats completely exhausts the obsolete inventory, but profit has dropped significantly. We cannot expect the full $456,900 in profit obtained earlier if we want to use all the engines. However, we might want to see how many engines can be used if we require a $456,000 profit (within $900 of the maximum possible). Try this with either the Excel Solver or What's*Best!* as follows:

1. Create a new >= constraint with cell A6 on the left, and $456,000 on the right.

2. Re-optimize the model.

Re-optimization results in a $456,000 profit and five remaining engines. This process of alternatively selecting new objectives while imposing constraints on old ones allows a great deal of managerial flexibility in using optimization.

Market Limitations

Suppose it turns out that the engines will not become obsolete after all. However, the marketing department points out that the demand for the various boat types is limited as shown in the following table:

	Large Sailboat	Motorboat	Small Sailboat	Sailboard
Market limit (units)	160	130	170	150

Recall that the current optimal production involves 370 sailboards, far more than can be sold.

EXERCISE
7.1

BOAT MARKET LIMITATIONS

Retrieve BOATSOPT.xls, the optimized production plan saved before the experiment of maximizing engine usage.

a.   Place these market limits in row 4 of the BOATSOPT worksheet.

b.   Add constraints to the current model to ensure that each boat's production figures do not exceed their associated market limits.

c.   What are the new production figures and total profit?

d.   Re-save BOATSOPT.xls.

The D's of Optimization: Dual Values

The Economic Value of Limited Resources

Looking at the optimized model with market constraints, you should see the following usage of scarce resources.

Raw materials	Usage	On hand
Sailcloth	700	700
Glass fiber	1370	1380
Epoxy resin	1200	1280
Aluminum	920	1100
Engines	120	120

The sailcloth and engines have been completely exhausted. How much would you profit from additional units of each resource? The answer lies in what are known as *dual values*, or *shadow prices*. Proceed as follows to find them.

TUTORIAL: FINDING DUAL VALUES

Excel Solver

1. Re-optimize the model by clicking the **Solve** button.

2. When the Solver Results dialog appears, select the **Sensitivity** report.

What's*Best!*

1. Select blank cells J10:J14 in which to store the dual values.

2. Invoke the **WB! Advanced Dual** command. The Dual dialog box appears.

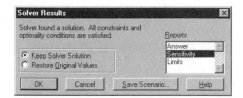

3. Click OK to generate the report, which will be found on a separate worksheet of the workbook.

Name	Final Value	Shadow Price
Sailcloth Usage	700	300
Glass Fiber Usage	1,370	0
Epoxy Resin Usage	1,200	0
Aluminum Usage	920	0
Engines Usage	120	1,050

The column labeled "Shadow Prices" displays the economic value of additional units of each resource. If the Assume Linear Model option had not been used with the solver, this column would have been labeled "Lagrange Multipliers."

3. With the cursor in the Report Information In: field, select the constraint cells H10:H14 then click **OK**.

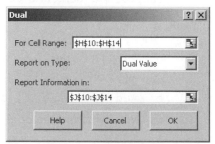

4. Formulas with values equaling 0 will appear in cells J10:J14. Re-optimize the model with the **WB! Solve** command. The dual values will appear in cells J10:J14 as shown.

	J10		=WBDUAL(H10,300)	
	A	**G**	**H**	**I**	**J**
9	**Raw Materials**	**Usage**		**On Hand**	
10	Sailcloth	700	=<=	700	300
11	Glass Fiber	1,370	<=	1,380	0
12	Epoxy Resin	1,200	<=	1,280	0
13	Aluminum	920	<=	1,100	0
14	Engines	120	=<=	120	1050

What the Dual Values Mean

Notice that you have not run out of glass fiber, epoxy resin, or aluminum. Because you have enough already, you can't increase profit by getting more. Hence they have a dual value equal to 0. Sailcloth and engines, on the other hand, are both in short supply. Additional supply of either of these items taken one at a time would increase profit by $300 or $1,050 per unit. This is very valuable information if you are planning to purchase additional raw materials to continue production. Taken in this context, the quote from Mother Goose that began this chapter says, in effect, that a horseshoe nail's dual value was one kingdom. We will discuss dual values further in the next chapter.

EXERCISE
7.2   Determining the Profitability of a New Boat Type

Suppose the marketing department thinks it can sell as many as 100 sailing dinghies at $850 profit per unit, where each sailing dinghy requires two units each of sailcloth, glass fiber, and epoxy resin.

a. Would it be profitable to add the sailing dingy to the product line? Why or why not?

b. Add the sailing dingy to the lineup and find the new optimal production.

c. Now what are the dual values of the resources?

BASIC OPTIMIZATION EXAMPLES

Since its introduction shortly after World War II, linear programming has produced literally thousands of applications. Although those in the following list represent a small fraction of problem types to which this technique can be applied, a few important classes have been covered. The associated worksheets can be expanded, tailored, and combined to encompass a wide variety of real-world applications. The models discussed include the following:

- **Product Mix.** Allocating limited raw materials into various products for maximum profit.

- **Blending.** Mixing ingredients to meet blend requirements at minimum cost.

- **Staff Scheduling.** Meeting staff needs at minimum cost.

- **Transportation.** Shipping goods from sources to demand points at minimum cost.

- **Network Flow Models.** A generalization of the transportation model in which material flows through complex networks or pipelines.

The files are supplied in formats for the Excel Solver and for What's*Best!* The Solver versions use the Assume Linear Model option[1] and have inequality signs entered in place of the *What'sBest!* inequality formulas for clarity. The What's*Best!* versions have "W" appended to the file names. For most small problems the Excel Solver and What's*Best!* perform similarly, but each has its own advantage in some cases. These will be pointed out as they arise.

---

[1]The Excel Solver defaults to nonlinear optimization. If you know that your model is linear, you should always select Assume Linear Model from the Options dialog box to take advantage of the LP algorithm. If the model turns out to be nonlinear, you will get an error message. What's*Best!* detects whether or not the model is linear, then automatically applies the appropriate algorithm. The error screen will optionally display a warning for nonlinear formulas in case they are not intentional.

Product Mix

In product mix problems, the objective of optimization is to find a most profitable allocation of a set of limited resources over a set of desired products or activities. The BOATS model discussed in the tutorial earlier in this chapter is an example of this problem type. Industrial LP software can now solve such models involving tens of thousands of products and resources.

EXERCISE
7. 3   **MANUFACTURING ATHLETIC SHOES**

A firm manufactures three types of athletic shoes: Basketball with a $10 per pair profit, Running with a $9 per pair profit, and Tennis with a $7.50 per pair profit. The resources consumed per pair of shoes and the quantities available are shown in the following table.

Resources	Basketball	Running	Tennis	Available
Canvas	2	1	1	12,000
Labor hours	4	2	2	21,000
Machine hours	2	3	2	19,500
Rubber	2	1	2	16,500

a. What production quantities maximize profit?

b. Given optimal production, what is the economic value to the firm of each of the resources ?

Blending

Blending problems are an important class of linear programs. They occur in the production of gasoline and other petroleum products, chemicals, paints, alloys, fertilizers, and processed foods. Unlike the product mix problem in which a single set of raw materials could be combined into many different types of products, here a single type of product can be produced from many different combinations of raw materials. In blending problems, the objective is generally to minimize cost per unit of final product, and the constraints are to enforce correct proportions of ingredients.

In the following example, various constituents are blended to form a metal alloy. The chemical requirements are that the alloy must contain at least 9% of element A and between 6.5% and 11% of element B.

The raw materials that can be used in this alloy are three ores—with chemical analysis shown in the following figure, and the element A in its pure form.

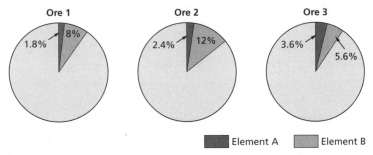

The costs of the raw materials are shown here. Notice that element A in its pure form is far more expensive than any of the ores. The objective is to meet the chemical requirements at the minimum cost per ton.

Raw material	Cost per ton
Ore 1	$50
Ore 2	$60
Ore 3	$40
Element A	$8,000

Exploring the Blending Model. Retrieve BLEND.xls for the Excel Solver or BLENDW.xls for What's*Best!*. The key elements of the model are as follows:

■ The percentage of each raw material used is stored in the range C3:F3.

■ Cost per ton of each raw material are in C4:F4.

■ The total cost per ton of the blend in cell F10 is the SUMPRODUCT of C3:F3 and C4:F4.

■ The sum of C3:F3 is in C12. This must total 100% to ensure we have accounted for all raw materials in the blend.

■ The percentage of element A in the blend in cell C15 is the SUMPRODUCT of C3:F3 and C6:F6. *Note:* do not confuse the percentage of pure element A purchased (cell F3) with the percentage of element A in the final blend (cell C15).

■ The percentage of element B in the blend in cell C19 is the SUMPRODUCT of C3:F3 and C7:F7.

■ A pie chart displays the percentage of each of the raw materials in the blend.

The ABC's of the Blending Model

A. ***The adjustable cells***, C3:F3 represent the percentage of each raw material used in the alloy.

B. ***The best solution*** is that which minimizes total cost per ton in cell F10.

C. ***The constraints*** are as follows:

- The percentages must sum to 100%.

- The blend must contain at least 9% Element A.

- The blend must contain between 6.5% and 11% Element B.

- The adjustable cells are constrained to be greater than or equal to zero. This is the default in What's*Best!*. With the Solver you may set these constraints explicitly or use the Assume Non-Negative option.

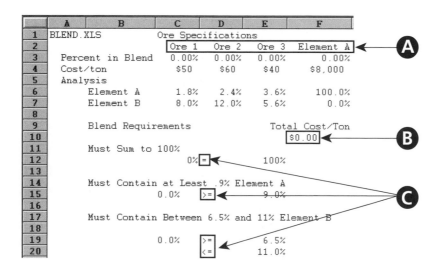

EXERCISE

7.4   OPTIMIZING THE BLENDING MODEL

a.   Optimize the blending model that has already been set up. What are the proportions of raw material that will yield minimum cost?

b.   Find the dual values on the constraints, and interpret their meaning. See Chapter 8 for further discussion of dual values.

Blending models are used extensively in the petroleum and chemical industry, and also in the production of fertilizers and animal feed as in the following example.

BLENDING FEEDMIX

An animal feed is to be blended from four types of grain. The final blend must have sufficient quantities of three nutrients as shown in the following table.

	Nutrient A	Nutrient B	Nutrient C
Units required per bushel	5	8	35

Each grain has a different concentration of these nutrients as shown in the following table.

	Nutrient units per bushel			
Grain type	**1**	**2**	**3**	**4**
Nutrient A	2.2	3.4	7.2	1.5
Nutrient B	2.3	5.6	11.1	1.3
Nutrient C	12.0	11.9	41.8	52.1

If the four grains cost $25, $40, $75, and $80 per bushel respectively, what blend will result in the lowest cost feed that meets the nutritional requirements?

Staff Scheduling

In staff scheduling problems, the objective of optimization is to meet specified manpower requirements at minimum cost. Generally, the schedule must meet certain conditions—such as those imposed by regulations or union contracts involving shift length, number of work breaks, or maximum overtime hours.

This example involves a business with daily staff requirements that range from 120 to 190 people, depending on varying work loads each day of the week, as shown in the following figure:

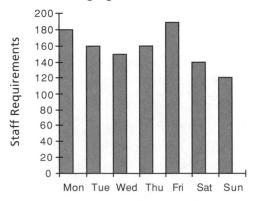

In addition, a labor union requirement must be met which stipulates that employees work a five-consecutive-day workweek followed by two days off. Thus, the allowable shifts are Monday through Friday, Tuesday through Saturday, Wednesday through Sunday, and so on. Each employee earns $500 per week.

Exploring the Scheduling Model. Retrieve STAFF.xls for the Excel Solver or STAFFW.xls for What's*Best!*.

The model's key elements are as follows:

▪ The number of people hired to start on each day is shown in cells F8:F14.

▪ The number of people on duty each day of the week (cells C8:C14) is the sum of the number of employees starting that day and each of the previous four days.

▪ The total number hired is the sum of F8:F14 in cell F15.

▪ The total cost is the total number hired times the cost per week, in cell F19.

▪ A graph shows both the staff needs and staff size.

Because 180 people are needed on Monday, enter 180 in cell F8 (the number starting Monday). You will see that cells C8:C12 now all contain 180, reflecting the union requirement that employees work a five day shift. The formula in column C for any given day is simply the sum of the number of employees starting that day and those starting each of the previous four days.

The graph now shows just the right number of employees on Monday, but a few too many on Tuesday through Thursday. Friday is understaffed by 10, and Saturday and Sunday are unstaffed. Enter 10 in cell F12 (the number starting Friday). You should now have adequate coverage on Monday through Friday, but will still be short 130 on Saturday and 110 on Sunday. Next, enter 130 in cell F13 (the number starting Saturday), and view the graph.

The good news is that the staff needs have been met each day of the week. The bad news is that the employees hired to start Saturday would work until the following Wednesday. As you can see from the graph, this solution is so over-staffed Monday through Wednesday that people would be sitting on each other's laps! Also notice that the total cost is $160,000.

The ABC's of the Scheduling Model.

A. ***The adjustable cells***, F8:F14 are the number of employees starting each day.

B. ***The best solution*** is that which minimizes total cost, cell F19.

C. ***The constraints*** are as follows:

 • Daily staff size is constrained to be at least as great as the staff need.

- The adjustable cells are constrained to be greater than or equal to zero. This must be explicitly specified with the Solver[2] but is the default in What's*Best!*.

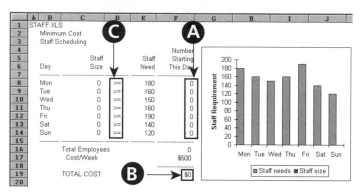

EXERCISE 7.6 STAFF SCHEDULING

a. See if you can improve the previous solution by adjusting cells F8:F14 by hand before optimizing the model. Remember as you do so that the staff size must remain at least as large as each day's staff needs.

b. Optimize the model. How do the graph and total cost differ from the solution you found by hand?

EXERCISE 7.7 GENERALIZING STAFF.XLS: COVERING PROBLEMS

The previous scheduling model provides graphic proof of the effectiveness of optimization for this kind of problem. As formulated, however, it does not generalize easily. Suppose, for example, that the union is requesting a four-day work week with three days off in a row instead of the current two. For the model to accommodate these new work rules, you would have to change all formulas in C8:C14. This exercise is to generalize STAFF.xls so that the work patterns are stored as data.

a. Modify STAFF.xls so that any allowable seven-day work patterns can be entered without changing any formulas. The work patterns will be entered as a range with a row for each day and a column for each allowable pattern. The data for the current work rules should appear as shown below in the worksheet.

---

[2]In Excel 97, it is convenient to use the Assume Non-Negative option to impose this constraint.

	Allowable Patterns: 1 = on, 0 = off						
Pattern	1	2	3	4	5	6	7
Monday	1	0	0	1	1	1	1
Tuesday	1	1	0	0	1	1	1
Wednesday	1	1	1	0	0	1	1
Thursday	1	1	1	1	0	0	1
Friday	1	1	1	1	1	0	0
Saturday	0	1	1	1	1	1	0
Sunday	0	0	1	1	1	1	1

The 1's and 0's signify whether or not a given pattern requires working on a given day. Thus pattern 2 is off Monday, on Tuesday, and so on. Now remove the current adjustable cells and replace them with cells denoting the number hired for each work pattern. Next, you will need to replace the staff size expressions for each day with SUMPRODUCT formulas involving the number hired for each pattern and the rows of the pattern data. Test your model to make sure that it gives the same answer as before.

b. What happens to labor costs if the four-day work week is adopted without reducing the $500 per week cost? If you get fractional answers for the number of each pattern to hire, round the results up to the nearest integer.

c. Suppose the union agrees that the pay for a four-day work week should only be 4/5ths the pay for a five-day work week. How would labor costs differ from the original five-day work week?

Problems of this type in which a set of patterns is used to cover a demand are known as *covering problems*. They are useful in many different optimization settings, such as the following example.

7.8   THE CUTTING STOCK PROBLEM

A supplier of sheet steel cuts stock in various widths from 100" rolls. Current demand in feet is shown below by width.

Width in Inches	15	18	25	35
Demand in Feet	1450	967	3000	1020

The rolls can be cut using any of the four patterns shown in the following figure.

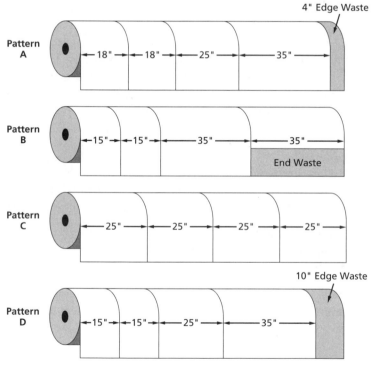

In the process of cutting, two kinds of waste can occur. Edge waste occurs for the entire length cut from a pattern that sum to less than 100 inches (A and D for example). End waste can occur with any of the patterns, and corresponds to the amount of any width for which more than the demand was produced. The cost penalty of edge waste is $1.50 per inch foot while end waste, being a useful width, imposes a smaller penalty of $0.75 per inch foot.

a.   Build an optimization model to determine the quantity of each pattern to cut to meet demand with minimum total (edge plus end) waste cost. Assume that the rolls are much longer than the total quantities being cut, so you won't run out of material with any pattern.

b. Come up with a new pattern, which when added to the current four, results in an improved optimum cost. *Hint:* Look at the dual values from part a.

Transportation

This problem is the simplest of a class known as network problems. These generally involve the shipping of goods through transportation networks, or of oil or gas through systems of pipelines.

In this model, two steel mills supply three manufacturing plants. Each plant has a demand for steel that must be met, and each steel mill has limited manufacturing capacity as shown in the schematic below.

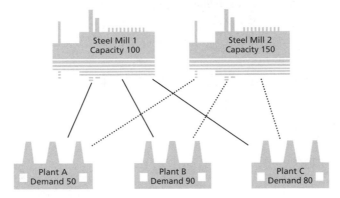

The unit shipping costs from the mills to each plant are shown in the following table.

To:	From:	
	Steel Mill 1	**Steel Mill 2**
Plant A	$200	$500
Plant B	$300	$400
Plant C	$500	$600

The objective is to minimize shipping cost while meeting all demand without exceeding steel mill capacity.

Exploring the Transportation Model. Retrieve TRANS.xls for the Excel Solver and TRANSW.xls for What's*Best!*.

The model's key elements are as follows:

■ The amount shipped from each mill to each plant is stored in the range B6:C8.

■ The shipping costs per unit are stored in the range B16:C18.

- The total shipping cost in cell G14 is the SUMPRODUCT (B6:C8,B16:C18).
- The total shipments by plant are calculated in cells E6:E8.
- The total production by mills are stored in cells B10:C10.

The ABC's of the Transportation Model.

A. **The _adjustable cells_**, B6:C8 represent the amount shipped from each mill to each plant.

B. **The _best solution_** is that which minimizes total shipping cost, cell G14.

C. **The _constraints_** are as follows:

- The total shipped to each plant is at least as great as the demand.
- The total shipped from each mill does not exceed its capacity.
- The adjustable cells are constrained to be greater than or equal to zero. This is the default in What's_Best!_, but is specified with the Assume Non-Negative option with the Solver.

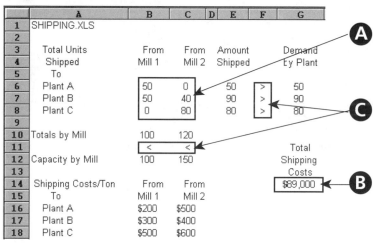

	A	B	C	D	E	F	G
1	SHIPPING.XLS						
2							
3	Total Units	From	From		Amount		Demand
4	Shipped	Mill 1	Mill 2		Shipped		Ey Plant
5	To						
6	Plant A	50	0		50	>	50
7	Plant B	50	40		90	>	90
8	Plant C	0	80		80	>	80
9							
10	Totals by Mill	100	120				
11		<	<				Total
12	Capacity by Mill	100	150				Shipping
13							Costs
14	Shipping Costs/Ton	From	From				$89,000
15	To	Mill 1	Mill 2				
16	Plant A	$200	$500				
17	Plant B	$300	$400				
18	Plant C	$500	$600				

EXERCISE 7.9

TRANSPORTATION BETWEEN STEEL MILLS AND PLANTS

Optimize the transportation model that has already been set up. What is the minimal shipping cost that meets demand without exceeding steel mill capacity?

EXERCISE
7.10   DISASTER RELIEF

A major earthquake has hit a developing nation, leaving thousands of people homeless. They are located in four refugee camps with the following immediate requirements for food, medicine, and other emergency supplies.

	Camp A	Camp B	Camp C	Camp D
Tons Required	10	5	10	20

Supplies are available in two neighboring countries, with 25 tons in country 1 and 20 tons in country 2.

The shipping cost per ton from the two countries to each of the four camps is shown in the following table.

	From:	
To:	**Country 1**	**Country 2**
Camp A	$100	$150
Camp B	$150	$200
Camp C	$200	$300
Camp D	$300	$400

Determine the most cost effective allocation of emergency supplies to camps.

Network Flow Models

Network flow models are a generalization of the transportation model discussed earlier. Intermediate nodes are allowed between the sources of supply and the demand points. There may be capacity constraints on individual arcs within the network that limit the hourly or daily flow. Also, flow can be permitted in either direction over the arcs. Network models have the useful property that if the source flow and the capacity constraints are integers, then the LP optimized flow along all arcs will be integers.

The following figure is a schematic representation of an oil pipeline network. There is a supply or *source* of oil at oil field (1) and a consumption point or *sink* at the refinery (6). The following figure shows each pipeline's distance in miles, hourly capacity, and cost per unit flow that can differ in each direction.

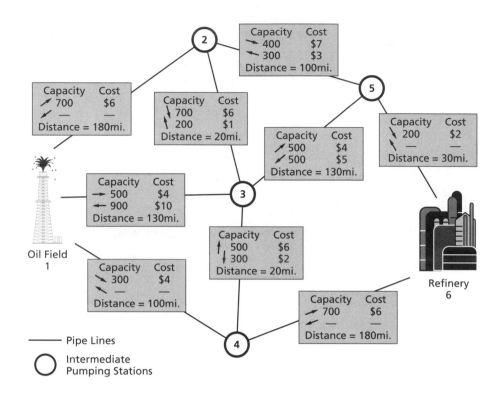

At each network node, one of four things can happen:

- There can be a source of oil coming into the network, such as an oil field.

- There can be a sink, a place where oil gets consumed, such as a refinery.

- There can be flow **to** that node from other nodes.

- There can be flow **from** that node to other nodes.

You might have several objectives in using such a model. We will start by determining the network's overall capacity. That is, the maximum flow possible from the source to the sink.

Exploring the Network Flow Model. This formulation for network flow problems was inspired by an approach suggested by Donald Plane (Plane, 1994). Retrieve NETFLOW.xls for the Excel Solver. The Excel solver model formulation uses the DSUM formula. What's*Best!* cannot process DSUM, but does work with a related formula, SUMIF. A formulation suggested by Cliff Ragsdale of Virginia Polytechnic Institute is used in NETFLOWW.xls. You are encouraged to explore both models, as DSUM and SUMIF are important and interesting formulas each in its own right.

The model has two major sections: the arc data and the node summary.

Arc data is specified in cells A3:F20. This range contains one row for each arc in the network. The key elements are the following:

■ The node the arc comes from, column A.

■ The node the arc goes to, column B.

■ The amount of oil flowing per hour through the arc, column C.

■ The maximum hourly flow capacity through the arc, column E.

■ The unit pumping cost of flow through the arc, column F.

■ The distance in miles of the arc, column G.

■ The hourly cost of the current flow in cell C1, calculated as SUMPRODUCT ($C$3:$C$20,F3:F20).

	A	B	C	D	E	F	G
1	Total Cost		$0				
2	From	To	Flow		Capacity	Cost/Unit	Distance
3	1	2	0	<=	700	$6	180
4	1	3	0	<=	500	$4	130
5	1	4	0	<=	300	$4	100
6	2	1	0	<=	0	$0	180
7	2	3	0	<=	700	$6	20
8	2	5	0	<=	400	$7	100
9	3	1	0	<=	900	$10	130
10	3	2	0	<=	200	$1	20
11	3	4	0	<=	300	$2	20
12	3	5	0	<=	500	$4	130
13	4	1	0	<=	0	$0	100
14	4	3	0	<=	500	$6	20
15	4	6	0	<=	700	$6	180
16	5	2	0	<=	300	$3	100
17	5	3	0	<=	500	$5	130
18	5	6	0	<=	200	$2	30
19	6	4	0	<=	0	$0	180
20	6	5	0	<=	0	$0	30
21	Insert New Arcs Here						

The Node Summary is specified in cells I25:O37. This range contains one column for each node in the network. Each column contains the following:

■ The flow entering the node from a source (if one is present at that node), row 28.

■ The flow coming to the node from other nodes, row 29.

■ The total flow entering the node, row 30.

■ The flow leaving the node through a sink (if one is present at that node), row 35.

■ The flow leaving the node to other nodes, row 36. This is similar to the formula in row 29.

■ The total flow leaving the node, row 37.

Excel Solver: These values are calculated using formulas of the form DSUM(Arc-Data,"Flow",L26:L27). See your Excel documentation or Help file for an explanation of DSUM.

What's*Best!*: These values are calculated using formulas of the form = SUMIF(TO or FROM,J$24,FLOW). See your Excel documentation or Help file for an explanation of SUMIF.

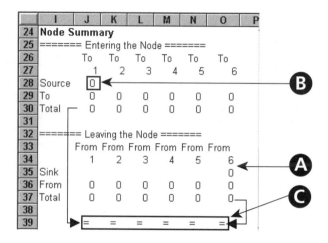

The ABC's of the Network Flow Model.

A. *The **a**djustable cells* are the following:

- The flow through each of the arcs, cells C3:C20.

- The source at node 1, cell J28.

- The sink at node 6, cell O35.

B. *The **b**est solution* is that which maximizes either the source at node 1, or the sink at node 6: we have used cell J28. Note that the objective function is an adjustable cell, not a formula.

C. *The **c**onstraints* are the following:

- The total flow down the arcs, C3:C20, must not exceed the capacities, E3:E20.

- The total flow into each node, J30:O30, must equal the total flow out of that node, J37:O37, to prevent the pipes from bursting. These are known as conservation constraints.

- The adjustable cells are constrained to be greater than or equal to zero.

Three Related Network Flow Problems

Network flow models form the basis of a number of interesting optimization problems, three of which follow:

- *Maximum Flow Problem.* What is the overall capacity of the network? The objective is to determine the maximum flow possible from the source to the sink.

- *Minimum Cost Problem.* What is the cheapest way to achieve it? The objective is to determine how much oil to flow down each arc to achieve the maximum flow.

- *Shortest Path Problem.* What is the shortest path between the source and the sink? The objective is to find the shortest set of arcs that connect the source to the sink; for example, for laying a communication line.

The network flow problem presented earlier is an example of the maximum flow problem. Minor modifications are needed for the minimum cost and shortest path problems, as demonstrated in the following exercises.

EXERCISE

7.11   MAXIMUM FLOW THROUGH A NETWORK

Optimize the network flow model to find the maximum hourly flow of oil that can be supported over the network between the field and refinery. This information is critical in planning for future oil field development.

Explore the flow through the various arcs. What is the total hourly flow through the network from source to sink? You should see a total hourly flow through the network from source to sink of 800 units. What is the hourly cost?

EXERCISE

7.12   MINIMUM COST AT MAXIMUM FLOW

Modify the maximum flow model to determine whether the solution found in Exercise 7.11 represents the lowest cost way to flow 800 units through this network. If not, what is the minimum cost solution?

EXERCISE

7.13   SHORTEST PATH PROBLEM

Suppose it is necessary to lay a phone line from the oil field to the refinery. The line is to be laid over the pipelines because the land is already leased. We require the shortest path along the arcs, that starts at node 1 and ends at node 6. *Hint:* Start with the minimum cost problem and limit the flow from the source to the sink to 1 unit, then create a new cell to calculate total distance.

Conclusion

This chapter has introduced some important classes of linear optimization models. Once these are understood, they may be modified or expanded to solve a wide variety of problems. In the next chapter, we will explore some extensions of optimization, and show how small models may be combined to form larger ones.

END OF CHAPTER EXERCISES

7.14   OPTIMAL ADVERTISING MIX

Your firm is planning a cable television advertising campaign aimed at three demographic groups; single adult males, single adult females, and married couples. The campaign requires 500,000 viewers among the single males, and 200,000 viewers in each of the other two groups. Five channels are available, each with its own audience demographics. The table below shows the number of viewers of each type per $1,000 of advertising for each of the five channels. That is, $2000 spent on channel 2 would reach 200 Single Men, 1800 Single Women, and 4,000 couples, etc.

	Single Men	Single Women	Couples
Channel 1	300	850	1200
Channel 2	100	900	2000
Channel 3	0	1200	800
Channel 4	2000	0	200
Channel 5	750	500	500

Find the minimum cost media purchase that will meet your goals for each of the three demographic groups.

7.15   ALLOCATING PEACE-KEEPING UNITS

The United Nations must decide how to allocate five peace-keeping units to five separate missions. The suitability of assigning any particular unit to any mission is based on many factors which have been summarized by a score between 1 and 3—with 3 signifying the highest suitability to the mission and 1 the lowest.

	Unit 1	Unit 2	Unit 3	Unit 4	Unit 5
Mission A	1	3	3	1	1
Mission B	3	1	1	2	1
Mission C	1	1	1	1	2
Mission D	2	1	2	2	2
Mission E	2	2	2	1	1

Find the assignment of units to missions which maximizes the sum of the assigned suitabilities. *Hint:* This problem is known as the Assignment Problem, and it is very similar to the transportation problem. In fact, the quickest way to solve this is to start with TRANS.xls and make a few modifications.

7.16   STAMPING PARTS

A fabrication plant must stamp the following shapes from sheets of steel.

First they must arrange the shapes on the sheets to form patterns to be cut. Then they must cut enough of the various patterns to meet the demand for each shape. Three possible patterns are shown below.

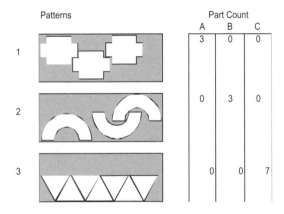

a.   How many sheets would be required to fill a demand of 100 of part A, 75 of part B, and 60 of part C using just the current three patterns? *Hint:* You should be able to do this in your head, or at most with pencil and paper.

b.   Next, use optimization to try to minimize the number of sheets required to fill the demand above. The file PARTS.xls contains the various shapes that may be cut and pasted to form patterns for your model. You may rotate the parts (180 degrees only), but must not change the size of either the parts or the sheets from which they are to be cut. You may use as many patterns as you like, and need not use the three original patterns. If you get fractional answers, you may round up or specify integer answers as discussed in Chapter 8. *Hint:* This is a variant of the cutting stock problem.

8 ■■■■■■■■■■■■■■■■■■■■■■■■■■■■■■■■

Extensions of Optimization

The final test for a theory is its capacity to solve the problems which originated it.

GEORGE DANTZIG, FATHER OF LINEAR PROGRAMMING

The technique of linear programming was developed in 1947 by George Dantzig. He first came up with a simple characterization that brought a tremendous class of problems under a single roof. He also devised the powerful simplex algorithm to potentially solve them all in one fell swoop. The quote above is from the preface to his book *Linear Programming and Extensions.*

As you attempt to solve real-world problems with linear programming, additional complications arise for which the theory of optimization has been extended. For example:

- Optimization might not give integer answers. No one would produce 5.75 large sailboats and 1.5 motorboats. The good news is that variables can be specified to take on integer values. The bad news is that the optimization process may be greatly slowed down by doing so.

- Real-world problems are seldom solved in isolation. You would not decide how to produce sailboats at a factory in a single time period without also being concerned about how this would apply to production in future time periods.

- Many aspects of the problem might be uncertain. Optimizing for "average" conditions might not be optimal under *any* real life conditions. Stochastic optimization attempts to optimize over a set of uncertain scenarios.

- Some important problems, particularly those in financial portfolio optimization, are not linear and require nonlinear programming.

- Traditionally, optimization models required rigid mathematical formulation, which was foreign to most managers. The latest versions of the Excel Solver and What's*Best!* go a long way toward relaxing this requirement.

■ ■ ■ OVERVIEW

Extending the Application of Optimization

We extend the concepts of the last chapter to cover:

■ **Integer Models:** Models in which fractional solutions cannot be tolerated.

■ **Combining Optimization Models:** Simple optimization models can be viewed as objects that can be combined to form more complex models. Examples include multi-time period and vertically integrated models.

■ **Optimization Under Uncertainty:** Problems with uncertain inputs are solved with stochastic optimization.

■ **Nonlinear Optimization:** An important class of financial portfolio problems require nonlinear optimization, as do certain data-fitting techniques.

Common Errors in Optimization Models

A few of the most common errors in model formulation are discussed for linear and nonlinear problems.

The Basics of Optimization Theory

To discuss the theory behind optimization, we examine a very simple model in some detail.

EXTENDING THE APPLICATION OF OPTIMIZATION

Integer Variables

As mentioned in the last chapter, network optimization models return integer (whole number) answers when the sources and sinks are integers. This is not true of optimization problems in general. In many cases, if you get fractional answers, rounding to the closest integers that do not violate the constraints can provide a good solution. However, there are situations, especially when the desired number is a small integer, when rounding might not give satisfactory results. The good news is that there are techniques that force optimization to give integer answers. The bad news is that these techniques can greatly slow down the solution process. Thus, it is generally not practical to solve problems with a large number of integer variables.

As an example of a situation where you would want only integer answers, suppose you have decided to run away from home and can take only those personal possessions that will fit in your knapsack. You have ranked all the items according to both value and size. The problem of selecting the most valuable set of items that will fit is known as the *knapsack problem.* This is not such an easy problem because if you take the most valuable thing, your portable TV, there isn't room for anything else. And obviously, you require an integer answer. No one wants to hit the road with half a portable TV and two-thirds of a teddy bear!

Similar problems arise in stocking limited shelf space in a store with items of various sizes and profit margins, or, as in the next example, loading a truck.

Optimal Truck Loading

A firm is loading six types of items of different weights and values into a truck with a 10,000 pound load capacity. Management wants to know the most valuable set of cargo that can be loaded without exceeding the weight limit. In this example, we will assume that there is a large number of each item, so you can load as many as you like of any one item.

Exploring the Model. Retrieve TRUCK.xls for the Excel Solver and TRUCKW.xls for What's*Best!*.

The model's key elements are as follows:

- The value of each item that can be loaded, B6:B11.

- The weight of each item that can be loaded, C6:C11.

- The number of each item to load on the truck, D6:D11.

- The total value of the load in cell A15 is SUMPRODUCT (B6:B11,D6:D11).

- The total weight of the load in cell C15 is SUMPRODUCT (C6:C11,D6:D11).

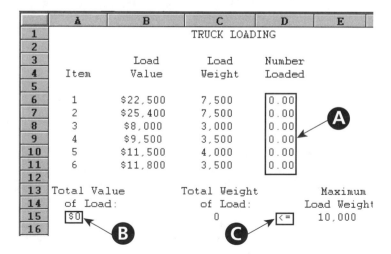

The ABC's of the Truck Loading Model.

A. *The **a**djustable cells,* D6:D11 represent the number of each type of item loaded.

B. *The **b**est solution* is that which maximizes the total value of the loaded items A15.

C. *The **c**onstraints* are as follows:

- The total weight of the items loaded must not exceed the capacity of the truck.

- The adjustable cells are constrained to be greater than or equal to zero. This must be done explicitly with the Solver[1] but is the default in What's*Best!*.

TUTORIAL: OPTIMIZING TRUCK.XLS/TRUCKW.XLS

Optimize this model with the Solve command and you will get a fractional solution that suggests loading 1.33 of item 2, yielding a $33,867 value. Round this down to one unit of item 2 and the value drops to $25,400. There is an integer load with a significantly higher value. Can you find it by hand? To specify that the adjustable cells take on integer values, proceed as follows:

Excel Solver

1. Bring up the Solver dialog box, and add a constraint.

2. Select D6:D11 for the left hand side of the constraint, and Int for the type of constraint, then click **OK.**

What's*Best!*

1. Select cells D6:D11, then invoke the **WB! Integer** command. The following dialog box appears. A name is required for each integer. Type a name in the **Integer Names in Workbook** field.

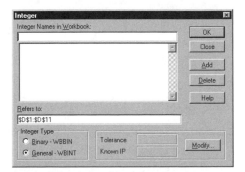

2. **General** specifies that any number of each item can be loaded on the truck (**Binary** would have implied 0 or 1). Click **OK.**

---

[1] In Excel 97, you can use the Assume Non-Negative option to impose this constraint.

Now re-optimize the model. You should see a completely new set of items loaded with a higher value than the $25,400 that was found through rounding the initial solution.

The Fixed-Cost Problem

An area in which integer variables are even more important is that of Yes/No decisions. This is summed up by the old adage that there is no such thing as being "a little bit pregnant." Undoubtedly there are parents who wish they could have had 1/3 of a baby, heard 1/3 of the crying, bought 1/3 of a crib, changed 1/3 the number of diapers, and so on.

Similar Yes/No decisions arise in business when you must incur a fixed cost of some kind before engaging in an activity. This is known as a *fixed-cost problem.*

Let's return to the boat manufacturing problem but introduce a new wrinkle. Suppose it has just been determined that to produce any large sailboats, it is necessary to replace a piece of manufacturing equipment for $14,000. Thus, if any large sailboats are produced at all, $14,000 must be subtracted from the profit cell.

The obvious way to solve this problem is to:

1) create a cell in the model with the following formula:

    =IF(C2>0,14000,0), where C2 is the production quantity of Large Sailboats
    and

2) subtract this result from the profit formula in cell A6.

Obvious maybe, but as of the first edition of *Insight.xla*, the available optimization software was unable to correctly interpret IF statements in the context of optimization. As of the 2nd edition, new features in What's*Best!* and the Premium Solver solve this problem in different ways. What follows is a discussion of how to model fixed costs with each of the solvers as of this writing. But as this is in an area of evolving technology, further improvements are likely. The technique for the standard Excel Solver, using FIXCOST.xls, will work in all environments, although it is more complex to use. Those with a keen interest in optimization techniques are urged to study all three approaches discussed below.

Premium Solver

1) Create the IF statement and modified profit formula described above.

2) Set the solver type to **Standard Evolutionary**.

3) Constrain the changing cells to Integer (note that unlike traditional optimization methods, the Integer constraint actually speeds up the Evolutionary solver rather than slowing it down).

4) Select the **Linear Local Gradient** option.

The Evolutionary solver is a heuristic algorithm, which you may recall from the discussion in Chapter 7, is analogous to walking versus riding a horse or driving a car. However, it has the advantage of being able to find improved solutions to almost *any* problem that can be expressed in the spreadsheet. The above problem was essentially a linear program with an added IF statement. Recalling the discussion of Chapter 7, in which linear problems are analogous to paved roads, the Linear Local Gradient option allows the algorithm to slip on a pair of roller blades when it comes to asphalt.

If you do not wish to explore the traditional approach for solving this problem, skip to exercise 8.1 below.

What'sBest!
1) Create the IF statement and modified profit formula described above and optimize as usual.

2) Make sure that **Linearization** is turned on under General Options

What'sBest! "linearizes" the model, automatically creating additional integer variables and constraints similar to those discussed in FIXCOST.xla below. Using the analogy of Chapter 7, this is an automobile which can pave its own road through jagged mountains. The result is that optimal results are achieved using high speed traditional optimization methods. For additional information consult What'sBest! Help on the Delta and Big M coefficients that control details of the linearization.

If you do not wish to explore the traditional approach for solving this problem, skip to exercise 8.1 below.

Standard Solver
Keep the settings the same as they were for creating BOATSOPT.xls.

FIXCOST.xls models an activity for which there is a fixed cost when the activity is undertaken and a variable cost per unit of activity thereafter as follows:

Total Cost = Fixed Cost + Variable Cost X Number of Units of Activity

The contents of FIXCOST.xls can be copied into any desired worksheet.

Exploring the Model
Retrieve FIXCOST.xls if you use the Excel Solver and FIXCOSTW.xls if you wish to investigate this model with What'sBest!

The model's key elements are described in the following list. The cell names given are for the FIXCOST file itself. Actual cell names depend on where the module is copied into other worksheets.

- *Fixed Cost:* G7. This is the fixed cost incurred if the activity is undertaken.

- *Variable Cost Per Unit:* G8. You can also input a variable or marginal cost associated with the activity.

■ *Maximum:* G9. This should contain an upper limit on the level of the activity. It is most effective to enter a number somewhat higher than the maximum level of activity you believe to be possible.

■ *Activity:* G10. This cell must be equal to the level of the activity on which the fixed cost is being imposed. It should contain the formula =CELL, where CELL is the adjustable cell containing the activity in the worksheet to which FIXCOST has been copied.

Program cells that force the fixed cost to be incurred are as follows:

■ *Yes/No Cell:* G14. This is a changing or adjustable cell. It must be forced to take on the values of 0 (No) or 1 (Yes).

■ Cell G15 calculates Max Activity * Yes/No, or =G9 * G14.

■ Cells E16 and G16 are set up to constrain Activity <= Max * Yes/No. Thus, if the Yes/No cell is 0, the activity must be 0. If the Yes/No cell =1 then the activity can be as great as Max.

Module output is as follows:

■ Cell G18 contains a formula for the total cost associated with the activity, that is,

$$\text{Fixed Cost * Yes/No + Variable Cost * Activity, or} = \text{G7 * G14 + G8 * G10.}$$

This cell must be subtracted from the formula in your profit cell to make sure the economic impact of the fixed cost is incorporated into the optimization.

Combining FIXCOST.xls with BOATSOPT.xls

We will now combine this module with BOATSOPT.xls (the optimized boat production model saved earlier) to model the $14,000 fixed cost for producing large sailboats. We will complete the following four procedures in this process: paste a copy of FIXCOST.xls into BOATSOPT.xls; link input cells in the copy of FIXCOST to cells in the BOATSOPT model; respecify the ABC's of optimization; and optimize the model.

If you want to save the fixed-cost version of this model, use a different file name, as we will use BOATSOPT.xls again further on.

TUTORIAL: COPYING THE FIXED-COST MODULE[2]

1 Retrieve FIXCOST.xls (FIXCOSTW.xls if you are using What's*Best!*).

2 Select the entire contents of cells A1:G20, and copy it to the clipboard with the **Edit Copy** command.

3 Retrieve BOATSOPT.xls, position the cursor in cell J1[2] and paste the contents of the clipboard.

[2]When used with What's*Best!*, it is more convenient to paste FIXCOSTW.xls into its own sheet within the workbook.

TUTORIAL: SPECIFYING THE INPUTS

1   Enter the $14,000 fixed cost in cell P7. We are not concerned with variable cost in this model, so P8 should be left at 0.

2   We will assume that the production of large sailboats will not exceed 200 under any conditions. Enter 200 in cell P9.

3   Place the cursor in cell P10 and type "=". Move the cursor to C2, the number of large sailboats to be produced, then click Enter. Cell P10 should now contain =C2.

TUTORIAL: MODIFYING THE ABC'S[3]

Excel Solver

1. In the Solver dialog box, add the Yes/No cell to the changing cells as shown below.

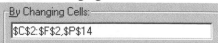

2. Constrain the Yes/No cell to integer.[3]

3. Constrain the Yes/No cell not to exceed 1.

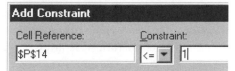

4. Constrain cell N16 not to exceed P16. This constraint ensures that there will be no activity if the Yes/No variable = 0.

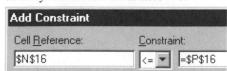

5. Edit the total profit in cell A6 by subtracting the fixed cost. The formula should now read: =SUMPRODUCT (C2:F2, C3:F3) – P18

What's*Best!*

1. Select the Yes/No cell, P14 then invoke the **WB! Integer** command. Don't forget to put a name in the **Integer Names in Workbook** field.

2. Click **Binary** to specify that the Yes/No variable can only take on the values 0 or 1. Click **OK.**

3. Edit the total profit in cell A6 by subtracting the fixed cost. The formula should now read: =SUMPRODUCT (C2:F2, C3:F3) – P18.

---

[3]In Excel 97 and above, steps 2 and 3 can be replaced by specifying the Bin constraint type.

Optimize the Model. Re-optimize the model and you should find the following production and profit figures. Notice that it is no longer optimal to produce large sailboats.

	Large Sailboat	Motorboat	Small Sailboat	Sailboard
Production quantity	0	120	170	150
Profit per unit	$1,200	$1,050	$930	$750
Demand	160	130	170	150
Total Profit $396,600				

EXERCISE 8.1

Determining the Critical Fixed Cost

Suppose the fixed cost were not yet known. It would still be useful to know the fixed cost just below which, large sailboats would be produced, and just above which, they would not be produced.

Combining Optimization Models: An Object Oriented Approach

Traditionally, optimization models have been developed and described in terms of algebraic representations. This has often led to an *algebraic curtain* separating management from management science. In contrast, all the classes of optimization mo-dels presented so far have been expressed in terms of small fully functioning spreadsheet models that I refer to as the *developmental necessities of applications,* or DNA for short. They can be expanded and modified to fit a wide array of small, real-world situations.

A practical way to create complex models is to combine and modify the DNA of simpler models (dare I call this recombinant DNA?).

In the last chapter, we saw that the Excel Solver allowed a more elegant formulation of the network model because it could interpret the DSUM formula. When it comes to the technique of combining models, What's*Best!* is more convenient for two reasons:

■ All variables and constraints are part of the model itself instead of being defined in a dialog box. Thus, when two or more models are combined it is not necessary to respecify them.

■ Models can be built across different worksheets within the same workbook. This keeps the combined model from getting difficult to manage.

We now present two situations in which it makes sense to combine models.

Multi-period Models

With the exception of the scheduling model, all optimization examples addressed so far have modeled a single period in time. Most important management decisions, however, must consider the effect of actions in one time period on future periods. Models of this type are known as multi-period models, and often have their basis in simple one-period models. We will describe how the boat production model introduced earlier can be replicated to reflect two time periods.

TUTORIAL: BUILDING A TWO-PERIOD MODEL

If you completed the boat production tutorial, then the results were saved as BOATSOPT.xls. This contains a single time period of production, say the first half of the year. We will now split this one time period into a distinct first and second quarter. This version of BOATSOPT will reflect two refinements:

▪ The total demand for the various boats is the same, but differs by quarter as shown in the following table.

Market Limit	Large Sailboat	Motorboat	Small Sailboat	Sailboard
Q1	80	65	85	45
Q2	80	65	85	105

▪ Additional sailcloth can be ordered in the first quarter at $50 per unit that will arrive in time for second quarter production.

Create two quarters by following the these steps:

1 Retrieve BOATSOPT.xls.

2 Copy A1:I14 to the clipboard with the **Edit Copy** command.

3 With the cursor in cell A16, paste the clipboard. The original copy of the model represents the first quarter. This second copy represents the second quarter. *Note:* If you are using What's*Best!* you will get a more manageable model if you paste the second model into cell A1 of a new worksheet. Now each worksheet represents a different time period. You will, of course need to modify some of the following cell references.

4 Change labels in cells A5 and A20 to Q1 Profit and Q2 Profit respectively. Make the necessary changes to each quarter by following these steps:

5 Change market demands in rows 4 and 19 to reflect the Q1 and Q2 figures in the previous table.

6 Inspect the formula for the total usage of sailcloth in the second quarter, cell G25. Notice that because of the absolute ($) cell addressing, it still refers to first quarter production (C2:F2). Change this formula to =SUMPRODUCT (C$17:F$17,C25:F25) to reference second quarter production. If you are using What's*Best!* and build your model across two worksheets you will not have this problem.

7 Copy cell G25 to G26:G29 to complete usage formulas for the other raw materials.

8 The raw materials on hand in the second quarter must equal those originally on hand in the first quarter minus those used in the first quarter. Change the amount On Hand in I25 to =I10–G10. If you have built your model across two worksheets, then the On Hand formula in cell I10 on the second sheet is =Sheet1!I10–Sheet1!G10. You do not need to type "Sheet1! Etc.". Simply type "=" into the cell to start the formula, then tab to sheet 1 and click on cell I10, then "-" and so on to complete the formula.

9 Copy the formula just created down for the remaining raw materials. Now, model the sailcloth purchase by following these steps:

10 Place a 0 in cell J10 to represent the amount of sailcloth to purchase in the first quarter.

11 Enter 50 in cell K10 for the cost per unit of sailcloth.

12 Edit the formula for the sailcloth On Hand in the second quarter to add in the first quarter purchase of sailcloth (J10). And finally, create a new total profit formula by following these steps:

13 In cell B1, enter total profit equal to first quarter profit plus second quarter profit minus the cost of the first quarter sailcloth purchase. The formula should be = A6+A21–J10*K10 for the single sheet model. For the two-sheet model, this formula will be =A6+Sheet2!A6 –J10*K10.

14 Specify B1 as the objective to maximize.

Next we will specify variables and constraints then optimize the model.

SPECIFYING VARIABLES AND CONSTRAINTS

Excel Solver

15. In the Solver dialog box, add the second quarter production and Sailcloth purchase to the changing cells as shown below.

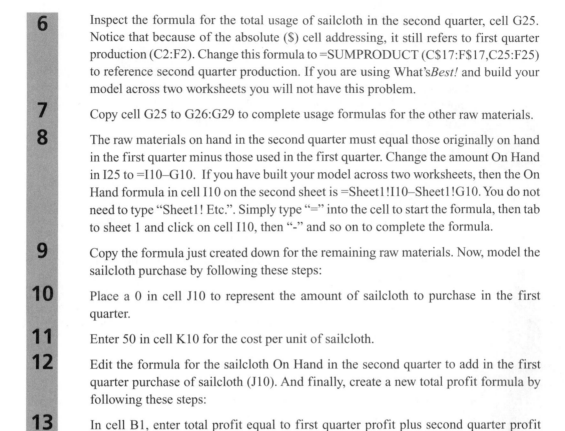

By Changing Cells:

$C$2:$F$2,$C$17:$F$17,$J$10

What's*Best!*

15. Select J10, the quantity of sailcloth to purchase in first quarter, then invoke the **WB! Adjustable** command.

Excel Solver (continued)

16. Add nonnegativity constraints for both the second quarter production (C17:F17) and sailcloth purchase (J10).

17. Constrain the second quarter usage not to exceed the amount on hand.

What's Best! (continued)

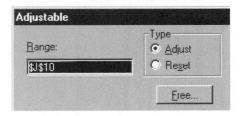

16. All other adjustable cells and constraints were preserved when the second copy of the model was pasted into place.

Optimize. When you optimize, you should get a total profit of $409,850, with a purchase of five units of sailcloth. But if you look at the second quarter production you will see 11.25 large sailboats. Round this down to 11, and you will have a profit of $409,550. Is this the optimal integer solution?

EXERCISE
8.2   INTEGER PRODUCTION AMOUNTS

Specify that both first and second quarter production take on integer values and re-optimize.

EXERCISE
8.3   ADDITIONAL MOTORS

Suppose you could purchase additional motors for $500 in the first quarter for second quarter delivery. What would the profit be?

Two-Period Supply Chain Model

This problem is a generalization of the transportation problem modeled in TRANS.xls. Instead of two steel mills supplying three plants, we now have three warehouses supplying four customers. More important, you must make decisions in two time periods. In period 1, we must decide how much to stock at each warehouse. In period 2, we must decide how much to ship from each warehouse to each customer. This problem's schematic is shown in the following figure.

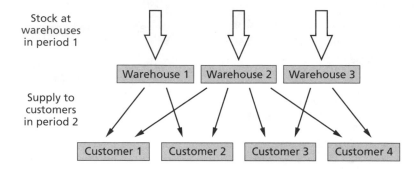

For each unit stocked at a warehouse in period one, there is an inventory cost shown in the following table.

	Warehouse 1	**Warehouse 2**	**Warehouse 3**
Inventory Cost per Unit	$1.00	$1.25	$1.00

The unit shipping cost from the warehouse to the customers is shown in the following table:

	Shipping Cost/Unit		
	Warehouse 1	**Warehouse 2**	**Warehouse 3**
Customer 1	$2.00	$2.50	
Customer 2	$1.00	$1.50	
Customer 3		$1.50	$1.00
Customer 4		$2.00	$1.50

The objective is to find stocking levels in period 1 and shipping routes in period 2 that minimize total cost (inventory plus shipping) while meeting customer demand, and without shipping more from any warehouse in period two than was stocked in period one.

Exploring the Model. Retrieve SUPPLY.xls for the Excel Solver or SUPPLYW.xls for What's*Best!*.

SUPPLYW.xls takes advantage of the fact that What's*Best!* can optimize across worksheets. It has one sheet for each time period. SUPPLY.xls, formatted for the Excel Solver, is similar in structure, but stored on a single sheet. SUPPLYW.xls is described here. The model's key elements are the following:

Period 1

■ The amount stocked at each warehouse in period 1 appears in the range B4:D4.

■ The inventory costs per unit are stored in B5:D5.

■ The total inventory cost in cell B9 is calculated as SUMPRODUCT(B4:D4,B5:D5).

■ The total shipping cost from period 2 in cell D9 is 'Period 2'!F17.

■ The total cost (inventory plus shipping) appears in cell C11.

Period 2

■ The amount shipped from each warehouse to each customer is stored in the range B6:D9. *Note:* Not all customers can be supplied from any given warehouse, blank cells denote nonexistent routes.

■ The shipping costs per unit appear in the range B19:D22.

■ The total shipping cost in cell F17 is the SUMPRODUCT (B6:D9,B19:D22).

■ The total shipments by warehouse are calculated in cells B11:D11.

■ The stocks available at each warehouse from period 1 appear in cells B13:D13.

■ The total shipments to each customer are stored in cells F6:F9.

The cell row references will be different on SUPPLY.xls (the Solver version).

The ABC's of the Supply Chain Model.

A. *The adjustable cells*

   1. B4:D4 in period 1 represent the amount stocked at each warehouse.

   2. B6:D9 in period 2 are the quantities shipped between warehouses and customers.

B. *The best solution* is that which minimizes total cost (inventory plus shipping), in cell C11 of period 1.

C. *The constraints* are the following:

   1. The total shipped to each customer is at least as great as the demand.

   2. The total shipped from each warehouse in period 2 does not exceed that stocked in period 1.

   3. The adjustable cells are constrained to be greater than or equal to zero.

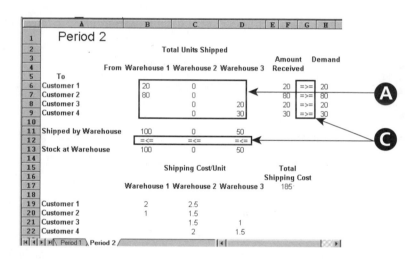

Vertically Integrated Models

We saw in the two-period boat manufacturing example how worksheet BOATSOPT.xls can be recombined with itself to create a multiperiod model. In the next exercise, you will combine BOATSOPT.xls and TRANS.xls to create a vertically integrated model that addresses both profit from manufacturing and the cost of transporting resources.

EXERCISE
8.4   Combining a Production and Transportation Model

Suppose the boat manufacturer has plants in three countries, each producing the same line of boats. The unit profit and demand vary by country as shown in the following table.

Country		Large Sailboat	Motorboat	Small Sailboat	Sailboard
A	Profit/unit	$1,200	$1,050	$930	$750
	Demand	160	130	170	150
B	Profit/unit	$1,100	$1,000	$900	$500
	Demand	120	120	180	160
C	Profit/unit	$1,400	$1,000	$950	$800
	Demand	50	80	180	140

The corporation orders all its aluminum from two mills. The combination of shipping cost and tariffs between the two mills and three countries is shown in the following table with the mills' capacities.

		Shipping Cost and Profits From:	
		Mill 1	Mill 2
To:	A	$100	$75
	B	$90	$80
	C	$70	$50
Capacity by Mill		1,000	1,500

Each plant's starting inventories are shown in the following table.

	A	B	C
Sailcloth	700	720	800
Glass Fiber	1,380	1,400	1,200
Epoxy Resin	1,280	1,300	1,100
Engines	120	130	90

Model this situation by combining TRANS.xls with three copies of BOATSOPT.xls in the same worksheet.

Hints:

■ Your objective should be to maximize the sum of the profit from the three plants minus the shipping cost.

■ If you build the model in a single worksheet for the Excel Solver, remove the absolute ($)cell references from the usage formulas before copying BOATSOPT.xls. If you arc using What'sBest!, keep the transportation model and each of the production models on its own sheet.

- You no longer need constraints requiring that a given amount be shipped to each plant. The model will decide how much to ship to maximize profit.

A possible single sheet layout is shown in the following figure where Excel's auditing tools have been used to show how the models have been tied together.

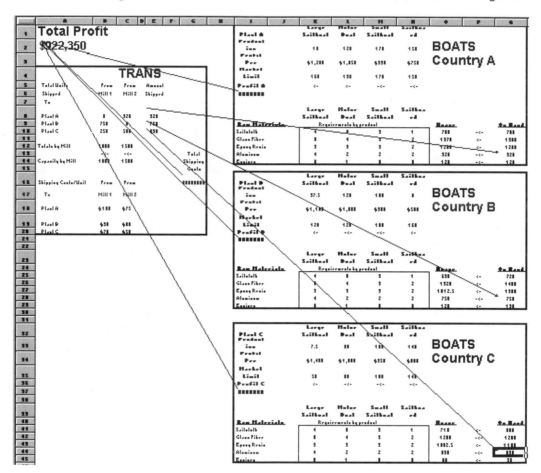

Optimization Under Uncertainty

This next example revisits the two-period supply chain model. This time, however, the demand in period 2 is not known with certainty. A linear program that incorporates uncertainty, such as this one does, is known as a ***stochastic linear program.*** This model was jointly developed with Gerd Infanger. For a thorough explanation of stochastic linear programming, see Infanger (1994).

Retrieve SUPPLYU.xls for the Excel Solver or SUPPLYUW.xls for What's*Best!*. Recall that in this model we are uncertain about the quantity of demand. Specifically, the marketing department is fairly certain about overall demand, but does not know whether it will be heavier among West Coast customers (1 and 2) or East Coast customers (3 and 4).

The two contingencies are referred to as scenario 1 and scenario 2 as outlined in the following table.

	Demand by Scenario		
	Scenario 1	Scenario 2	Average
Customer 1	10	30	20
Customer 2	70	90	80
Customer 3	30	10	20
Customer 4	40	20	30

The average demand is simply that used in the previous (deterministic) version of the supply chain problem. As discussed in the chapters on simulation, it is a common, but usually erroneous, practice to use averages of uncertain numbers in place of probability distributions.

Here we have approximated the complete distribution of demand with only two scenarios. This is quite simplistic, but we can conceptually extend this approach to much larger numbers of scenarios. In the defense of simplicity, however, don't forget that Paul Revere only needed two scenarios (one if by land or two if by sea) to adequately prepare the colonial forces for the British offensive.

In general, the scenarios used in stochastic linear programming can simply be states of the world that management believes are likely. Scenarios can also be generated by Monte Carlo simulation or other automated means.

SUPPLYU.xls differs from SUPPLY.xls in the following respects:

- In period 1, we must now decide how much to stock at each warehouse without knowing what the customer demands will be in period 2.

- In period 2, we will now make different shipping decisions depending on which scenario occurred.

- We must allow for the fact that, given certain stocking decisions in period 1, it might not be possible to satisfy customer demand under both scenarios. Therefore, we will introduce cells to measure lost sales if supply falls short of demand.

- We will also introduce formulas that calculate the average shipping costs and lost sales across both scenarios.

We now have conflicting objectives of minimizing average cost and average lost sales. Our approach will be to explore the trade-offs between these two, by minimizing one while constraining the other.

Exploring the Model. SUPPLYUW.xls again takes advantage of multiple worksheets. It has one sheet for time period 1 and a separate sheet for each of the two scenarios of period 2. SUPPLYU.xls, formatted for the Excel Solver is similar in structure, but is stored on a single sheet. SUPPLYUW.xls is described below. Key differences from the deterministic supply model are as follows:

Period 1

- The total shipping cost from period 2 in cell D9 has been replaced by the average shipping cost over both scenarios: ('Period 2 – Scenario 1'!F17+'Period 2 – Scenario 2'!F17)/2.

- The average lost sales over both scenarios appears in D13, as

  ('Period 2 – Scenario 1'!E13 + 'Period 2 – Scenario 2'!E13) / 2.

Period 2

- Period 2 is now represented by two work sheets, one for each scenario.

- Cells E6:E9 have been added to track lost sales for each customer under each scenario.

- Total lost sales for the scenario appear in E13.

- In the event that a customer's entire demand is not met by the warehouses, the remainder of the order will be lost to competitors. Thus the totals received by each customer (F6:F9) are now expressed as the sum of those delivered from the warehouses plus lost sales. In the case of customer 1, for example, this is SUM(B6:E6).

- The only difference between the two scenarios in this example is the customer demand in cells H6:H9. However, it would have been possible for any factor—such as shipping costs, or even whether or not a particular shipping route was open—to vary across scenarios.

Changes to the ABC's.
A. ***The adjustable cells***

  The lost sales E6:E9 must be made adjustable so they will automatically take up the slack left by unfulfilled demand.

B. and C.

  There are two potential objectives for this model: the minimization of costs or lost sales. Load the model and optimize it to minimize total average cost. The good news is that you should get a cost of zero, the bad news is that you have simultaneously lost all your sales. Next try minimizing average lost sales. This time the good news is that there are no lost sales, but the bad news is that costs are quite high. As you can see, there is a trade-off between average cost and average lost sales. Either of these can be chosen as an objective with the other limited by a constraint.

EXERCISE
8.5

GENERATING A TRADE-OFF CURVE

How do we deal with these conflicting objectives? Cost, of course, is measured in money. Lost sales are measured not only in money, but also good will on which it is difficult to place monetary value. In such situations, it is useful to perform repeated optimizations on one of the two objectives while increasingly constraining the other. This creates a trade-off curve between the two that can assist management in making a final decision. Proceed as follows:

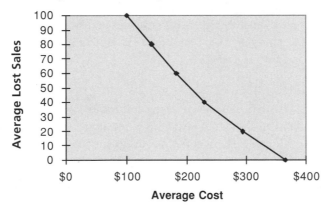

a.   Constrain average lost sales to be <= 100 and then minimize average cost. Copy the resulting values of cost and lost sales into blank cells at the bottom of the worksheet using **Paste Special Values.**

b.   Repeat this experiment, tightening the constraint on lost sales to 80, 60, 40, 20 and finally 0, copying the results below those of part a.

c.   Move the column of lost sales results just to the left of the cost results, then create a scatterplot of the data. Use the second scatterplot format, which connects the points with a line, to display the trade-off curve between lost sales and cost.

d.   What expected cost and lost sales would have resulted from using the stocking levels specified by the deterministic model?

Nonlinear Optimization

Financial Portfolio Optimization

In the 1950s, Harry Markowitz pointed out that there are generally trade-offs between the expected return and the risk (often measured in variance) of an investment portfolio. He went on to develop a method to determine the least risky portfolio that met a required rate of return.[5]

By *investment instrument,* we mean a single stock or other investment with known statistical behavior. By *investment portfolio,* we mean a mix of investment instruments. We will start our discussion with a portfolio containing only two instruments and then describe a worksheet model with three instruments.

An investment's *expected return* is the percentage return you would expect on average from that investment. For example, an expected 10% return would imply an average return of $1.10 for each dollar invested. The expected returns of our two hypothetical instruments will be denoted by r_1 and r_2.

Let x_i denote the percentage of the portfolio in instrument i. Because these are percentages, the sum of x_1 and x_2 must total 100%, that is, $x_1 + x_2 = 1$. The expected return of the portfolio as a whole is

$$E_p = x_1 r_1 + x_2 r_2$$

The contours of E_p are shown in the following figure for the three possible relationships between r_1 and r_2. A contour is a line along which the expected return is constant. In this figure, the heavier the line, the greater the expected value. That is, all combinations of x_1 and x_2 lying on a thin line yield the same low expected return, and all those combinations lying on a thicker line yield the same higher expected return.

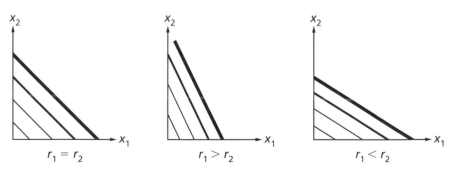

An investment's *risk* is often measured by its variance. Variance turns out to be a nonlinear function of the elements in the portfolio, hence the need for nonlinear optimization.

---

[5] This discussion assumes some familiarity with statistical dependence, for which you might want to review Chapter 3.

The variance of the two instruments under discussion are denoted by σ^2_1 and σ^2_2 respectively. The covariance of the two returns, a measure of the degree to which one return goes up or down when the other goes up or down, is denoted by σ_{12}, and can be found using the COVAR function in Excel. See Chapter 3 for more information on covariance.

The variance or risk of the portfolio as a whole can be shown to be

$$\sigma^2_p = x^2_1\sigma^2_1 + x^2_2\sigma^2_2 + 2x_1x_2\sigma_{12}$$

The risk contours as measured by σ^2_p are shown in the following figure under several conditions. Because this is a nonlinear function, the contours are curves rather than straight lines. The heavier the line, the greater the risk. All combinations of x_1 and x_2 lying on a thin line result in the same low risk, and all those combinations lying on a thicker line result in a higher risk.

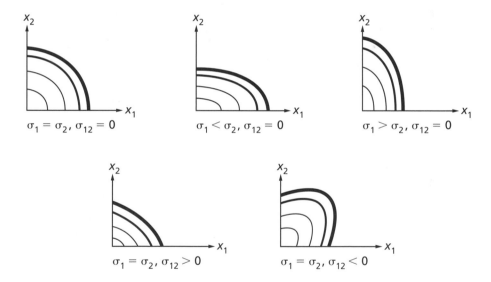

Consider a case in which $r_1 < r_2$, and σ_1, σ_2, $\sigma_{12} = 0$. The following figure superimposes both the expected return contours (black straight lines) and risk contours (shaded curved lines). Because $x_1 + x_2 = 1$, our choices of portfolio are limited to the thick textured line.

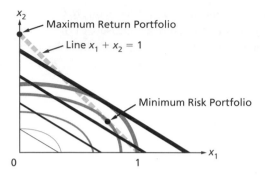

The portfolios yielding maximum return and minimum risk are marked. Any point on the line between these two portfolios will yield intermediate values of return and risk, which could reasonably be favored by people with different preferences for risk. Note that any portfolio to the southeast (that is down and to the right) of the minimum risk portfolio offers **decreased** return at **increased** risk and is therefore not sensible regardless of one's risk preference. For an arbitrary number of instruments, the variance of the portfolio is $\sigma^2_p = x \cdot Q \cdot x^T$, where Q is the covariance matrix, x is the vector of investment percentages, and x^T is x transpose.[6]

Exploring the Model. Retrieve MARKWTZ.xls for the Excel Solver or MARKWTZW.xls for What's*Best!*.

The model's key elements are the following:

- Cells A10:C10 contain *x,* the vector of percentages of the three investment instruments to be included in the portfolio.

- Cells A13:C13 contain *r,* the vector of expected returns of reach instrument.

- The covariance matrix **Q** in cells A16:C18 is defined as follows:

$$Q = \begin{matrix} \sigma^2_1 & \sigma_{12} & \sigma_{13} \\ \sigma_{21} & \sigma^2_2 & \sigma_{23} \\ \sigma_{31} & \sigma_{32} & \sigma^2_3 \end{matrix}$$

- Cells E16:G16 contain **x.Q.**
  Excel Solver: The calculation uses the MMULT array formula.
  What's*Best!*: The calculation uses addition and multiplication.

- Cells E5 and G5 contain the actual expected return and required expected return of the portfolio.

- Finally, cell E7 contains the risk of the portfolio as measured by the variance, **x.Q.x.**

---

[6]You can run the model without understanding what this means. See Luenberger (1997) for a further explanation.

The ABC's of the Portfolio Model.

A. ***The adjustable cells,*** A10:C10, are the percentages of each instrument in the portfolio.

B. ***The best solution*** is that which minimizes the risk of the portfolio, cell E7.

C. ***The constraints*** are as follows:

  1. Because the adjustable cells represent percentages, their sum must equal 1.

  2. The expected return is required to be at least a specified minimum.

  3. The adjustable cells are constrained to be greater than or equal to zero.

Additional constraints can be added to limit the percentage of the portfolio devoted to any particular instrument or class of instruments.

The Efficient Frontier: Parameterized Optimization

Every possible investment opportunity, including individual instruments as well as portfolios, has both an expected return and a risk. In theory, we could plot all investments relative to these two measures. Suppose that each plotted investment opportunity were the head of a nail. Imagine stretching a piece of string across the nail heads as shown in the following figure. Let x be any investment opportunity that touches the string.

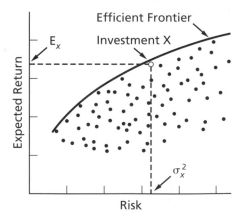

Its expected return and variance are labeled E_x and σ^2_x. It should be apparent from the figure that no other investment with expected return greater than or equal to E_x has risk lower than σ^2_x and that no other investment with variance less than or equal to σ^2_x has an expected return higher than E_x.

Thus, an investment such as x is said to be efficient, and the line formed by the string is known as the ***efficient frontier***. Depending on an investor's willingness to trade higher risk for a higher expected return, an investment at any point on the efficient frontier might be reasonable, whereas an investment away from the frontier is generally not reasonable. An efficient investment can be found at any point on the frontier by combining other investments.

An optimal solution of the portfolio model yields one point on the efficient frontier. By repeatedly solving the model while incrementally changing the constraint on expected return, the frontier can be plotted out. This is known as parametric or parameterized optimization.

EXERCISE
8.6   PARAMETERIZED PORTFOLIO OPTIMIZATION

Repeatedly optimize the portfolio model for required returns of 10%, 12%, 14%, 16%, 18%, and 20%. After each optimization, copy the expected return and variance to a blank range in the worksheet (*Hint:* Use **Edit Paste Special Values**). Then graph all five values with an XY plot to display the efficient frontier.

EXERCISE
8.7   VISUAL BASIC MACRO FOR PARAMETERIZED PORTFOLIO OPTIMIZATION

Write a Visual Basic macro to perform the parameterized optimization and graphing.

Curve Fitting

A common nonlinear problem involves fitting a curve to data. As an example, consider the time series extrapolation technique of Exponential Smoothing discussed in Chapter 5, "Forecasting."

Exponential Smoothing involves adjusting one or more parameters in a forecasting model to minimize the mean squared error between the model and the actual data. Exercise 5.5 describes how to apply nonlinear optimization to the exponential smoothing models to minimize mean squared error. Use the built-in solver in Excel to change alpha and beta to minimize the MSE. *Note:* Alpha and beta must be constrained to be between 0 and 1.

Combinatorial Optimization

A classic combinatorial problem is the Traveling Salesman Problem, which involves visiting a set of cities and returning home, in the minimal distance. Suppose, for example that a tourist agency in Anchorage is planning a promotional tour to publicize its Alaskan vacations. To get broad coverage, it has decided to send its representatives to Atlanta, Chicago, Denver, Houston, Los Angeles, New York and San Francisco before returning home. How should the cities be sequenced to minimize the total air travel? Clearly visiting the cities in alphabetical order is inefficient as shown in the illustration.

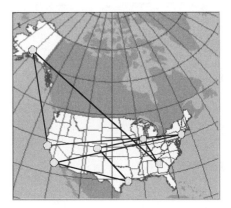

In analyzing this problem, the first question to ask is how many distinct trip sequences there are for this 8 city Traveling Salesman Problem (note the home city counts toward the 8). This is just the number of different orderings (permutations) of the 7 cities excluding the home city. Starting from Anchorage there are 7 possible choices for the first city to visit. For each of these 7 choices, there are 6 choices for the 2nd city to visit, 5 for the 3rd, and so on. By the time we have selected the 6th city to visit, there is only one remaining choice for the 7th, where upon we must return home. Thus the number of possible sequences is:

$$7 * 6 * 5 * 4 * 3 * 2 * 1 = 5,040$$

This is known mathematically as 7 factorial and is written as 7! or =Fact(7) in Excel. However, these 5040 sequences are not all distinct because they include both the clockwise and counter clockwise versions of each trip. So in actuality there are only 7!/2 = 2520 distinct sequences. It would not be difficult to program a computer to simply search all of these sequences for the shortest trip. However, even though there are just a finite number of things to evaluate, N factorial (N!) grows incredibly fast with N. Imagine a computer that could evaluate the total distance of 1 billion sequences per second (that's faster than the computers as of this writing). The table below shows the time it would take for various values of N, to evaluate all N!/2 sequences.

Complete Evaluation Times for N-City Traveling Salesman Problem

N	N!	Complete Evaluation	Time Units	
1	1	Less than 1	Second	
2	2	Less than 1	Second	
3	6	Less than 1	Second	
4	24	Less than 1	Second	
5	120	Less than 1	Second	
6	720	Less than 1	Second	
7	5040	Less than 1	Second	
8	40320	Less than 1	Second	
9	362880	Less than 1	Second	
10	3628800	Less than 1	Second	
11	39916800	Less than 1	Second	
12	479001600	Less than 1	Second	
13	6227020800	3	Seconds	
14	87178291200	44	Seconds	
15	1307674368000	11	Minutes	
16	20922789888000	3	Hours	
17	355687428096000	2	Days	
18	6402373705728000	1.25	Months	
19	121645100408832000	2	Years	
20	2432902008176640000	4	Decades	
21	51090942171709400000	8	Centuries	
22	1124000727777610000000	18	Millennia	
23	25852016738885000000000	410	Millennia	
24	620448401733239000000000	9.8	Million Years	
25	15511210043331000000000000	1	Estimated Time Since Origin of Dinosaurs	
26	403291461126606000000000000	1.4	Estimated Time Since Origin of Earth	
27	10888869450418400000000000000	17	Estimated Time Since Origin of Universe	

Even those readers who believe in repeated reincarnation until the end of time would be ill-advised to wait for the complete evaluation of a 27 city problem. But it is not just the astronomical number of potential solutions that make the Traveling Salesman Problem notorious. Certain linear programming problems also have vast numbers of potential solutions. But whereas LP problems can be solved extremely quickly by the simplex algorithm, there is no known algorithm for solving the Traveling Salesman Problem whose runtime doesn't grow roughly like the numbers in the table above. This doesn't mean we can't find "good" solutions to large problems. But it does mean that we can't guarantee to find the absolute shortest route, or even if we did happen to find the shortest one by luck, there would be no way to know for sure that we had found it.

This problem requires the Evolutionary algorithm of the Premium Solver.

Exploring the Model: Retrieve TSP.xls

This model makes extensive use of VLOOKUP and INDEX formulas which are powerful in their own right. The key elements are:

- Cells C4:C11 (range name **Sequence**) contain the current sequence in which the cities will be visited. Note that C12 = C4 to force the trip to end where it started. Cell B4 contains the length of the current sequence. Note the VLOOKUP formulas in cells D4:D12 that place the name of the appropriate city next to its number in column C.

- Cells F3:R11 contain the data for the problem. This includes the numbers and names of the cities and their map coordinates in cells F4:I11 (range name **Coordinates**) and the matrix of inter-city distances in cells K4:R11 (range name **Matrix**).

- Cell N16:O24 contain VLOOKUP formulas resulting in the sequence of xy data points that appear in the graph. Cells N37:O40 contain four xy points plotted without lines or markers on the graph to control scaling of the X and Y axes.

- Cells P17:P24 contain INDEX formulas calculating the intercity distances between the pairs of adjacent cities in the current sequence.

The ABC's of the Traveling Salesman Problem.

A. **The _a_djustable cells,** C4:C11, the sequence of the cities.

B. **The _b_est solution** is that which minimizes the total distance in cell B4.

C. **The only _c_onstraint** is that no city is left out of the sequence. This is specified in the Evolutionary solver with the "alldifferent" constraint which keeps any of the cities from being repeated, and ensures that the adjustable cells remain a permutation of the original numbers.

COMMON ERRORS IN OPTIMIZATION MODELS

Two common problem areas in formulating linear programming models involve nonlinear formulas and improper constraints.

Linear and Nonlinear Formulas

The great problem-solving power of linear programming, as the name suggests, is based on linear formulas. As discussed earlier, the Excel Solver defaults to nonlinear optimization. If you know that your model is linear, you should select Assume Linear Model from the Options dialog box to take advantage of the LP algorithm. If the model turns out to be nonlinear, you will get an error message. What's*Best!* detects whether or not the model is linear, then automatically applies the appropriate algorithm. The What's*Best!* error screen will optionally display a warning for nonlinear formulas in case they are not intentional.

What Are Linear Formulas?

In their simplest form, linear formulas are "straight line" relationships. For example, suppose you are buying tomatoes at $1.50 per pound. The formula for your bill (B) for the amount of tomatoes purchased (T) is B = 1.5*T. This formula's graph is a straight line and shown in the following figure. Hence, the name "linear."

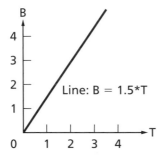

In this example, there is only one input value, the pounds of tomatoes purchased, but the concept of linearity also applies to more than one input variable. For instance, suppose that in addition to tomatoes we purchased potatoes at $0.75 per pound and apples at $1.25 per pound. The corresponding formula for the bill (B) is: B=1.5*T + .75*P + 1.25*A, where T, P, and A are the pounds purchased of tomatoes, potatoes, and apples, respectively. This formula is also said to be linear because it is the sum of three linear relationships. Because this formula has three input variables, however, it is not possible to visualize it as a straight line graph.

Rules for Writing Linear Formulas

Linear formulas can be built from simpler linear formulas according to the following rules:

- Adjustable cells can be multiplied or divided by numbers to form linear formulas.

- Two or more linear formulas can be joined together by **+**, **-** , or **SUM** to form a new linear formula.

- Linear formulas can be joined to *any* formula that does **not** depend directly or indirectly on an adjustable cell, by +, -, *, /, or **SUM** to form a new linear formula.

- If A is a range of adjustable cells and B is a range of constant numbers, then =SUMPRODUCT (Range A, Range B) is a linear formula.

- DSUM, SUMIF, and some other formulas can be linear depending on which arguments are adjustable cells. These will be interpreted correctly by the Excel Solver but not necessarily by What's*Best!*.

Examples of Linear and Nonlinear Formulas

A few examples of both linear and nonlinear formulas are shown in the following table. Cells A1 through A3 are adjustable cells. Cells B1 through B3 are nonadjustable (fixed) cells.

Linear Formulas	Nonlinear Formulas
=A1*B1	=A1*A2
=A1/B1	=B1/A1
=A1*B1+A2*B2	=A1^2
=A1*SQRT(B1)	=SQRT(A1)
=SUM(A1:A3)	=LOG(A1)
=SUM(A1:A3)*SQRT(B1)	=EXP(A1)
=SUMPRODUCT(A1:A3, B1:B3)	

When in doubt about a formula, try optimizing. If it is nonlinear and the Solver Option is set to Assume Linear Model, you will get an error message. What's*Best!* will return a warning message unless warnings are turned off.

Improper Constraints

Too many constraints create **infeasible** solutions. Suppose you add a constraint that contradicts one or more of the existing constraints. In the BOATS problem, for example, if you add the requirement that the number of large sailboats to be produced must be greater than 200, you will get a message that the problem is infeasible. This is because the new constraint violates both the market limit and usage constraints.

In contrast, too few constraints create unbounded solutions. Suppose you forget to include usage or market constraints in the BOATS production planning problem. Then there is no limit on the production and profit can also be increased without limit by producing an infinite number of boats. In such cases, you will get an error message indicating that the problem is ***unbounded.*** This message may also indicate that you maximized the wrong cell or incorrectly maximized the objective cell, when in fact you really wanted to minimize it.

Local Maxima or Minima in Nonlinear Optimization

Unlike linear optimization, which nearly always gets an optimal solution if there is one, nonlinear optimization often gets stuck at local maxima or minima. It is therefore important to test your solution by making several runs, with different starting values of the adjustable or changing cells.

THE BASICS OF OPTIMIZATION THEORY

To discuss the theory behind optimization, we will examine a very simple model in some detail.

Optimizing a Simplified BOAT Problem

Consider a simplified version of the BOATS problem with only two possible products and three raw materials. This is stored in BOAT.xls as discussed in Chapter 1. Recall that the production was optimized in Chapter 1 using a data table to maximize profit without exceeding the usage of raw materials.

EXERCISE

8.8 OPTIMIZING BOAT.XLS

Optimize this model using the Excel Solver or What's*Best!*. The results should appear as shown in the following figure.

	A	B	C	D	E	F	G
1			Large Sailboat	Motor Boat			
2	Production Quantity		65	120			
3	Profit Per Unit		$1,200	$1,000			
4	Market Limit						
5	Total Profit						
6	$198,000						
7							
8			Large Sailboat	Motor Boat			
9	Raw Materials		Requirements by product		Usage		On Hand
10	Sailcloth		4	0	260	<=	400
11	Glass Fiber		8	4	1,000	=<=	1,000
12	Engines		0	1	120	=<=	120

The Algebraic Expression of the BOAT Model

Traditionally, linear optimization problems have been expressed algebraically. The BOAT model can be expressed as follows, where L and M denote the number of large sailboats and motor boats produced respectively. The defining elements in this representation are as follows:

- The objective coefficients

- The constraint coefficients

- The constraint limits

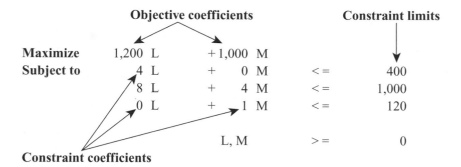

Tableau Representation

Remarkably, every linear optimization problem can be expressed in this same form. The only thing that varies from model to model are the number of variables, objective coefficients, constraint coefficients, and constraint limits.

Because of this, linear programming problems were traditionally expressed as the coefficients only in a representation known as a *tableau* as shown in the following table. Although it is possible to create a tableau for any linear problem, it is not an intuitive notation for use by managers. Today, spreadsheets and specialized optimization languages (AMPL, GAMS, LINGO) are most commonly used to express optimization problems.

Tableau for BOAT

1200	1,000	
4	0	400
8	4	1000
0	1	120

A Geometric View of Optimization: TABLEAU.xls

TABLEAU.xls provides a geometrical interpretation of the simplified production problem modeled by BOATS_2.xls.

■ FUNDAMENTALS 8-1

Tableau

Every linear problem can be expressed as a *tableau* that consists of the objective coefficients, constraint coefficients, and constraint limits.

■ FUNDAMENTALS 8-2

Feasible Region

The set of values that satisfy all constraints is known as the *feasible region.*

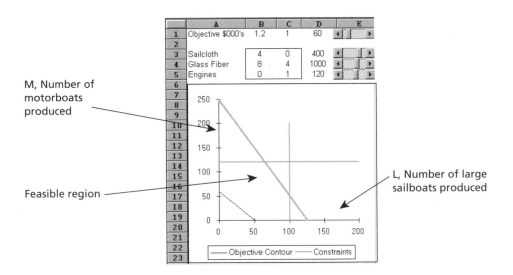

M, Number of motorboats produced

Feasible region

L, Number of large sailboats produced

The Constraint Contours and Feasible Region. The thick lines (in green in the worksheet) denote *constraint contours.* That is, each line represents a production combination along which one of the resources would be completely exhausted. Specifically,

- The vertical line at L=100 means that 100 large sailboats would consume all 400 units of resource 1, sailcloth.

- The diagonal line running from L=125 to M=250 indicates that all 1000 units of resource 2, glass fiber, would be consumed by production anywhere on the line.

- The horizontal line at M=120 means that 120 motorboats would consume all of resource 3, motors.

▪ FUNDAMENTALS 8-3

Contours

- A *contour* is a line in the plane over which a function takes on a constant value.

- For linear functions, the contours are straight.

- In a linear program with two variables, combinations of values that exactly meet constraints define contours.

▪ FUNDAMENTALS 8-4

Corner Solutions

If a linear problem has an optimal solution at all, there will always be one in a corner.

The Feasible Region. The region bounded by the axes and these solid lines represents the only feasible combinations of production and is known as the *feasible region.*

By moving the slide bars, you can see how the feasible region is affected by changes in the quantity of raw materials. If you make large changes to the numbers in the worksheet, you may need to adjust the scale factor in cell C26 to properly adjust the graph. Be sure to return numbers to their original values before proceeding. Compare the feasible region to the data table generated in the tutorial of Chapter 1.

The Objective Contour. The thin line on the graph (in blue in the worksheet) denotes the objective contour, that is, the combinations of large sailboats on the horizontal axis and motorboats on the vertical axis that result in the objective value displayed in $000's in cell D1. In the example shown, the line runs from 50 on the L axis to 60 on the M axis. This means that 50 units at $1,200 or 60 units at $1,000, or any linear combination in between will result in $60,000.

Corner Solutions. The optimal solutions to linear problems are at corners where constraint contours intersect.

Use the slide bar to increase the objective value to $120,000 and observe how the contour moves out while staying parallel with the original line. Now move it all the way to $300,000. The objective contour has moved outside of the feasible region. This objective cannot be achieved with the raw materials on hand.

How high can you raise the objective before you leave the feasible region? At $198,000, the objective just intersects the corner of the feasible region where the motor and glass fiber constraints intersect as shown in the following figure. It is not possible for any contour to take on higher value without leaving the feasible region, hence this corner is the optimal solution.

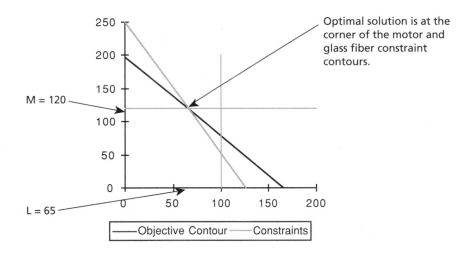

EXERCISE

8.9   CORNER SOLUTIONS FOR LARGE SAILBOATS

To test your understanding of corner solutions, answer the following questions by observing the graph in TABLEAU.xls. Start with the original coefficients in the worksheet, but with the objective set to $198,000.

a. Increase the profit per unit for large sailboats beyond $1,200.

b. What happens to the angle of the objective contour?

c. For what profit per unit does another corner also become optimal?

d. Approximately what value of profit can be obtained with this profit per unit for large sailboats?

e. How many optimal solutions are there now?

f.   Approximately what production figures does the new corner represent?

g.   How many optimal solutions are there if you increase the profit per unit of large sailboats a little further?

More Variables and Constraints

Variables Correspond to Dimensions. The number of decision variables (adjustable cells) corresponds to the dimension of the feasible region. In the BOAT model, there are two decision variables and, hence, a two-dimensional feasible region. If a third boat type were added to the model, the feasible region would be three dimensional and might look like the following figure.

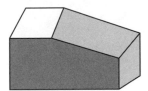

If there are more than three decision variables, then the feasible region cannot be visualized directly. But the concept is still useful.

Constraints Correspond to Boundary Lines. Each boundary line of the feasible region corresponds to a constraint as shown in the graph in TABLEAU.xls. If more linear constraints were added, the feasible region would be bounded by more straight lines, perhaps like the following figure.

Linear versus Nonlinear Problems

These geometrical concepts illuminate some of the important differences between linear and nonlinear optimization problems.

Linear Problems

For ***linear*** problems, the ***boundary*** lines of the feasible region and ***contours*** of the objective function are ***straight lines*** (or flat planes in three dimensions, or hyper planes in higher dimensions).

There are always ***solutions*** to linear problems in corners of the feasible region. This is a generalization of the fact that a ball-bearing in a tilted cardboard box rolls to the lowest corner. For certain angles of the box, there might be two corners and an edge or even a whole side of the box that is lowest.

The famous linear programming simplex algorithm developed by George Dantzig in 1947 in effect rolls a mathematical ball bearing from corner to corner of a high-dimensioned box.

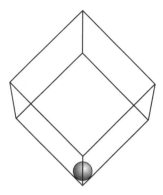

Nonlinear Problems

For *nonlinear* problems, some of the *boundary* lines of the feasible region or the *contours* of the objective function, or both, are curved lines (or curved planes in three dimensions, or curved hyper planes in higher dimensions).

The *solutions* can be anywhere in the feasible region. This is because nonlinear problems can take many forms, unlike linear problems that are always generalizations of a ball bearing acted on by gravity within a cardboard box. For example, a problem with a nonlinear objective formula and linear constraint formulas would be more like a ball-bearing in a box acted on by one or more magnets.

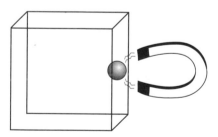

A problem with a linear objective formula but nonlinear constraints would be analogous to a smooth bowl in which the bearing slowly spirals to the bottom, or worse yet, like a rubber glove in which the bearing gets trapped in the thumb and never gets to the lowest point at all. The bowl represents a *convex* problem, whereas the glove is an example of a *nonconvex* problem.

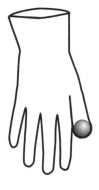
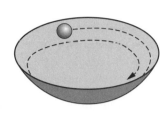

More on Dual Values

As we have seen, optimization can help you *maximize* profit or *minimize* cost given your *current* resource limitations and performance requirements. Dual values help you plan beyond the current environment, by indicating *rewards* or *penalties* associated with *changes* in your resource limitations and performance requirements.

Specific types of dual values for linear problems are *shadow prices* and *reduced costs.* The dual values for nonlinear problems are called *Lagrange multipliers.*

We can output the ranges over which shadow prices and reduced costs are valid. In general, it is not possible to determine the ranges over which Lagrange multipliers are valid.

Dual Value of a Constraint Cell—Shadow Price. Loosely stated, dual values let you assess the impact on your objective cell of tightening or relaxing a constraint in your model. For example, in the BOATS tutorial we found that the limit on sailcloth created a binding constraint. Additional sailcloth would increase profit by $300 per unit. That is, the shadow price of sailcloth was $300. The shadow price of a constraint that is not tight must always be 0 because loosening it further would have no effect.

■ FUNDAMENTALS 8-5

Dual Values

- A *dual value* is the reward associated with relaxing a constraint or, equivalently, the penalty associated with tightening a constraint.

- For linear problems, a dual value associated with the nonnegativity constraint of a variable is called a *reduced cost,* any other dual value is called a *shadow price.*

- For nonlinear problems, a dual value is called a *Lagrange multiplier.*

Dual Value of an Adjustable or Changing Cell—Reduced Cost. Dual values can be found for adjustable cells in the same manner as for constraint cells. Remember that adjustable cells are usually constrained to be greater than or equal to zero. Therefore, an adjustable cell forced to 0 during optimization is a tight constraint. Tightening this constraint further by one unit corresponds to constraining the adjustable cell to be at least +1. In other words, we engaged in one unit of the associated activity even though it was not optimal to do so. The penalty of this non- optimal activity is reflected in the dual value, which in this context is referred to as a *reduced cost.*

Dual Values for Models Containing Integer Variables. Dual values do not give dependable information with models containing integer variables. The Excel Solver will not display them at all if integer constraints are present.

EXERCISE
8.10   Reduced Cost on Large Sailboats

Before market limits were imposed on the BOATS problem, no large sailboats were produced. The reduced cost on large sailboats indicates the amount that the profit per unit needs to be increased before they could be profitably produced. Remove the market limit constraint from BOATSOPT and find all the reduced costs.

Reward/Penalty Interpretation of Dual Values

We are now ready to state more generally the interpretation of dual values. Dual values pertain to all adjustable cells and to all constraint cells in models that do *not* contain integer variables. There can be a non-zero dual value associated with each constraint that is tight—that is, met exactly—after optimization. Remember that adjustable cells are usually constrained to be greater than or equal to zero. In this case, any adjustable cell that equals zero after optimization is also considered to be a tight constraint.

The dual value can be interpreted either as a *reward* for relaxing a constraint or *penalty* for tightening a constraint.

Under the first interpretation, the dual value is the *amount* by which the objective cell would change if the constraint in question is relaxed by one unit. Examples include the increase in profit given one additional unit of a limited resource, or the decrease in cost given a unit reduction of a performance requirement.

Under the second interpretation, the dual value is the *negative amount* by which the objective cell would change if the constraint in question is tightened by one unit. Examples include the decrease in profit given one less unit of a limited resource, or the increase in cost given a unit increase in a performance requirement.

Valid Ranges for Dual Values

Going back to BOATSOPT.xls, recall that each additional unit of sailcloth contributed $300 to profit. How many additional units could be purchased before this number changed? This is known as the dual value's upper range or allowable increase.

Conversely, if sailcloth currently in stock were lost, how many units would it take before the penalty for lost cloth changed from $300 per unit. This is known as the dual value's lower range or allowable decrease.

With the Excel Solver, the ranges can be read from the sensitivity report. With What's*Best!,* range information can be requested from the Dual dialog box.

EXERCISE
8.11   DUAL VALUE RANGES

Find the upper and lower ranges for the dual values of BOATSOPT.

Conclusion

As we have seen, the possibilities for optimization are endless. However, with complex situations, there is a danger that the problem you are trying to solve might change before you finish the optimization model. Such models, although intellectually satisfying, fail George Dantzig's test that began this chapter.

END OF CHAPTER EXERCISES

8.12   OPERATION OF A HEALTHCARE FACILITY

A large health care facility has limited resources available per week, as shown in the table below.

Resource	Units /wk
ICU Beds	400
Routine Beds	620
Anesthesiology	890
Radiology	525
OR Rooms	680
Equipment	580

The facility is set up to perform six types of procedures, which make use of the resources in various amounts as shown below.

Procedure	1	2	3	4	5	6
		Resource Requirements				
ICU Beds	1	4	0	4	2	0
Routine Beds	1	4	1	4	3	4
Anesthesia	0	3	8	0	1	0
Radiology	2	0	1	2	1	5
OR Rooms	2	4	2	2	2	4
Equipment	4	5	3	0	1	0

The CFO of the organization is concerned with the revenue generated by the procedures:

Procedure	1	2	3	4	5	6
Revenue	$3,000	$4,500	$2,400	$2,600	$2,000	$3,000

The medical staff is more concerned with the healthcare benefits to the municipality, and has established its own ranking on a scale of 1 to 10 in this regard:

Procedure	1	2	3	4	5	6
HB Rank	4	3	5	3	10	7

a. The CFO wants to perform the mix of procedures that maximizes revenue. Find this mix. (You may round down any fractional answers).

b. The medical staff wants to maximize healthcare benefits. What mix of procedures accomplishes this?

c. If the organization picks solution a, the medical staff will be furious. If they pick solution b, the CFO will quit. However, this is not an "either or" situation. A set of optimal compromises may be found as follows.

   1. Maximum revenue.

   2. Constrain revenue at this maximum

3. Maximize healthcare benefits and record both the revenue and benefits using **paste special values**.

4. Lower the constraint on revenue and repeat step 3.

5. When you reach the point that further reductions in revenue do not increase benefits, quit and graph the optimal trade-off curve between revenue and benefits. The potential all or nothing fight between the financial and medical staff over solutions a or b has now been reduced to a tug of war along this trade-off curve.

8.13 **PLANT LOCATION**

A distributor of industrial chemicals with demand in six major cities is in the process of setting up several manufacturing plants. It has five potential locations to choose from. The final choice of plant locations will be based on three factors: the monthly operating costs and capacities, which vary from location to location, and also the shipping costs to the demand cities. This information is summarized in the tables below.

	Monthly Fixed Cost	Monthly Capacity in Tons
Location 1	$7,500	18
Location 2	$3,500	24
Location 3	$5,000	27
Location 4	$4,000	22
Location 5	$3,000	31

Shipping costs per ton between the proposed plant locations and demand cities

	Location 1	Location 2	Location 3	Location 4	Location 5	Monthly Demand:
City 1	1600	1500	2000	400	900	10
City 2	400	1900	2400	1400	1600	8
City 3	700	1000	1400	500	700	12
City 4	1600	100	500	1000	500	6
City 5	1200	500	900	700	300	8
City 6	2800	1200	800	2300	1800	11

Find the locations where the plants should be opened so as to minimize monthly operating costs while meeting customer demand.

8.14   OPTIMAL AIRLIFT OF SUPPLIES

The military must carry large supply containers to 6 destinations. The expected number of containers required at the destinations is shown below.

Destination	Expected Number Required by Destination					
	A	B	C	D	E	F
Exp. Number	10	10	4	3	15	14

Missions

Small, medium and large aircraft are available to fly various missions covering the six destinations. The missions along with their costs in $000's are shown in the mission table below. The number of missions flown by a given aircraft type is limited by the total availability of that type. The figures under Destination Coverage are the numbers of containers that mission will deliver to the various destinations. For example mission 7 may be viewed schematically as follows.

Schematic of Mission 7

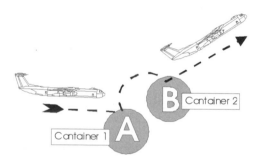

Mission Table

	Total Available		Destination Coverage					
Small Aircraft	20		A	B	C	D	E	F
	Mission	Cost						
	1	40	1					
	2	60		1				
	3	40			1			
	4	50				1		
	5	30					1	
	6	40						1

Thus a small aircraft can carry a single container to any destination, and 20 such aircraft are available during the time period in question.

	Total Available		Destination Coverage					
Medium Aircraft	15		A	B	C	D	E	F
	Mission	Cost						
	7	70	1	1				
	8	70		1	1			
	9	60			1	1		
	10	50				1	1	
	11	80					1	1
	12	50	2					
	13	60		2				
	14	50			2			
	15	60				2		
	16	50					2	
	17	50						2

A medium sized aircraft can either carry one container to two destinations or two containers to a single destination.

	Total Available		Destination Coverage					
Large Aircraft	4		A	B	C	D	E	F
	Mission	Cost						
	18	120	2					2
	19	100			2		2	
	20	90			2	2		
	21	110				2	2	
	22	130					2	2
	23	100	4					
	24	90			4			
	25	90				4		
	26	80					4	
	27	100						4

a. It is practical for large aircraft to carry two containers to two destinations or four containers to a single destination, but large aircraft cannot be landed at destination B. Also, they do not carry enough fuel to land at more than two destinations. *Note:* the 27 missions listed above do not represent every possible mission, but merely a representative sample.

b. Create a deterministic optimization model to minimize the cost of delivering the expected number of containers to each location using the current 27 missions. The data above are stored in AIRCRAFT.xls.

c. Reduce the cost still further by introducing new missions.

d. In many military situations, the actual number of containers required at a given location might be highly uncertain. Suppose that military strategists believe there are five equally likely requirement scenarios, shown below.

Scenario	Actual Requirement by Scenario					
	A	B	C	D	E	F
1	20	0	4	3	14	20
2	20	0	5	2	14	8
3	10	10	3	4	16	11
4	0	20	4	2	14	13
5	0	20	4	4	17	18

Create a stochastic optimization model which takes account of the uncertain requirement scenarios as outlined below.

Create a shortfall penalty cell for each destination under each scenario, analogous to the "lost sales" penalties in SUPPLYU.xls. For example, if the strategy called for sending 10 containers to destination A, the shortfall penalty at A would be 10 under scenarios 1 and 2, and 0 under the remaining three scenarios. This would result in an average penalty over all scenarios at destination A, of 20/5 = 4. The total average penalty would be found by taking into account all six locations.

Perform the following analysis with your model:

i. Find the set of missions that minimize cost and record the average shortfall.

ii. Find the set of missions that minimize average shortfall and record the cost.

iii. Calculate the trade off curve between the cost of the missions and the average penalty, as was done with SUPPLYU.xls.

e. Recall the inventory problem of chapter 3 in which parameterized simulation was used to find the stocking level that resulted in minimum average cost. It is possible to solve this problem as a stochastic LP as follows.

The stocking level becomes a variable cell.

Then for each row of the historical inventory levels create new formulas and variables as shown below (What's*Best!* format has been used for the constraints as it clearly indicates the cells involved).

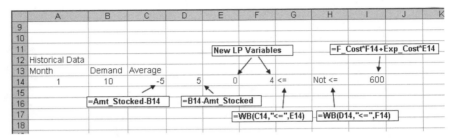

For each scenario, the formula in column C will be greater than zero only if the demand was less than the amount stocked. This will force the variable in column E to be greater than 0 by the same amount due to the constraint in column G. The formula in column D will only be positive if the demand was greater than the amount stocked, with a similar effect on the variable in column F due to the constraint in column H. Thus, for each demand scenario, either column E will display the excess inventory, or column F will display the shortfall. In either case, the formula in column I will calculate the cost for that scenario. Find the stocking level that minimizes average cost by minimizing the average of column I.

Appendix A ■■■■■■■■■■■■■■■■■■■

Queuing Equations: QUEUE.xla and Q_NET.xla

USER INPUTS

The following variables and formulas apply to both QUEUE.xla and Q_NET.xla. However, with Q_NET.xla, much of the structure is repeated for each station in the queuing network.

Maximum Run Time. The simulation will run until time equals the max run time.

Mean Interarrival Time and Mean Service Time. The simulation assumes exponential distributions. ***Note***: Mean interarrival time must be greater than mean service time or the queue length will eventually become infinite.

Initial State. This screen contains the values used to initialize the simulation, there are no formulas. To reach stability more quickly, you can enter any starting values in the current screen after initialization and before running. To specify permanent changes in the initial conditions, you can edit the initial screen.

FORMULAS

The following formulas appear in the *next state* worksheet of QUEUE.xls. Multiple columns of these formulas appear in Q_NET.xls. They are quite complex and need not be understood in detail to run simulations. However, if you want to modify the models as suggested in some of the exercises, you will need to understand at least some of these.

Queue Statistics

Time. Time is determined from the next event, a system arrival or a departure. The next event is generated by taking the minimum of the next arrival time and the next service time. These appear in the section labeled Next Event Times.

Time = MIN(SRVC_TIM_NXT,ARIVL_TIM_NXT)

Queue Length. The queue length increases by one when the server is busy and an arrival occurs. It decreases by one when there is a departure unless the length is already 0 (see Status Indicators below).

Queue Length = (Q_LENGTH + (BUSY*ARIVL_NXT)) –
((DEPRTR_NXT*Q_LENGTH)<>0)

Number Served. The total number served increases by one for a departure from the system (see Status Indicators below).

Number Served = SERVED + DEPRTR_NXT

Total Wait Time. The total wait time is the current total wait time plus the queue length multiplied by the time between the current and the next events.

Total Wait Time = TTL_WAIT_TM+Q_LENGTH*(TM_NXT-TM)

Average Wait Time. The average waiting time in the queue is the total waiting time divided by the number served.

Avg Wait Time = IF(OR(TM = 0,SERVED = 0),0, TTL_WAIT_TM / SERVED)

Average Queue Length. The average queue length is calculated by dividing the total wait time by time.

Avg Queue Length = TTL_WAIT_TM /TM_NXT

Average Through-Put. The average through-put equals the total number served divided by the time.

Avg Through-Put = SERVED_NXT/TM_NXT

Maximum Queue Length. The maximum queue length takes the maximum of the current maximum queue length and the queue length in the next state.

Max Queue Length = MAX(MAX_L,Q_LENGTH_NXT)

Status Indicators

The Status Indicators signify a true or false statement. A "1" indicates the statement is true, and a "0" indicates the statement is false.

Server Busy. This formula defines the status of the server in the next state. If there is an arrival in the next state, then the server *is busy* (−1). If there is no arrival in the next state, and if there is a departure and the queue length is 0, the server is *not busy* (=0). In any other case, the busy indicator in the next state is the same as that in the current state (=BUSY).

$$\text{Server Busy} = \text{IF(ARIVL\_NXT} = 1,1,\text{IF(AND(DEPRTR\_NXT} = 1,\text{Q\_LENGTH} = 0),0,\text{BUSY))}$$

Arrival. An arrival occurs if the next *arrival* time equals the next time. This is a Boolean formula that equals 0 or 1 depending on the truth value of the equality.

$$\text{Arrival} = \text{TM\_NXT=ARIVL\_TIM\_NXT}$$

Departure. A departure occurs only when the next service time equals the next time and the server is busy. This is a compound Boolean expression.

$$\text{Departure} = ((\text{TM\_NXT} = \text{SRVC\_TIM\_NXT}) * \text{BUSY}) <> 0$$

Next Event Times

The service and system arrival times determine when the next event will occur. These are drawn from an exponential distribution with mean interarrival time and mean service time set by the user.

The exponential random variable is generated by evaluating the inverse cumulative distribution function with a uniformly distributed random argument. Thus

$$-\text{M} * \text{LN(RAND())}$$

yields an exponentially distributed random variable with mean M (Bratley, Fox, and Schrage, 1987, or Law and Kelton, 1991). This expression appears in both the service time (M=SERVICE_MEAN) and arrival time (M=SYSARRVMEAN) formulas. It can be replaced by other random number generators if appropriate.

Service Time. Service time refers to the time at which the customer presently being served will depart the system, allowing the queue length to be reduced. If the server in the current state is not busy, the next service time is set to 10^8. Otherwise, if the current service time is 10^8 or there is a current departure, then the next service time is set to the current time plus an exponential random variable with mean =

SERVICE_MEAN. In all other cases, the next service time is replaced with the current service time.

Service Time = IF(BUSY = 0,10^8,

IF(OR(SRVC_TIME = 10^8,DEPRTR = 1),

TM + (–SERVICE_MEAN * LN(RAND())),SRVC_TIME))

System Arrival. The system arrival time refers to the time at which the next customer arrives. If the current arrival time is less than the current time or the queue length is 0, the next system arrival time is set to the current time plus an exponential random variable with mean = SYSARRVMEAN. In all other cases, the next system arrival time is replaced with the current system arrival time.

System Arrival = IF(OR(ARIVL_TIME <= TM,Q_LENGTH = 0),

TM + (–SYSARRVMEAN * LN(RAND())),ARIVL_TIME)

Traffic Flow Equations

Q_NET.xls has a column of these formulas for each station plus formulas to control the flow of traffic between stations. Following are summaries:

Transition Matrix. The probability of going to station *j* after leaving station *i* is found in the *ith* row and *jth* column. Station *0* denotes system arrival, the final station denotes system exit. You can input these probabilities directly as either numbers or formulas that depend on the current states of the various queues. *Note:* The rows of this matrix must always sum to 1.

From and To Calculations. Cells B13 and B14 on the next event worksheet contain formulas specifying the station the next event is coming *From* and going *To*. The *From* formula depends on cells in row 19, which indicate which station has triggered the current event. The *To* formula involves a lookup table based on the cumulative probability distribution across the rows of the transition matrix. This is stored on its own worksheet.

FIRE.xls

FIRE.xls and its macros can be modified to simulate a wide variety of simple situations. However, numerous commercial packages are available to perform discrete event simulation on a much larger scale. Some of these contain graphics depicting the current state of the simulation.

Appendix B ■■■■■■■■■■■■■■■■■■■

Two-Parameter Exponential Smoothing for Estimating Trends

One-parameter exponential smoothing does not accurately track time series with a trend. For time series with either a ***constant*** or ***slowly varying trend***, two-parameter exponential smoothing is appropriate.

The Formulas

One-parameter exponential smoothing uses a single parameter to smooth random fluctuations in a series that is assumed to have a constant or slowly changing mean. In two-parameter exponential smoothing, of which there are several kinds, a second parameter is added to smooth random fluctuations in the *trend* of a series that is assumed to be constant or slowly changing. The parameters are referred to as α (alpha) and β (beta). The approach used in XLForecast is modeled after Gardner (1985, 1992).

The two-parameter smoothing routine in XLForecast makes its initial estimate of the trend by performing linear regression on the data, then the smoothing proceeds to adapt the trend to fluctuations in the data. As with one-parameter smoothing, the data is divided into a warm-up and forecast period.

Linear regression is performed on the warm-up period with the resulting Y-intercept and slope used as the initial level and trend. α and β can be adjusted to minimize the Mean Square Error (MSE) over the period. *Note:* This model is much more sensitive to changes in β than it is to changes in α. Good starting values for α and β are 0.1 and .01 respectively.

Remember that the forecast for period t in one-parameter exponential smoothing is

$$F(t) = F(t-1) + \alpha E(t-1),$$

where

$$E(t-1) = Y(t-1) - F(t-1)$$

is the error of the forecast at time $t-1$.

Two-parameter exponential smoothing models $F(t)$ as the sum of two parts, a level $S(t)$, and a trend $T(t)$. This is based on the following formulas:

$$F(t) = S(t-1) + T(t-1)$$

where

$$S(t) = F(t) + \alpha * E(t),$$

$$T(t) = T(t-1) + \beta * E(t),$$

$$E(t-1) = Y(t-1) - F(t-1)$$

and where α and β are smoothing parameters between 0 and 1.

To get the model started, linear regression is performed on the sample, whereupon **S(0)** and **T(0)** are set to the Y-intercept and slope of the regression line respectively.

Future Forecasts

If you have n data points, then using these formulas, the forecast for period $n+1$ is

$$F(n+1) = S(n) + T(n)$$

Because **Y(t)** is assumed to have either a constant or slowly changing trend, we would expect the series to increase by the trend amount for each time period. Hence, for all future time periods the formula is

$$F(t) = F(t-1) + T(n), t > n + 1$$

Note: Because both a level and a derivative are being forecast, you should not rely on a forecast many periods into the future.

The Effect of Changes in α ***and*** β**.** If α and β are both set to 0, then for each *t*, *S(t)=F(t)* and *T(t)=T(0)*. In this case, this model reduces to a linear regression of *Y* against *t*. Because β has a significant effect on the slope of the above model, it is much more sensitive to this parameter than it is to changes in α. Good starting values of α and β are 0.1 and .01, respectively.

Seasonal Data

When a time series displays repeating seasonal fluctuations, the data should be deseasonalized or seasonally adjusted before other forecasting techniques are applied. A forecast based on the deseasonalized data can then be made using exponential smoothing. Finally, this forecast is reseasonalized to get the desired result. Deseasonalization is generally not performed unless you have at least three full seasons of data. XLForecast.xla assumes that one full season is 12 months. Deseasonalizing and reseasonalizing are accomplished as follows:

1. Calculate seasonality factors for each month, indicating that month's percentage of the average monthly total for the series, as follows:

$$S_j = \frac{12}{N} \sum_{i=1}^{N} \frac{Y_{ij}}{A_i}, \ j = 1\ldots12$$

where N is the number of complete years worth of data, Y_{ij} is the value of the time series $Y(t)$ in month j of year i, and A_i is the annual total of the series in year i. *Note:* A perfectly average month will have a seasonality factor of 1.0.

2. Calculate the deseasonalized data by dividing the data in each month by its corresponding seasonality factor. Use the following formula:

$$D_{ij} = \frac{Y_{ij}}{S_j}, \ i = 1\ldots N, \ j = 1\ldots12$$

Notice that if some month j of the time series data consistently had very small or zero values, that the S would be very small or zero and lead to instabilities in this equation.

3. A 12-month forecast, f_j is made of the D's, using one- or two-parameter exponential smoothing.

4. Find the final forecast F_j by multiplying each month of the future forecast by its corresponding seasonality factor, as specified in the following equation:

$$F_j = S_j f_j, \ j = 1\ldots12$$

Appendix C ■■■■■■■■■■■■■■■■

Software Command Reference

OUTLINE OF REFERENCE

XLSim®
QUEUE and Q_NET
Extend™
XLForecast™
XLTree™
OPTIMIZATION SOFTWARE

XLSim®

XLSim is a Monte Carlo simulation add-in for Excel 97 or higher. It is provided in several editions with different limitations. Use the **Simulate About** command to determine your edition. Limitations are described further on in this section.

Note: If you are upgrading from SIM.xla, SIM25k, or an earlier version of XLSim, be sure to use the **Freeze** command followed by the **Thaw** command to convert your models.

To access XLSim, run Excel and open XLSim.xla from the File menu.

Auto Load Option. If you want XLSim.xla to load every time you launch Excel, follow these steps:

1. Select **Add-ins** from the **Tools** menu in Excel.
2. Select **XLSim.xla** from the list of **Add-ins** and click **OK**.
3. You can later go back and deselect XLSim.xla from the **Add-in** menu to prevent Excel from loading it automatically.

Note: When too many add-ins are attached to Excel, they tend to interfere with each other, sometimes freezing Excel. We recommend that you minimize the number of add-ins used in conjunction with XLSim. Use the Tools Add-ins menu from Excel, and remove the check marks from those add-ins not needed. In particular, if you have previously used SIM.xla, cSIM or SIM25k, make sure to unload them before using XLSim. Then exit and restart Excel.

Menu and Dialog Boxes

Once XLSim.xla is loaded, the **Simulate** menu will appear.

- **Simulation** initiates a simulation run, allowing you to select output cells and set the number of trials.
- **Parameterized Sim** repeatedly runs the same simulation of a single output cell while changing the value of a specific parameter of the model.
- **Data Range** generates statistics and graphs based on a data range in a worksheet.
- **Graphs** creates histograms and cumulative graphs of the simulation data.
- **Common Graphs** creates histograms and cumulative graphs of multiple series on the same axis. It also generates Series Graphs.
- **Freeze** is used before saving a spreadsheet model to create a static version that may be viewed by those without XLSim.
- **Thaw** is used to re-activate a frozen model. *Note:* If the random number formulas display #NAME?, execute a Freeze followed by a Thaw and resave the model[1].
- **View Trials** displays the actual simulation data and convergence graphs.
- **Remove XLSim** closes XLSim and (optionally) removes it from the Tools Add-Ins startup list.
- **Help** accesses the help files.
- **Tutorial** (Commercial edition only) accesses the XLSim tutorial.
- **About** identifies edition, version and limitations of XLSim.

[1] This occurs when a model created with one version of XLSim is viewed on another machine with a different version of XLSim, or one of its predecessors such as SIM.xla or SIM25k.xla.

Simulation

The following dialog box will appear when you select **Simulation** from the menu.

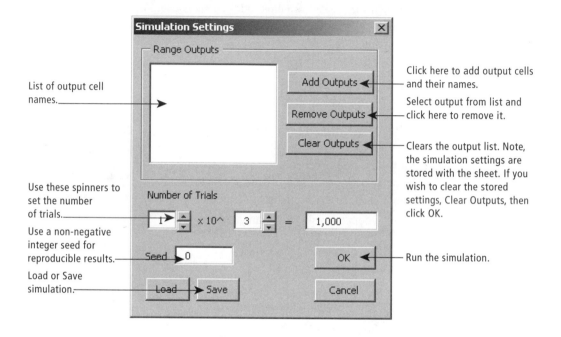

List of output cell names.

Click here to add output cells and their names.

Select output from list and click here to remove it.

Clears the output list. Note, the simulation settings are stored with the sheet. If you wish to clear the stored settings, Clear Outputs, then click OK.

Use these spinners to set the number of trials.

Use a non-negative integer seed for reproducible results.

Load or Save simulation.

Run the simulation.

After clicking the "Add Outputs" button, the following dialog box appears.

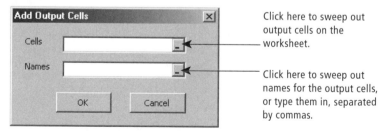

Click here to sweep out output cells on the worksheet.

Click here to sweep out names for the output cells, or type them in, separated by commas.

Parameterized Sim

The following dialog box will appear when you select **Parameterized Sim**.

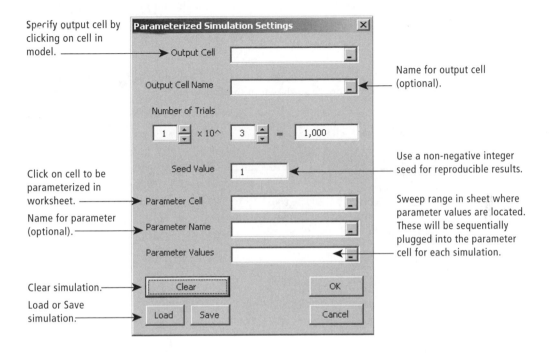

Specify output cell by clicking on cell in model.
→ Output Cell

Name for output cell (optional).
→ Output Cell Name

Number of Trials

Use a non-negative integer seed for reproducible results.
→ Seed Value

Click on cell to be parameterized in worksheet.
→ Parameter Cell

Sweep range in sheet where parameter values are located. These will be sequentially plugged into the parameter cell for each simulation.
→ Parameter Values

Name for parameter (optional).
→ Parameter Name

Clear simulation.
→ Clear

Load or Save simulation.
→ Load Save

Data Range

This command is used when you want to read in data from a worksheet and analyze it with XLSim. The results are in the same format as if you had run a simulation. For example, it provides a histogram in which you can adjust the number of bins (unlike Excel's histogram in the Analysis Tools). The following dialog box will appear when you select **Data Range** from the **Simulate** menu.

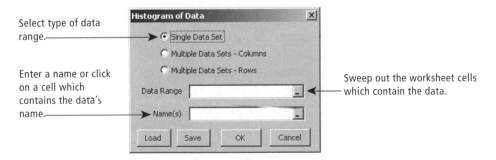

Select type of data range.
→ Single Data Set

Enter a name or click on a cell which contains the data's name.
→ Name(s)

Sweep out the worksheet cells which contain the data.
→ Data Range

Simulation Results

XLSim.xla can produce the following outputs: statistics, histograms, cumulative graphs and parameterized graphs. All outputs are Excel cells and graphs and can be edited with standard Excel commands.

Statistics

After completion of the simulation, statistics are displayed for each output cell. **Simulation** statistics appear as shown in the following figure.

	Cost	Revenue	Profit
Average	0.9981	2.46959	0.4928
Std Dev	0.5797	1.42586	0.2875
Std Err	0.0183	0.04509	0.0091
Max	1.998	4.99356	0.9991
Min	0.0009	0.00335	0.0005
Percentiles			
5%	0.0968	0.26712	0.0571
10%	0.2006	0.45801	0.0945
15%	0.3222	0.73317	0.1395
20%	0.4136	0.9964	0.1866
25%	0.5068	1.23842	0.2476

For **Parameterized Simulation**, statistics will be displayed for each parameter value, as shown in the figure below. In this case the parameter is Demand and the output is Revenue.

Demand	Revenue 1	Revenue 2	Revenue 3	Revenue 4
Average	0.48831	1.00349	1.49173	1.92279
Std Dev	0.29159	0.57043	0.85709	1.16883
Std Err	0.00922	0.01804	0.0271	0.03696
Max	0.99833	1.99979	2.99998	3.99292
Min	0.00115	0.00062	0.00109	0.00297
Percentiles				
5%	0.05101	0.11308	0.15796	0.17586
10%	0.0909	0.21482	0.3079	0.31418
15%	0.13951	0.32049	0.46477	0.48176
20%	0.17898	0.40591	0.60087	0.69622
25%	0.23798	0.51818	0.76881	0.92066

Graphs

After a simulation, the outputs can be graphed using the **Graphs** command.

Click here to select which outputs to graph.

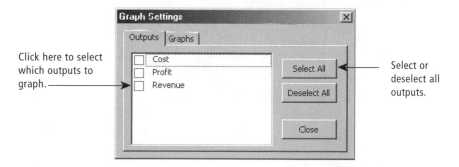

Select or deselect all outputs.

Once you have selected which outputs to graph, click on the Graphs tab at the top of the dialog box.

Select this option if all the outputs only take integer values (e.g., the roll of a die).

Controls the number of bins on the histogram.

Controls how many decimal places appear on the bin labels.

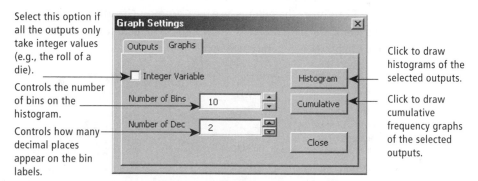

Click to draw histograms of the selected outputs.

Click to draw cumulative frequency graphs of the selected outputs.

Histogram and Cumulative Graph

A separate histogram and cumulative graph are created for each of the selected outputs. The histogram appears on a worksheet called *Output Name* H and the cumulative graph on a worksheet called *Output Name* C.

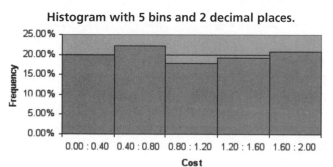

Histogram with 5 bins and 2 decimal places.

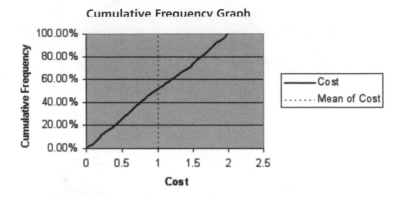

Common Graphs

Sometimes it is useful to compare the different outputs of a simulation side-by-side on the same set of axes. This is especially useful when you have run a parameterized simulation and would like to see the histogram of outputs for each of the parameter values. To compare the outputs, use the **Common Graphs** command on the **Simulate** menu. Once you have selected which outputs to include (using the Outputs tab), click on the Graphs tab, which brings up the following dialog box.

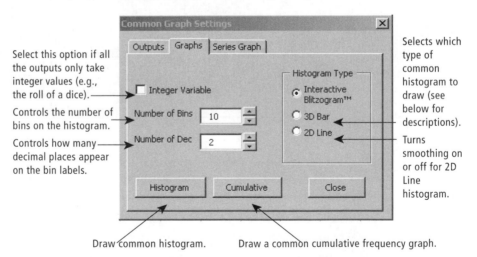

Interactive

This option produces a Blitzogram™ interactive histogram by placing graphs for each selected output on separate worksheets. The histograms all have the same axes so that a meaningful comparison can be made between them. The worksheets are called *Output Name* I, and can be paged through to create an animation effect using Ctrl-PgUp and Ctrl-PgDn.

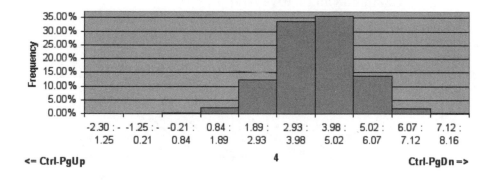

<= Ctrl-PgUp   4   Ctrl-PgDn =>

3D Bar

This option draws a 3D histogram showing all of the outputs on one set of axes.

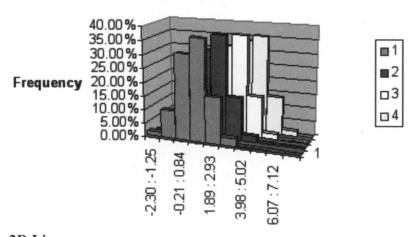

2D Line

This option also draws all outputs on one axis, but represents them as 2D lines.

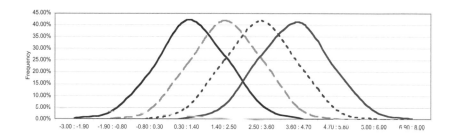

Common Cumulative Graph

The Cumulative button on the Common Graph dialog box draws the cumulative frequency graphs of the selected series all on the same axis.

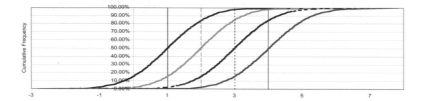

Series Graph

Series graphs plot the mean and specified confidence interval of the selected outputs on a common axis. They are often a useful way to present the results of a parameterized simulation. They are accessed using the Series Graph tab on the Common Graph dialog box.

Adjusts the size of the confidence interval on the graph. ———

Draws the series graph of the selected outputs. ———

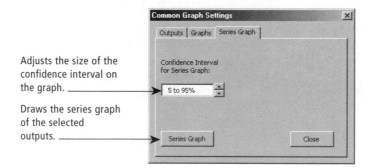

A series graph is useful for assessing expected value and the risk associated with various parameter values.

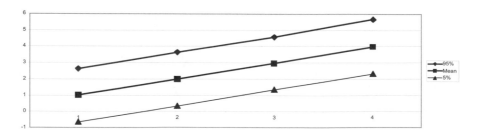

Freeze and Thaw

Use the **Freeze** command on the **Simulation** menu before you send an XLSim model to another user of XLSim. Freezing a workbook causes the random numbers to be replaced by their current value, and their formulas to be stored in the cell comments. Once a workbook is frozen it can be given to another user of XLSim who can use the **Thaw** command to restore the random number formulas and recreate the model. To update a model written with SIM.xla or SIM25k.xla, first Freeze it, then Thaw it. Freeze is also useful for providing static versions of simulation models for use by those without XLSim.

View Trials

You can view the results of the simulation trials by selecting **View Trials** from the **Simulation** menu. The following dialog box will appear.

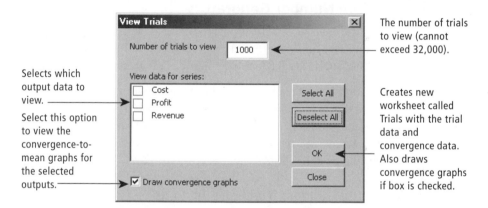

The trial data appears on a new worksheet, along with the convergence data, if the Draw convergence graph box is checked.

	A	B	C	D	E
1	Cost	Running Average		Revenue	Running Average
2	1.421437	1.421436667		0.880988	0.880987883
3	0.533269	0.977352709		4.137392	2.509189963
4	1.038948	0.997884532		4.833224	3.283007915
5	0.925556	0.97980243		0.773439	2.656260669
6	1.77784	1.139409947		1.472914	2.419591403

The convergence graphs appear on worksheets named *Output Name* Conv:

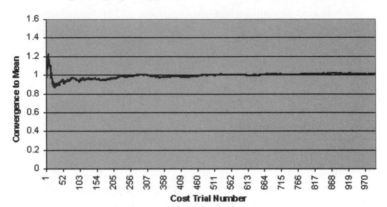

Random Number Generators

Make sure that XLSim.xla is open before entering random number generating functions or opening an Excel workbook which uses these functions. Open the **gen_FUNCTIONS.xls** file to see applications of the various functions.

Note: If the Freeze command is not used when models using add-in functions are moved between computers, occasionally **#NAME?** will appear. This means that the random number generation formula has not yet been recognized by the worksheet. If this occurs, use the **Freeze** command followed by the **Thaw** command, then re-save the model.

Inserting Random Number Functions

To place a random number generating function in the spreadsheet, place the cursor in the desired cell, then click on the **Function icon** or use the **Insert Function** command. You should see a screen, from which you select **Statistical** from the Function category list, and the desired function name from the Function name list.

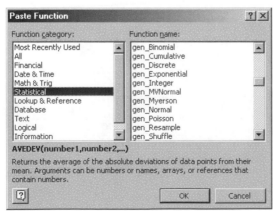

Click on **OK** and you will be prompted for the distribution's parameters. If, for example, you selected the function **gen_Normal**, you will be prompted for the Normal distribution's mean and standard deviation as shown below.

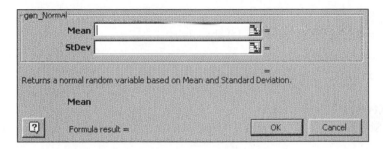

Fill in the requested parameters and click **OK**. Each time you press the calculate key—the **F9 key** in Windows and **Command=** in Macintosh—you should see a new random number generated in the cell.

Random Number Generating Functions

The following list shows random number generating functions available in XLSim.xla and their parameters. Be sure to investigate the **gen_FUNCTIONS.xls** file to see these functions in action.

- *gen_Binomial* (Number of Trials, Probability of Success)
- *gen_Cumulative* (Range of Cumulative Probabilities, Range of Associated Values)
- *gen_Discrete* (Range of Discrete Probabilities, Range of Associated Values)
- *gen_Exponential* (Mean)
- *gen_Integer* (Lower Integer, Upper Integer) returns integers uniformly distributed between Lower Integer and Upper Integer.
- *gen_Lognormal* (Mean, Standard Deviation) generates random variables whose natural log is normally distributed.
- *gen_MVLognormal* (vector of Means, Covariance matrix) generates a row of multivariate Lognormal random variables based on a column of means and a lower covariance matrix. This function must be entered as an array formula.
- *gen_MVnormal* (vector of Means, Covariance matrix)
- *gen_Myerson* (25th %, 50th %, 75th %, [Min], [Max]) generates random variables based on the quartiles of a distribution.
- *gen_Normal* (Mean, Standard Deviation)

- ***gen_Poisson*** (Mean)

- ***gen_Shuffle*** (Data Range) is an array formula that returns data in Range randomly shuffled.

- ***gen_Resample*** (Data Range) samples with replacement from the Data range.

- ***gen_Triang*** (Low, Most Likely, High)

- ***gen_Uniform*** (Lower, Upper) returns a continuous random variable uniformly distributed between Lower and Upper.

Software Limitations

XLSim is provided in both a Commercial and 10k edition as outlined in the table below.

XLSim Specifications		
Edition	Commercial[2]	10k
Iterations	1 Million	10 Thousand
Output Cells	50	5
Parameters	50	5

Check www.AnalyCorp.com for updates and upgrades. If more powerful Monte Carlo capability is required, consider @Risk from www.Palisade.com or Crystal Ball® from www.Decisioneering.com.

QUEUE.XLA AND Q_NET.XLA

QUEUE.xls

QUEUE.xla is used with QUEUE.xls to model a simple queue. Q_NET.xla is used with Q_NET.xls to model a queuing network. *QUEUE.xla and Q_NET.xla should not both be loaded at the same time.* Both QUEUE.xla and Q_NET.xla require Excel 5.0 or higher.

Running QUEUE.xla and Q_NET.xla. Launch Excel and open QUEUE.xla and QUEUE.xls or Q_NET.xla and Q_NET.xls from the **File** menu. QUEUE.xls and Q_NET.xls can be modified and saved under any desired file name. *Note:* Make sure your worksheet's calculation mode is set to automatic under **Tools Options** before running these add-ins.

Auto Load Option. If you want QUEUE.xla or Q_NET.xla to load every time you launch Excel, follow the steps below.

1. Select **Add-ins** from the **Tools** menu in Excel.

---

[2] More than 50 outputs and parameters may be specified, using the Commercial edition, if all outputs are not graphed.

2. Select QUEUE.xla or Q_NET.xla from the list of add-ins and click **OK**. You can later go back and deselect either of them from the **Add-in** menu to prevent Excel from loading them automatically. Do not load them both at once because they will not run correctly.

You will see the worksheet shown in the following figure when you open QUEUE.xls. Make sure that QUEUE.xla is opened first.

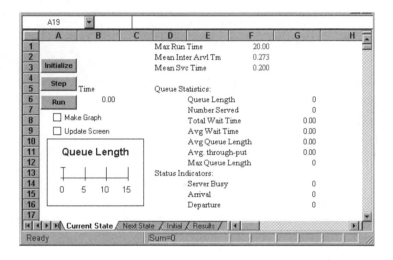

User Inputs

You must specify the maximum run time, mean interarrival time, mean service time, and initial state of the system

- ▪ *Maximum Run Time.* The simulation will run until time equals the maximum run time.

- ▪ *Mean Interarrival Time and Mean Service Time.* The simulation assumes exponential distributions. Note that mean interarrival time must be greater than mean service time or the queue length will eventually become infinite.

- ▪ *Initial State.* This screen contains the values used to initialize the simulation; there are no formulas. To reach stability more quickly, you can enter any starting values in the current screen after initialization and before running. To specify permanent changes in the initial conditions you can edit the initial screen.

Menu and Buttons

Once QUEUE.xla is loaded, the **Queue** menu will appear.

- ■ **Initialize** sets all counters to the initial state stored in the **Initial** tab of the workbook.

- ■ **Run Simulation** initiates a simulation run until time reaches Max Run Time and produces a graph of the queue length.

- ■ **Quick Run** performs the same function as **Run Simulation** but does not produce a graph.

- ■ **Single Step** advances the simulation to the next event.

- ■ **Quit** removes QUEUE.xla from memory and **Queue** from Excel's menu bar.

- ■ **Update Screen** toggles screen updating on and off.

You can access the Initialize, Single Step, and Run Simulation or Quick Run functions through either buttons or menus.

Output and Results

QUEUE.xls and Q_NET.xls generate *Queue Statistics, Status Indicators*, and *Next Event Times*. The formulas appear in the *next state* worksheet of QUEUE.xls. Multiple columns of these formulas appear in the *next state* worksheet Q_NET.xls. The formulas, detailed in Appendix A are quite complex, but you don't have to understand them in detail to run simulations. However, if you want to modify the models as suggested in some of the exercises, you should understand at least some of them.

Q_NET.xls

When you load Q_NET.xls, you will see the following worksheet. Make sure that Q_NET.xla is loaded first.

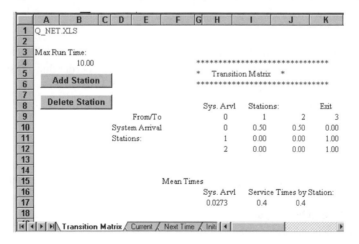

User Inputs

You must specify the maximum run time, mean interarrival, and mean service times for each station and the probabilities that characterize the network's traffic flow in Q_NET.xls's *Transition Matrix* worksheet, shown in the following figure.

The maximum run time, mean interarrival and mean service times have already been described in the discussion of QUEUE.xls's inputs. The *Transition Matrix* contains transition probabilities that describe the network flow. The rows of the probabilities in the transition matrix must sum to 1.

Menu and Buttons

Once QNET.xla is loaded, the **QNet** menu will appear. Most menu selections are the same as those in QUEUE.xla. The exceptions are shown in the following figure.

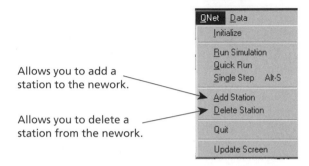

Allows you to add a station to the nework.

Allows you to delete a station from the nework.

EXTEND™

Extend is a discrete simulation package from ImagineThat Inc. (www.imaginethatinc.com). You can quickly assemble large models from Extends's pre-existing building blocks, or create new building blocks of your own. The complete Extend manual is included with this installation in Adobe Acrobat (.pdf) format. This can be accessed through the **start** menu (Windows) or the Extend installation folder (Macintosh) on your computer. Please consult this manual for complete information on Extend.

Using Extend

An Extend model is a document that contains components (called "blocks"), usually with connections between the blocks. Each block contains procedural information as well as data that you enter. After you create a model, you can modify it by adding blocks, moving connections, and changing the blocks' data.

Levels of use

You can use Extend on many levels:

■ Run pre-assembled models and explore alternatives by changing data in dialogs, Notebooks, or text files. If you work in a group environment, one user can create models for others to run . There is also a RunTime version available for distributing your pre-assembled models to others.

■ Assemble your own models from the blocks that come with Extend. Extend is shipped with libraries of blocks that handle both continuous and discrete event models, as well as specialized libraries for electronics and other fields. To assemble a model, pull blocks from menus of libraries and link connectors on the blocks.

- Create new blocks using the built-in ModL programming environment. You can also modify the blocks that come with Extend to work with your specific needs.

Extend helps you organize your model by letting you build your own hierarchical blocks containing subsystems. Thus, you don't have to start over when you need to build a model of a process which has elements in common with a previous model.

As you read this manual, you will see how Extend caters to the needs of users at all levels.

Extend Toolbar

Extend's toolbar provides quick access to the most commonly used functions. Each toolbar button has a menu equivalent. These can be found in the online Extend manual.

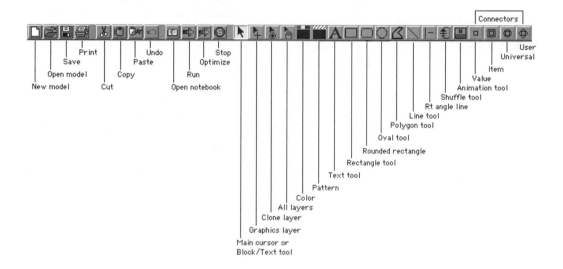

Commonly used blocks

Extend's blocks reside in libraries. By opening the appropriate library from the **Library** menu, these modeling components can be accessed. Below is a list of some commonly used blocks in Extend and the library that contains them. There are many more blocks in Extend that provide additional functions. These include the blocks required for simulating the steps in a process, reporting and plotting, calculation, or for utility functions such as communicating with Excel or providing debugging information. A complete listing of all of the blocks in each major library and their functionality can be found in the appendices of the Extend manual.

Block Icon	Block Name	Library	Description
	Activity, Delay	Discrete Event	Holds an item for a specified amount of delay time, then releases it. The delay time is the value in the dialog or, if connected, the value at the D connector when the item is received (the connector overrides the dialog). This block can be used for any kind of service delay. For example, you can use this block to represent red lights in traffic, the time it takes a clerk to wait on a customer, or multitasking CPU time.
	Activity, Multiple	Discrete Event	Holds many items and passes them out based on the delay and arrival time for each item. The item with the smallest delay and earliest arrival time is passed out first. The delay time for each item is set through the D connector or, if nothing is connected there, can be specified in the dialog. For example, this block can be used to represent a supermarket where customers arrive at different times and take a varying amount of time to shop. Customers who arrive earlier or only shop a little will leave first; customers who arrive later or shop a long time will leave last.
	Batch	Discrete Event	Allows items from several sources to be joined as a single item. This is useful for synchronizing resources and combining various parts of a job ("kitting"). In the dialog, you specify the number of items from each of the inputs that is required to produce one output item (one "kit"). You can also specify that items at one or more inputs will not be brought into the block until one or more of the other inputs has its requirements filled.
	Executive	Discrete Event	This block is the heart of each discrete event model and must be placed to the left of all other blocks in the model. It allows the duration of the simulation to be controlled by the end time or by another number specified in the dialog. Generally you will have no reason to change the default values in the dialog.
	Exit	Discrete Event	Passes items out of the simulation. The total number of items absorbed by this block is reported in its dialog and at the # connector.
	Generator	Discrete Event	Provides items for a discrete event simulation at specified interarrival times. Choose either a distribution on the left, or choose the empirical

Block Icon	Block Name	Library	Description
			distribution and enter probabilities in the table. Items can be created with a random distribution or at a constant rate of arrival. You can also specify the number of items output at each event in the dialog or at the V connector. The parameters for the distribution arrival times are set in the dialog. The random distributions include: beta, binomial, constant, empirical, Erlang, exponential, gamma, hyperexponential, log normal, normal, Pearson type V, Pearson type VI, Poisson, Triangular, uniform integer, uniform real, and Weibull. The empirical distribution may have up to 20 points and may be interpreted as a discrete, stepped, or interpolated distribution. The input connectors 1, 2, and 3 allow you to change the parameters of the random distribution as the simulation progresses.
	Get Attribute	Discrete Event	Displays and/or removes attributes on items, then passes the items through. The attribute value is shown in the dialog and output at the A connector. You can also use this block to clone the item based on the number in an attribute. As items are passed through the block, the block can either read or remove an attribute, and that attribute can be specified as the first attribute in the list or a named attribute. If the attribute is found, its value is reported in the dialog and sent through the A connector. The D connector outputs 1 if the attribute value has changed since the last value was read in.
	Queue, FIFO	Discrete Event	A first-in-first-out (FIFO) queue. The maximum length, which determines how many items the queue can hold, can be set in the dialog. You can specify that the simulation should stop when the queue is full (reaches the maximum length). You can also see the average queue length, average wait time, and utilization of the queue in the dialog.
	Queue, Priority	Discrete Event	A queue that releases items by priority. The item in the queue with the lowest numerical value for its priority will be released first. If the items in the queue all have the same priority, it becomes a first-in-first out (FIFO) queue. The maximum length, which determines how many items the queue can hold, can be set in the dialog. You can specify that the simulation should stop when the queue is full (reaches the maximum length).

Block Icon	Block Name	Library	Description
	Queue, Resource Pool	Discrete Event	A queue for resource pool units. Items wait until the specified number of resource pool units become available. The order of items in the queue is determined by the ranking rule in the dialog of the Resource Pool block. The maximum length, which determines how many items the queue can hold, can be set in the dialog. You can also see the average queue length, average wait time, and utilization of the queue in the dialog.
	Release Resource Pool	Discrete Event	Releases a resource pool as the item passes through. This pool of resource units can be released by either: - Choosing the "Release Resource Pool by name" radio button and entering the name of the Resource Pool block and the number of units to be released. - Choosing the "Release resource pool by attribute" radio button and specifying an attribute which has been set by a Queue, Resource Pool block.
	Resource Pool	Discrete Event	This block holds resource pool units to be used in a simulation. These units limit the capacity of a section of a model. For example, this could be used to represent a limited number of tables at a restaurant. Unlike the Resource block, the resource pool units are not items. They are variables which indicate how much of a constraining factor is available. The Resource Pool block works with the Queue, Resource Pool to allocate the pool of resources to items, and it works with the Release Resource Pool block to release the pool of resources.
	Select DE Output	Discrete Event	Selects the input item to be output at one of two output connectors based on a decision. The item at the input is passed through the selected output. The dialog has options for changing the outputs after a given number of items have passed and selecting based on the select connector. If the select connector is not used, you can have 1 out of every specified number of items go to the top connector or a random probability for each item to go to the top connector. If the select connector is used, the dialog has options for toggling (choosing the outputs sequentially each time select is activated), choosing the output based on the value at the select connector or specifying the probability of the top connector.

Block Icon	Block Name	Library	Description
	Set Attribute	Discrete Event	Sets the attributes of items passing through the block. Up to seven attribute names and values may be assigned to an item with each Set Attribute block. The attributes may add to or replace existing item attributes. You can specify the value of one of the attributes with the A connector. The value at the A connector overrides the corresponding value in the dialog. If the attribute name is already present on the item passing through, the old value will be stripped off, and the new value will be substituted for it.
	Unbatch	Discrete Event	Produces several items from a single input item. The number of items produced at each output are specified in the dialog. By default, this block holds its inputs until its outputs are used or another demand occurs at the connector. The attributes and priorities of the input item are copied to each output. If you selected preserve uniqueness in the Batch block and here, items will be output with their original properties (attributes and priorities) restored. This block can be used to break a message packet into component messages, route the same message to several places, or distribute copies of invoices.
	Decision	Generic	This block makes a decision based on the inputs and internal logic you define. The dialog lets you perform the following tests comparing A to B: greater than, greater than or equal to, equal to, less than, less than or equal to, and not equal. You can also test for A being an invalid number (noValue). The block compares the two inputs (A and B). If only the A input is connected, the block compares that value to the B value in the dialog. The block can also use hysteresis.
	Equation	Generic	Outputs the results of an equation entered in the dialog. The equation must be of the form "Result = formula;". You can use Extend's built-in operators and functions, and some or all of the input values as part of the equation. Each input must be named in the dialog in order to use it in the equation. You can use the default input value names (Var1, Var2, etc.) or specify new names. Extend will warn you if an input is used in the equation but it is not connected.

Block Icon	Block Name	Library	Description
	Input Random Number	Generic	Generates random integers or real numbers based on the selected distribution. You can use the dialog or the three inputs, one, two, and three to specify arguments for the distributions. You can select the type of distribution: Uniform (integer or real), Beta, Binomial, Erlang, Exponential, Gamma, Geometric, HyperExponential, LogLogistic, LogNormal, Neg. Binomial, Normal, Pearson type V, Pearson type VI, Poisson, Triangular, Weibull, and Empirical. The Empirical distribution uses a table of up to 50 values to generate a discrete, stepped, or interpolated empirical distribution.

XLForecast™

XLForecast is a basic time series analysis add-in for Excel 97 or higher. It makes use of 2 parameter exponential smoothing, and with seasonality.

To access XLForecast, run Excel and open XLForecast.xla from the **File** menu.

Auto Load Option. If you want XLForecast.xla to load every time you launch Excel, follow these steps:

1. Select **Add-ins** from the **Tools** menu in Excel.

2. Select XLForecast.xla from the list of add-ins and click **OK.**

3. You can later go back and deselect XLForecast.xla from the **Add-in** menu to prevent Excel from loading it automatically.

Menu

Once XLForecast.xla is loaded, the **Forecast** menu will appear.

Run Forecast

Once XLForecast.xla is loaded, the **Forecast** menu containing the following items will appear, as shown in the following figure:

Opens the run forecast dialog box. → Run Forecast

Closes XLForecast.xla and removes the **Forecast** menu. ← Close Forecast

Range containing
time series. ⟶

XLForecas.xla's calculations are discussed in the context of the motorcycle data within SERIES.xls. You should run a forecast on the motorcycle data before proceeding. Check the "Trended" and "Seasonal" options in the Forecast Parameters box and set the Holdout periods to 12.

The Results Worksheet. On this worksheet you adjust the parameters of the forecast and view a graph of the forecast.

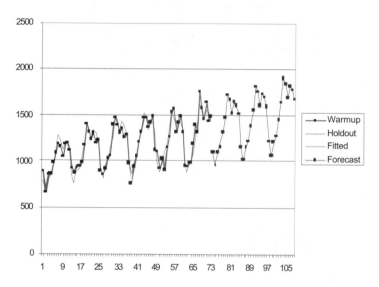

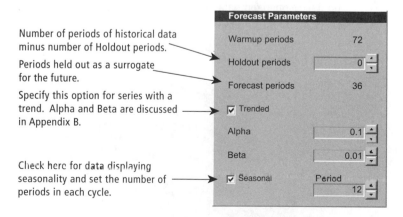

Number of periods of historical data minus number of Holdout periods.

Periods held out as a surrogate for the future.

Specify this option for series with a trend. Alpha and Beta are discussed in Appendix B.

Check here for data displaying seasonality and set the number of periods in each cycle.

The Calculations Worksheet. This worksheet contains the data used to generate the forecast graph. When you see "#N/A" it means there is no applicable data to be entered in that cell. Column B contains the original time series you selected and columns D and E (labeled 'Seasoned Data') break that time series into either warmup or holdout periods.

Season Factors. The season factors can be interpreted as percentages of an average month. The calculation of these factors is discussed below.

C	D	E	F	G	H	(
	Seasoned Data			**Deseasoned Data**		
	Warmup	**Holdout**		**Warmup**	**Holdout**	
	912	#N/A		1087.22	#N/A	
	1154	#N/A		1217.91	#N/A	
	1271	#N/A		1198.01	#N/A	
	1539	#N/A		1251.1	#N/A	
	1575	#N/A		1329.01	#N/A	
	1325	#N/A		1225.74	#N/A	
	1423	#N/A		1226.81	#N/A	
	1492	#N/A		1320.34	#N/A	
	1327	#N/A		1252.43	#N/A	
	#N/A	960		#N/A	1188.28	
	#N/A	954		#N/A	1358.78	
	#N/A	996		#N/A	1249.56	
	#N/A	1194		#N/A	1423.4	
	#N/A	1401		#N/A	1478.59	
	#N/A	1328		#N/A	1251.74	
	#N/A	1760		#N/A	1430.76	
	#N/A	1588		#N/A	1339.98	
	#N/A	1461		#N/A	1351.56	
	#N/A	1640		#N/A	1413.9	
	#N/A	1439		#N/A	1273.44	
	#N/A	1491		#N/A	1407.22	
	#N/A	#N/A		#N/A	#N/A	
	#N/A	#N/A		#N/A	#N/A	
	#N/A	#N/A		#N/A	#N/A	
	#N/A	#N/A		#N/A	#N/A	

	Season Factors
1	0.807890117
2	0.702099264
3	0.797077417
4	0.838834345
5	0.947523892
6	1.060924292
7	1.230118275
8	1.185093999
9	1.080976367
10	1.159914732
11	1.130010605
12	1.059536815
13	#N/A

January sales are 81% of an average month.

February sales are 71% of an average month, and so on.

The deseasonalized data is found by dividing each month of the seasoned data (original data) by the corresponding seasonality factor. You can use the Excel Chart Wizard to graph the original and deseasoned data side by side to observe the extent to which seasonality has been removed.

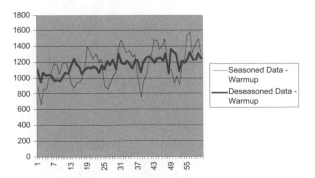

Deseasoned Model		Seasoned Model	
Fitted	Forecast	Fitted	Forecast
56	1256.259	#N/A	1488.785	#N/A
57	1265.594	#N/A	1368.077	#N/A
58	1263.271	#N/A	1465.287	#N/A
59	1260.923	#N/A	1424.856	#N/A
60	1268.756	#N/A	1344.294	#N/A
61	#N/A	1268.852	#N/A	1025.093
62	#N/A	1270.58	#N/A	892.0736
63	#N/A	1272.309	#N/A	1014.129
64	#N/A	1274.037	#N/A	1068.706

◄——— The model is also divided into seasoned and deseasoned data sets using the same season factors discussed earlier.

A model of the original time series is created and is divided into two parts—the fitted curve and the forecast. The fitted curve tries to follow the warm-up data as closely as possible while the forecast is an extrapolation of the fitted curve into the future. The forecast starts where the historical data ends minus any holdout periods. In this example, the historical data ended in period 72, minus 12 holdout periods means the forecast starts in period 61. We see that a point estimate of the forecast for the 61st period is 1025.093. We can improve upon this point estimate using simulation as described in the next section.

The **warm-up data** is used to calculate the forecast. It defaults to the entire data set, in which case the forecast is assumed to be for twelve months into the future. The **holdout data** is set aside at the end of the historical data as a surrogate for the future.

To find out how successful this forecast was for months 61 through 72, look at the Forecast graph as shown in the following figure. This shows that if we had used the first five years of data with this method to predict the sixth year, we would have significantly underestimated May sales.

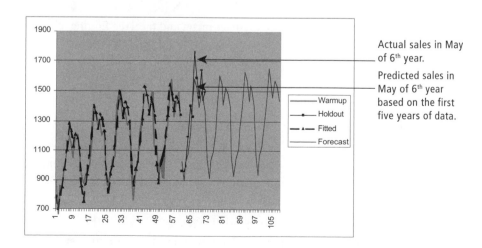

Actual sales in May of 6th year.

Predicted sales in May of 6th year based on the first five years of data.

Simulating the Future

Errors
125.6992
-50.9332
73.60919
13.29738
16.70363
-6.51747
-75.846
-65.6672
-75.9693
-14.9878
18.68171
4.422983

Live simulation of
upcoming period

Thaw to Activate

Deseasonalized forecast
for upcoming period   1268.852166

Seasonality factor
for upcoming period   0.807890117

The Simulation worksheet holds a series of random errors that allow you to create a distribution of the forecast for the next period (in our example, period 61). Load XLSim.xla and thaw the worksheet. Cell G4 is now activated and displays a forecast for period 61 that is no longer constant.

XLTree™

XLTree is a Decision Tree add-in for Excel 97 or higher. The Standard Edition is limited to 3 branches per node and a total depth of 4 nodes. The Commercial Edition is limited only by the limitations of Excel. Use the **Tree About** command to determine your edition.

Menu and Dialog Boxes

Once XLTree.xla is loaded the **Tree** menu and the Tree Editing toolbar will appear.

- **New** opens a new worksheet, prompts the user for the number of state variables (optional), and starts a new tree.

- **Add Decision Fork** adds a specified number of decision branches to the selected node in the tree.

- **Add Uncertainty Fork** adds a specified number of uncertainty branches to the selected node in the tree.

- **Node Labels** allows the user to add descriptions to nodes and to include state variables when creating a presentation of the tree. *Note:* the node labels are stored as cell comments.

- **Copy Node** copies the selected node.

- **Copy Subtree** copies the selected node and the subtree belonging to it.

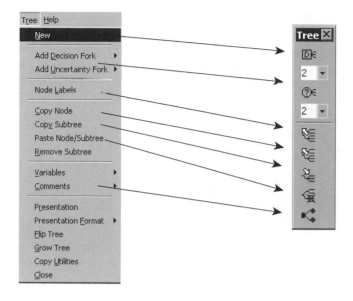

- **Paste Node/Subtree** pastes the node or subtree that was most recently copied.

- **Remove Subtree** deletes the portion of the tree extending from the selected node.

- **Variables** (**Show** or **Hide**) shows or hides state variable and joint probability columns.

- **Comments** (**Show** or **Hide**) shows or hides all comments in the workbook. This allows the Node Labels to be viewed.

- **Presentation** creates a graphical representation of the tree on the current worksheet based upon the formatting specified in the Presentation Format worksheet. The tree is created on a new worksheet labeled "Presentation".

- **Presentation Format (Save Current or Revert to Default)** allows the user to set the current formatting specified in the Presentation Format worksheet as the default, or to revert from a previously saved formatting back to the default formatting.

- **Flip Tree** changes the structure of symmetric trees by interchanging specified levels of the tree.

- **Grow Tree** copies the topmost subtree to lower branches with empty nodes. This is useful for creating large symmetric trees in just a few steps.

- **Copy Utilities** copies a utility function of the state variables from the topmost leaf of a tree into all other leaves.

- **Close** closes XLTree.xla and removes the **Tree** menu and the Tree Editing toolbar.

New. When the **New** command is invoked, the user is prompted to enter the number of state variables, if any, in the dialog box shown below. State variables, which will be discussed later, are not required for simple trees, in which case the field can be left at zero. When you click **OK**, a new worksheet containing the root of the new tree will be created.

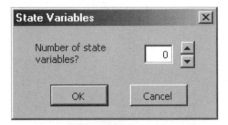

Add Decision Fork. From any empty leaf node (cell containing an asterisk "*") you can add a decision fork using either the **Tree** menu or the toolbar as shown in the following figure.

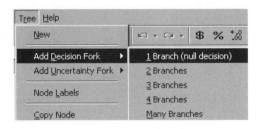
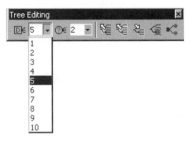

If you use the **Many Branches** option the following dialog box is displayed. *Note:* The Standard edition of XLTree is limited to 3 branches.

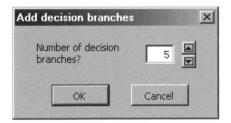

Add Uncertainty Fork. From any empty leaf node (cell containing an asterisk "*") you can add an uncertainty fork using either the **Tree** menu or the toolbar as shown in the following figure.

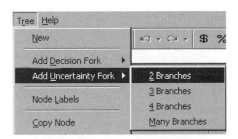

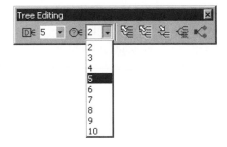

If you use the **Many Branches** option the following dialog box is displayed. *Note:* The Standard edition of XLTree is limited to 3 branches.

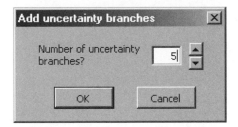

Node Labels. Node labels are used to display text and the values of state variables on nodes in presentations. Select a node in the tree and invoke the **Node labels** command to bring up the Node Properties dialog box below and enter a node description.

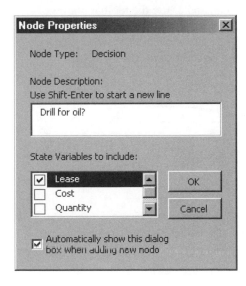

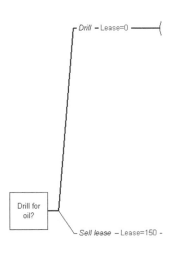

The figure on the previous page shows the root node of the wildcatter problem from Chapter 6. A short description of the decision node is added to the node, and appears in the presentation view of the tree if the appropriate formatting options are set on the Presentation Format worksheet. The "Lease" state variable is selected which allows the value of that variable to be displayed when a presentation is created.

Copy Node. 📝 This command copies the selected node, but not the nodes below it. The node can then be pasted using the **Paste Node/Subtree** command.

Copy Subtree. 📝 This command copies the selected node and all the nodes below it. The nodes can then be pasted using the **Paste Node/Subtree** command. In the figure below, with cell F2 selected, everything circled would be copied.

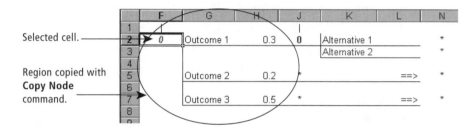

Paste Node/Subtree. 📝 Select an empty node (cell with asterisk "*") and invoke this command to paste the node or subtree that was most recently copied.

Remove Subtree. 📝 Select the topmost node in the subtree to be removed then invoke the **Remove Subtree** command or use the toolbar button.

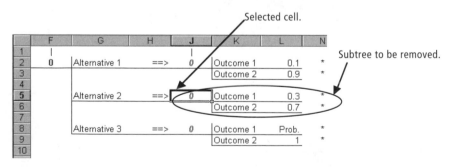

Variables (Show or Hide). When state variables are used, the **Variables, Hide** command can be used to hide the columns containing state variables and joint probabilities, making the structure of the tree easier to view. The **Variables, Show** command un-hides the state variable and joint probability columns.

Comments (Show or Hide). These commands are used to show or hide all comments that are attached to any cell in the workbook. It can be useful to show all comments to quickly edit the node description text in multiple nodes.

Presentation. This command creates a graphical representation of the tree on the current worksheet, based upon the formatting specified in the Presentation Format worksheet. The tree is created on a new worksheet labeled "Presentation".

The Presentation Format worksheet (bellow) allows for a wide variety of formatting options. There are three ways in which the format of the presentations may be changed:

1. Controls such as Radio Buttons and Check Boxes for specifying various options.

2. Excel formatting commands which may be applied to text and graphic objects in the Presentation Format worksheet using the Excel Drawing Toolbar.

3. Global Options

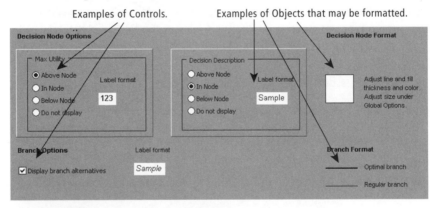

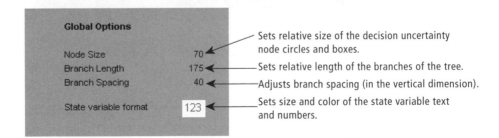

Note: If any utility values or state variables do not appear as they should (e.g., they appear as "##") when you create a presentation, check to make sure the columns which hold the original values on the Tree worksheet are wide enough to accommodate the formatted number. Also, in order for the joint probability values to appear on the presentation the **Variables, Show** command must first be used on the Tree worksheet.

The user is urged to thoroughly explore the Presentation Format worksheet and experiment freely with changing formats.

Presentation Format. When you find a presentation format that you particularly like you may save it as the new default. The **(Save Current or Revert to Default)** allows the user to set the current formatting specified in the Presentation Format worksheet as the default, or to revert from a previously saved formatting back to the default formatting.

Flip Tree

Flip Tree is used to interchange change levels within a symmetric tree (see Tree Flipping on page 342).

Grow Tree

Grow Tree is useful when creating large symmetric decision trees that have many similar branches. For example, suppose you are modeling a decision about which of three types of weather protection to use in the face of three types of weather. You could build this tree by filling in only the topmost branches as follows.

0	Wear Raincoat	==>	*0*	Sunshine	0.5	*
				Rain	0.4	*
				Hail	0.1	*
	Bring Umbrella			*	
	Raincoat & Umbrella			*	

The **Grow Tree** command quickly completes the tree as shown below.

0	Wear Raincoat	==>	*0*	Sunshine	0.5	*
				Rain	0.4	*
				Hail	0.1	*
	Bring Umbrella	==>	*0*	Sunshine	0.5	*
				Rain	0.4	*
				Hail	0.1	*
	Raincoat & Umbrella	==>	*0*	Sunshine	0.5	*
				Rain	0.4	*
				Hail	0.1	*

This command may also work on some asymmetric trees. A copy of the current tree is pasted into another worksheet named "_OldTree_" in case the grown tree does not come out as expected.

You can then go back and edit the details of the various branches to finish the tree. If you want to go back to the version of the tree before you grew it, delete the worksheet named "Tree" and change the worksheet named "_OldTree_" to "Tree". However, if you grow a tree more than once you won't be able to go back to your original tree, only to the version of the tree prior to the last use of the **Grow Tree** command. It is a good idea to save your model often as you modify the tree.

Copy Utilities. A utility function of the state variables can be entered as a formula in the topmost leaf node of the tree. With this formula in place, the **Copy Utility** command will copy it to the remaining leaf nodes. The tree will then evaluate automatically. *Note:* You must start with the cursor in the topmost leaf, and all leaf nodes must be in the same column to use the **Copy Utility** command. If they are not, use the 1 Branch (null decision) fork to extend leaf nodes to the same column. After the command is executed, the leaves of the tree will appear in **<u>Bold Underlined Green</u>** format in the Tree worksheet. Of course, they may be formatted any way you like in the presentation worksheet.

Close. The **close** command closes XLTree.xla and removes the **Tree** menu and the Tree Editing toolbar.

State Variables

You can use state variables to simplify the calculation of utilities at the leaf nodes of the tree. For example, suppose that utility can be expressed as Profit = Revenue – Cost, where Revenue and Cost take on different values on different branches of the tree. The following steps show how the utility can be calculated directly from the state variables.

1. In creating the tree one would specify two state variables. Var1 and Var2 would then be labeled Revenue and Cost.

Enter "Cost" here.

	B	C	D	E	F	G	H
1	|			Revenue	Var 2	JP	
2	*	Root	1			1	*
3							

2. When a branch occurs, the associated values of the state variables are entered.

Enter high Revenue value here

	H	I	J	K	L	M	N
1	|			Revenue	Cost	JP	
2	0	Hi Revenue	0.4	20	0	0.4	*
3		Lo Revenue	0.6	10	0	0.6	*
4							

Enter low Revenue value here.

Note: All subsequent branches will inherit the appropriate values of the state variables.

3. When all branching is completed, enter a utility formula based on the state variables for the topmost leaf of the tree. In this case, it is Profit = Hi Revenue – Hi Cost.

T2 ▼			=Q2-R2			
	N	**O**	**P**	**Q**	**R**	**S**	**T**

	N	O	P	Q	R	S	T
1	I			Revenue	Cost	JP	
2	7.5	Hi Cost	0.5	20	5	0.2	15
3		Lo Cost	0.5	20	3	0.2	*
4							
5	0	Hi Cost	0.5	10	5	0.3	*
6		Lo Cost	0.5	10	3	0.3	*
7							

4. Finally, with the cursor still in the topmost leaf, invoke the **Copy Utility** command to copy the formula in the topmost leaf to all other leaves. *Note:* All leaf nodes must be in the same column to use the **Copy Utility** command. If they are not, use the 1 Branch (null decision) fork to extend leaf nodes to the same column.

	N	O	P	Q	R	S	T
1	I			Revenue	Cost	JP	Utility
2	16	Hi Cost	0.5	20	5	0.2	15
3		Lo Cost	0.5	20	3	0.2	17
4							
5	6	Hi Cost	0.5	10	5	0.3	5
6		Lo Cost	0.5	10	3	0.3	7
7							

Tree Flipping

To understand tree flipping consider the diagnostic test for Some Rare Horrible Disease (SRHD) discussed in Chapter 6. The tree below represents first, the uncertainty that a person picked at random from the population is infected (+) or not infected (-). The second uncertainty, which clearly depends on the outcome of the first uncertainty, is whether that person displays a positive test for SRHD.

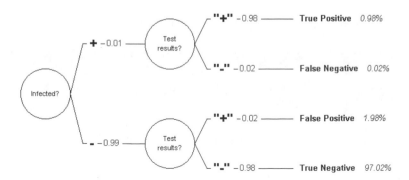

That is, the first level of the tree indicates that the infection rate in the population is only 1%. The next level of the tree indicates the probability that the test will give the correct diagnosis is 98% for both uninfected and infected members of the population. The final column on the right shows the joint probabilities of the four possible outcomes.

Suppose we wanted to know the probability that a person picked at random who tested positive was actually infected. In this case, the first uncertainty involves the test results while the second uncertainty is whether or not they are infected. The calculations of the probabilities on the branches of the flipped tree (as discussed in Chapter 6) are performed automatically by the **Flip Tree** command, and result in the tree below.

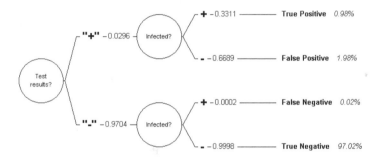

This indicates that a person picked at random who tests positive has only a 33% chance of actually being infected.

To flip a tree, first construct it in the standard manner. It is helpful to use **Node labels** to keep track of the probabilistic relations that are described by the nodes. Use the **Flip Tree** command to bring up the following dialog box:

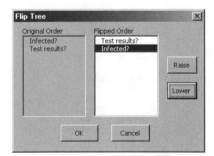

The Node Description text appears in the list box and the **Raise** and **Lower** buttons can be used to change the order in which you want the nodes to appear in the new tree.(If you have not used Node labels the Flipped Order box will display Level 1,

Level 2, etc.). Click "OK" and a new tree will be created on a worksheet named "Flipped Tree". You can create a presentation from this worksheet, as you can from any worksheet containing a tree. However, if you want to keep any presentation you have already created remember to rename it first. Tree flipping may have unpredictable results when applied to asymmetric trees, but a backup copy of the original tree is created as with Tree Growing.

OPTIMIZATION SOFTWARE

The two primary optimization packages available in spreadsheets are the Excel Solver, which ships with Excel, and What's*Best!*, a small version of which is included with INSIGHT. Larger versions of each product are available at www.Frontsys.com and www.Lindo.com, respectively.

The Excel Solver

The solver included with INSIGHT.xla is a small version of the premium solver. It has all the features of the standard Excel solver, but in addition includes an evolutionary solver which can provide approximate solutions to unsmooth and combinatorial problems. When using the evolutionary solver, the "All Different" constraint is available for solving problems such as the Traveling Salesman Problem in Chapter 8, which are described in terms of permutations. Once installed, the solver must be attached to Excel using the **Tools Add-Ins** command.

Menu and Dialog Boxes

Once installed and attached, the solver is invoked using the **Tools Solver** command. The following dialog box appears:

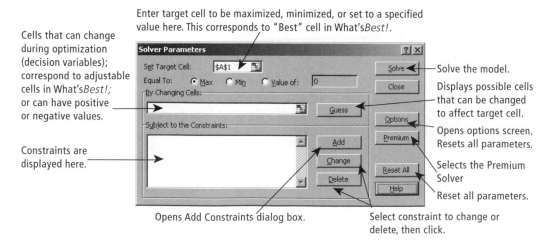

Enter target cell to be maximized, minimized, or set to a specified value here. This corresponds to "Best" cell in What's*Best!*.

Cells that can change during optimization (decision variables); correspond to adjustable cells in What's*Best!*; or can have positive or negative values.

Constraints are displayed here.

Solve the model.

Displays possible cells that can be changed to affect target cell.

Opens options screen. Resets all parameters.

Selects the Premium Solver

Reset all parameters.

Opens Add Constraints dialog box.

Select constraint to change or delete, then click.

When you add a constraint, the following dialog box appears. Select the ranges on both sides of the inequality. *Note:* along with inequalities, Integer or Binary Integer constraints are specified here.

Designate cell to take on integer values.

Select type of constraint here.

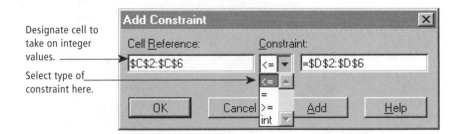

Once the solver has run, the Solver Results dialog box appears. Click the appropriate radio button to either keep the solver's solution or restore the original numbers in your model. Optionally, you may select one of the three listed reports.

Select to keep solver solutions in the model.

Allows you to save your problem for use with the Excel Scenario Manager.

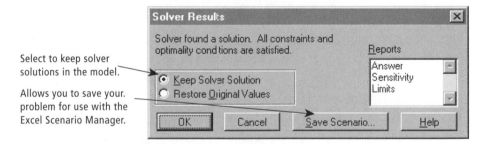

Reports

The following reports are available in the Solver Results dialog box:

- *Answer Report.* Lists information on original and final values of target and changing cells and constraints.

- *Sensitivity Report.* Reports on the sensitivity of the target cell to small change in the constraint levels. This contains similar information to the dual values in What's*Best!*.

- *Limits Report.* Lists the target cell and changing cells with their lower and upper limits.

Solver Options Dialog Box

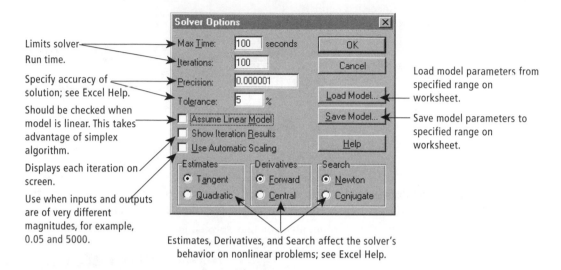

Limits solver Run time.

Specify accuracy of solution; see Excel Help.

Should be checked when model is linear. This takes advantage of simplex algorithm.

Displays each iteration on screen.

Use when inputs and outputs are of very different magnitudes, for example, 0.05 and 5000.

Load model parameters from specified range on worksheet.

Save model parameters to specified range on worksheet.

Estimates, Derivatives, and Search affect the solver's behavior on nonlinear problems; see Excel Help.

Note: In Excel 97 and above, the Assume Non Negative option defaults all changing cells to be greater than or equal to zero on optimization.

What's*Best!*®

Run the setup program from the INSIGHT disk and follow the instructions. Once What's*Best!* is installed a **WB!** menu and tool bar will appear.

- **Adjustable** specifies cells that can be adjusted during the optimization process (decision variables). These cells are colored blue so you can easily identify them.

- **Best** specifies the cell to be maximized or minimized.

- **Constrain** specifies the constraints.

- **Solve** solves the model.

- **Advanced | Dual** specifies cells to contain dual values and their ranges.

- **Integer** specifies cells to take on integer values.

- **Options** contains the five subcommands: **General, Linear Solver, Nonlinear Solver**, **Integer Pre-Solver**, and **Integer Solver** which open options dialog boxes.

- **Advanced** contains the two subcommands, **Dual** and **Omit,** to specify dual values and ranges to omit, respectively.

The icons associated with these commands are shown in the following figure.

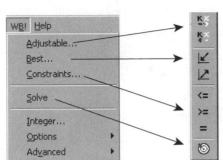

When the Adjustable dialog box appears (see below), highlight a range of cells that can be adjusted by the optimizer (decision variables). These correspond to the "changing" cells of the Excel solver. They are assumed to be non-negative unless designated as free.

Note: The text of the adjustable cells are colored blue, and they are given a custom font Style of Adjustable (see **Format I Style** on the Excel menu).

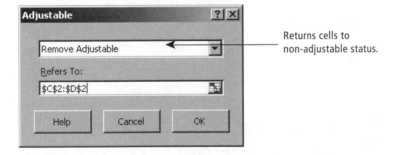

Returns cells to non-adjustable status.

When the **Best** dialog box appears, select the single cell to be maximized or minimized. This corresponds to the target cell of the Excel solver. If there is none, that is, you are merely trying to satisfy constraints, select "None" from the drop down box.

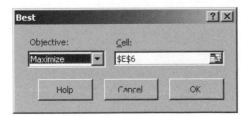

The **Constraints** command opens the following dialog box. Highlight cells to fill in both sides of the constraint type, and to specify the range used to store the constraint equations.

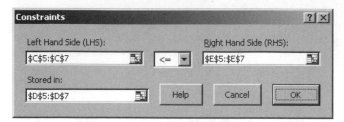

Note: If a range of columns is selected before you invoke the **Constraints** command, the three ranges in the dialog box will default appropriately, so that no further specification is required.

Formulas in the constraint range indicate whether the constraint is satisfied, tight, or not satisfied as shown in the following figure.

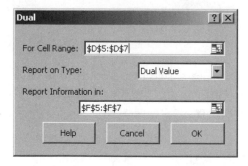

Dual opens a dialog box which is used to designate cells used to store dual values and ranges associated with specified constraints and adjustable cells. This information corresponds to the sensitivity report of the Excel Solver.

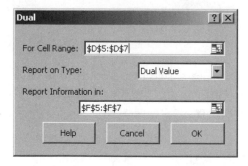

The **Integer** command opens a dialog box where the user designates cells to take on **integer** values in **Binary** (0,1) or **General** (0,1,2,3…) format. Ranges of integer cells must be named. See What's*Best!* help for additional information.

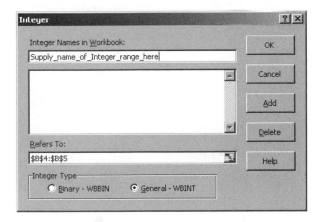

The 5 subcommands associated with the **Options** command are discussed in detail in What's*Best!* help.

References

@RISK. Palisade Corp., Newfield NY

Bratley, P, Fox, B. L. and Schrage, L. E. *A Guide to Simulation*. Springer-Verlag, 1987.

Brightman, Harvey J. *Statistics in Plain English*. South-Western, 1986.

Cancer Information Center of the National Cancer Institute, http://cis.nci.nih.gov/

Crystal Ball, Decisioneering Inc., Boulder, CO.

Dantzig, George B. *Linear Programming and Extensions*. Princeton University Press, 1963.

Dyson, Freeman. *Weapons and Hope*. New York: Harper & Row, 1984.

Efron, Bradley and Tibshirani, Robert J. *An Introduction to the Bootstrap*. Chapman & Hall, 1993.

Freedman, Russell. *The Wright Brothers, How They Invented the Airplane*. Holiday House, 1991.

Gardner, Everette S. Jr. "Exponential Smoothing: The State of the Art," *Journal of Forecasting*, 4 (1), (1986): 1–38.

Gardner, Everette S. Jr. *The Spreadsheet Operations Manager*. McGraw Hill. (1992): 10–13.

Gardner, Martin. "The Fantastic Combinations of John Conway's New Solitaire Game 'Life.'" *Scientific American*, (October 1970): 120-123.

Gonick, Larry and Smith Woollcott. *The Cartoon Guide to Statistics*. Harper, 1993.

Hertz, David B. "Risk Analysis in Capital Investment," *Harvard Business Review,* 57 (5), 1979.

Hillier, Frederick S. and Lieberman, Gerald J. *Introduction to Operations Research*, 1990.

Hull, John C. *Introduction to Futures & Options Markets*. Prentice Hall, 1991.

Infanger, Gerd. *Planning Under Uncertainty*. Boyd & Fraser, 1994.

Law, A. M. and Kelton, D. W. *Simulation Modeling & Analysis*. McGraw Hill, 1991.

Luenberger, David G. *Introduction to Dynamic Systems*. John Wiley, 1979.

——. *Investment Science*. Oxford University Press, 1997.

Markowitz, H. M. *Portfolio Selection, Efficient Diversification of Investments*. John Wiley, 1959.

Plane, Donald R. *Management Science A Spreadsheet Approach*. Boyd & Fraser, 1994.

Savage, Sam L. "The Flaw of Averages." *Harvard Business Review*, (November 2002): 20-21.

——. (a) *Blitzograms – Interactive Histograms*, Informs Transactions on Education. (January 2001). See http://ite.informs.org/vol1no2/Savage/Savage.html

——. (b) "Beat The Odds: Understand Uncertainty." *Optimize Magazine*, (December 2001)": 20-28. See http://www.optimizemag.com/issue/002/financial.htm.

——. "The Flaw of Averages", Soapbox column. *San Jose Mercury News*, October 8, 2000.

——. "Statistical Analysis for the Masses" in *Statistics and Public Policy*, edited by Bruce Spencer. Oxford University Press, 1996.

——. *Fundamental Analytic Spreadsheet Tools for Quantatative Management*. McGraw-Hill, 1993.

——. *The ABC's of Optimization using* What's*Best!*. General Optimization, 1985.

Simon, Julian L. *Resampling:The New Statistics*. Resampling Stats, Inc., 1974–1995.

Simon, J.L., Atkinson, D.T., and Shevokas, C. "Probability and Statistics: Experimental Results of a Radically Different Teaching Method." *American Mathematical Monthly*, 83 (9), (1976).

Tufte, Edward. *Visual Explanations*. Graphics Press, 1996.

Winston, Wayne L., Albright S. Christian, and Broadie, Mark. *Practical Management Science, Spreadsheet Modeling and Applications*. Duxbury Press, 1997.

Wolfram, Stephen. *A New Kind of Science*. Wolfram Media, 2002.

Index